Postcard History Series

Salisbury and Rowan County

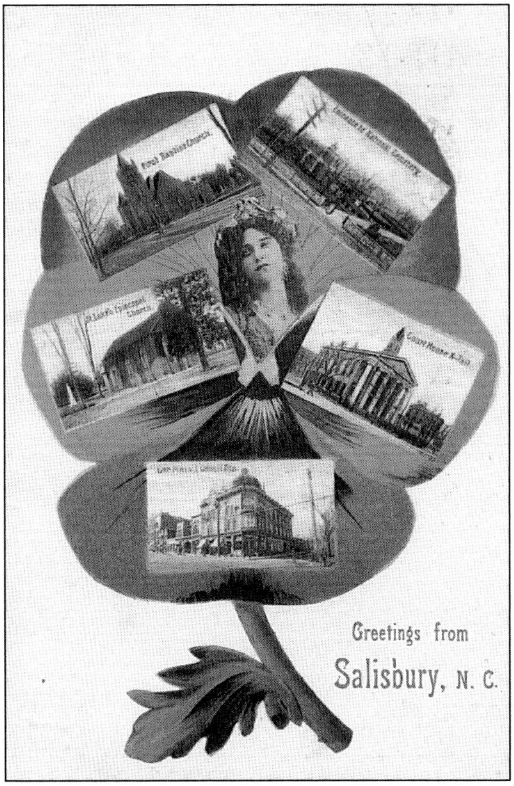

Greeting cards were very popular around the nation in the early 1900s. The Paul Koebler publishing firm, known as "PCK," was known for both the pansy-lady and the butterfly-lady formats. Local firms could send selected negatives to PCK to be printed in this form. The beautiful butterfly, shown here, was printed by W.T. Kluttz at the Hotel Vanderford and featured the Vanderford Hotel, the corner of Main and Council Streets, the Rowan County Courthouse and jail, and the Salisbury City Hall. The firm who sent in the pansy lady card is unknown. It highlights Salisbury's First Baptist Church, St. Luke's Episcopal Church, the National Cemetery, the courthouse and jail, and the corner of Main and Council Streets.

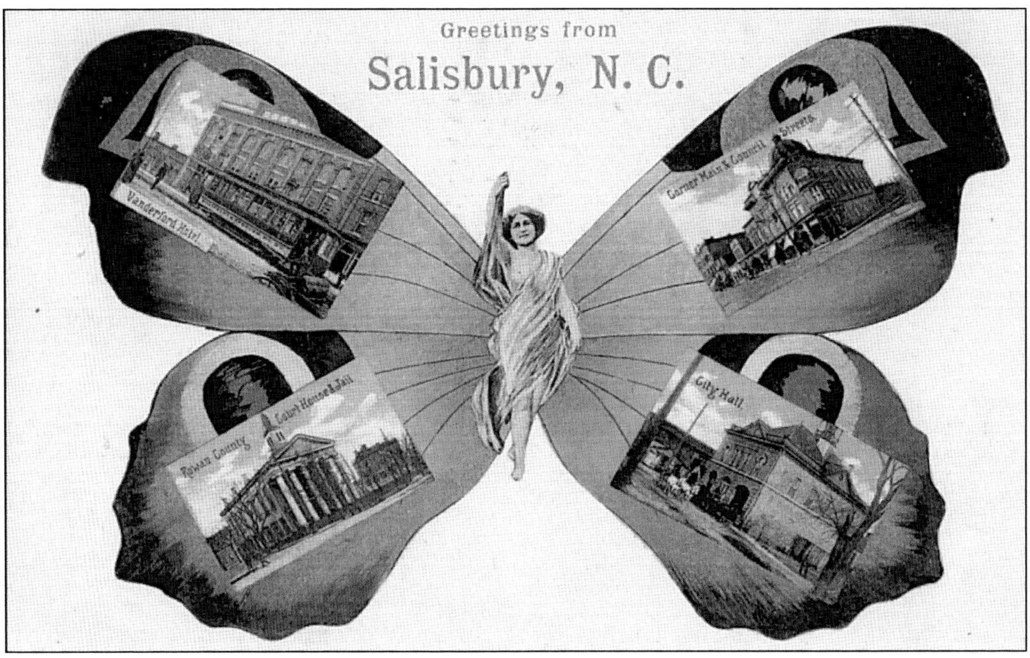

POSTCARD HISTORY SERIES

Salisbury and Rowan County

Susan Goodman Sides

ARCADIA PUBLISHING

ISBN 978-0-7385-0273-1

Published by Arcadia Publishing
Charleston, South Carolina

Printed in the United States of America

For all general information contact Arcadia Publishing at:
Telephone 843-853-2070
Fax 843-853-0044
E-mail sales@arcadiapublishing.com
For customer service and orders:
Toll-Free 1-888-313-2665

Visit us on the Internet at www.arcadiapublishing.com

*This book is dedicated to Alyssa, Sydney,
and Rivers Sides and Travis Goodman.
History begins in the heart!*

CONTENTS

ACKNOWLEDGMENTS

My sincere appreciation must be expressed to so many supportive friends. I want to thank each of the following for assisting me in this project: my parents, Mr. and Mrs. Greer Goodman; Dr. and Mrs. John R. Crawford III, whose support and encouragement have meant so much; J. Fred Corriher Jr.; Dr. Melvin Morgan; Rose Post; Mr. and Mrs. Ed Clement and the Historic Salisbury Foundation; Kay Hirst and the Rowan Museum; Mrs. Leo Wallace Jr.; Paul Bernhardt; Judy Haire; Arnold Snider; Norm Pierson; Dr. Mike Baranski; Mr. and Mrs. Steve Poteat; Charles Peacock; Mrs. Joe Taylor; John Beard; Clyde Overcash; Fred Kahn; Aileen Dekle; Joe Barbee; Mr. and Mrs. Ron Bowers; Bobby Rodgers; Elizabeth Summersett; Don Wooten; Ralph Wagoner; and Mrs. J. Van Hanford.

A few people have played a very significant role in this project. Kevin Cherry of the Rowan Public Library has shared his expertise, his vast knowledge, his patience, and his enthusiasm. Sue Corbin of Texas—you have a friend! Many have generously loaned cards from their collections, and their names appear in this book with their cards.

My daughter, Lori Sides, has worked daily on this project for months. She has researched, shown tireless energy, and handled the computer. She understood my vision from the beginning. This book would not exist without her.

INTRODUCTION

It is amazing to learn how much of a community's history can be seen through the medium of postcards. Many buildings, events, and scenes from the early 1900s were photographed, and these photographs now give us a glimpse of what Rowan County looked like nearly 100 years ago. Each image in this book is a postcard. The majority of the cards shown are Buerbaum cards but this book is not restricted to Buerbaums.

Much of our photographic history in Rowan County is attributed to Theodore Paas Buerbaum, who took photographs, had postcards printed, and then sold the cards in his bookstore on Main Street. The impetus to print this book was the acquisition of a collection of postcards that Buerbaum of Salisbury mailed to his nephew Carl Buerbaum of Dallas, Texas. Many of these had no written message but were simply mailed. Many others contain wonderful messages concerning Buerbaum's family or Rowan County events and people. Each of these cards is designated with "card" or "note" from Buerbaum.

Corresponding with Frances Winch, Buerbaum's granddaughter, has been a delightful pleasure. Mrs. Winch has shared so much personal information, and I am so appreciative. In a recent letter, Mrs. Winch stated, "Best wishes on your project on Theodore Paas Buerbaum. He would smile at the attention as he was a very quiet and unassuming man who ran a bookstore in Salisbury, NC. Incidentally, we all called him 'Papa,' even his wife."

It is my wish that this book be fun and informative, offering readers a glimpse of Rowan County yesterday and an explanation of how it came to be where it is today!

Susan Goodman Sides

One

Residences

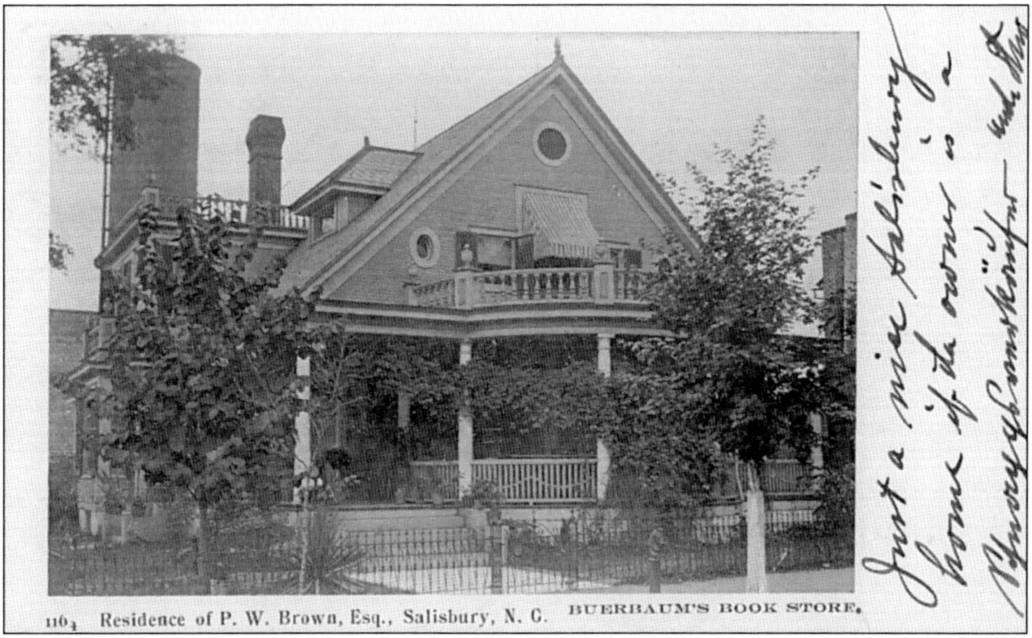

Salisbury's P.W. Brown owned one of the many distilleries located in Rowan County, and his White Elephant Saloon was located at 120 East Inniss Street. In one of his advertisements, Brown included the words, "All Nations Welcome, Except Carrie." Brown's home was located at 201 South Church Street. Buerbaum's German notation has not been interpreted, but he did say this was a "Nice Salisbury home."

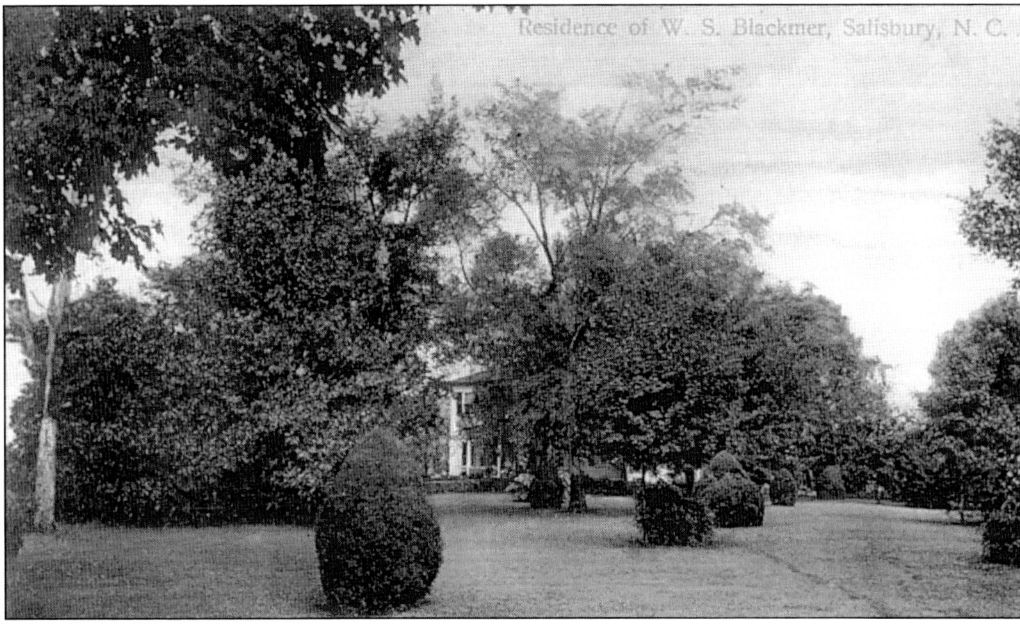

Walter S. Blackmer was employed in the retail clothing business and, later, in real estate. He was one of the best-known men in Salisbury and was father to Sidney—the Broadway, television, and movie star. Blackmer's home, shown here, was located at 425 West Horah Street.

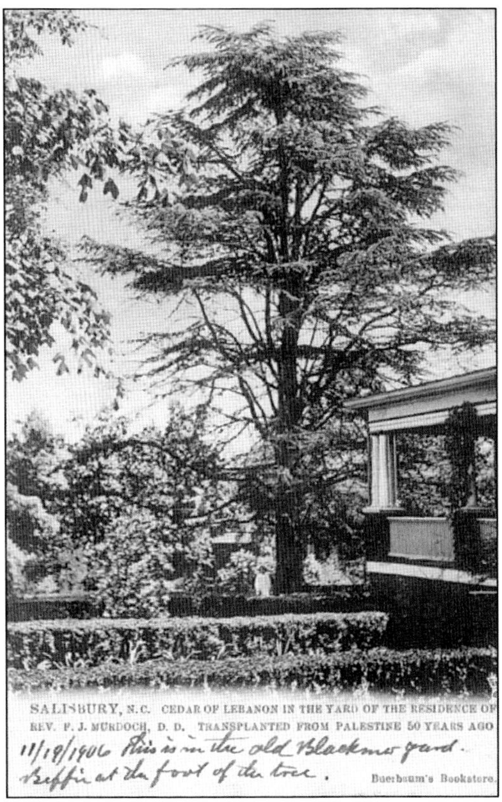

According to Buerbaum's note, this cedar tree was located in the old Blackmer yard. Luke Blackmer owned one half of the block at West Horah and South Church Streets. Blackmer, a native of Wheatland, New York, had divided loyalties during the Civil War. Too old to join the army of either side, he aided the suffering on both, by helping to organize Salisbury's Wayside Hospital for the Confederates and supplying books, food, and other supplies to Union POWs. Buerbaum's daughter, "Beffie," can be seen standing under the tree in this postcard.

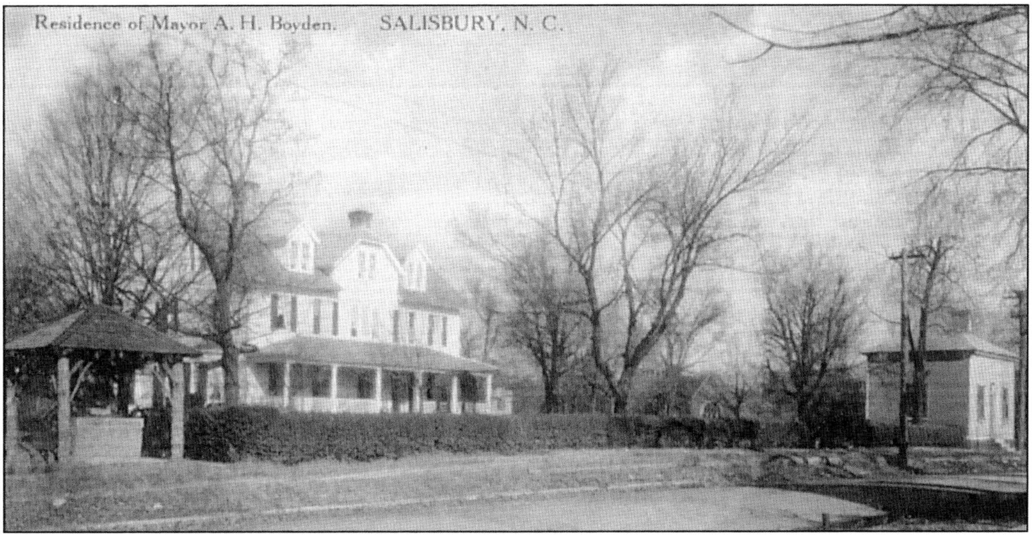

Erected on the site where Andrew Jackson studied law under Spruce Macay, this was home to Archibald Henderson. Henderson's daughter Jane married Nathaniel Boyden, a congressman and Supreme Court justice. Their son Archibald Henderson Boyden was chairman of the school board for 30 years, and Boyden High School was named in his honor. Boyden lived in this home until his death in 1929. The home was destroyed in 1949 to make way for the Rowan Public Library. The small building to the right was used as a law office by Archibald Henderson and Nathaniel Boyden and is still located on the Rowan Public Library property.

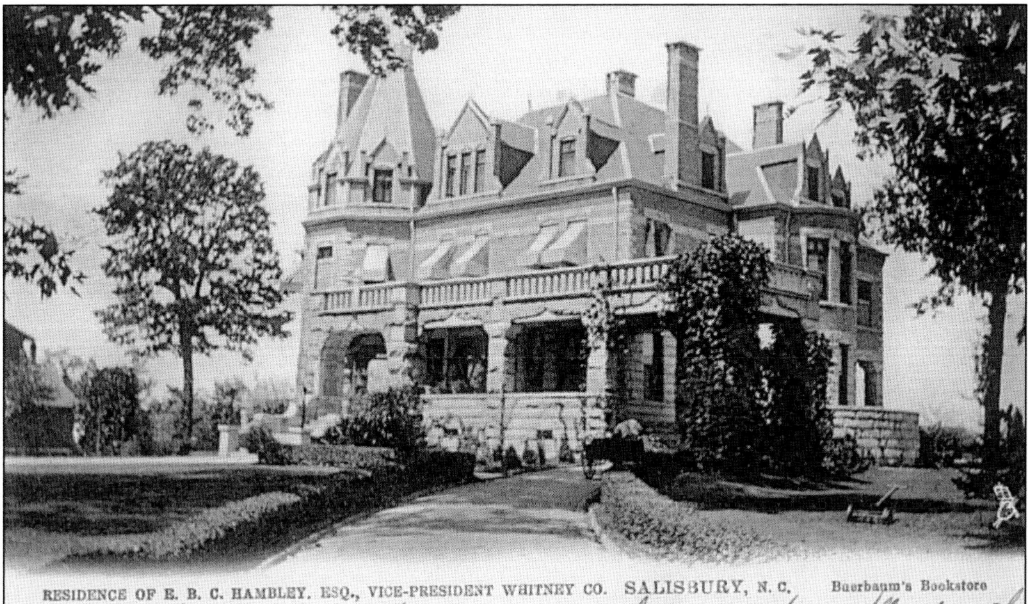

The Hambley-Wallace mansion was built in 1903. It was designed by Egbert Barry Cornwell Hambley, a mining engineer with the Whitney Company, and was erected by Alfred and Lee Lazenby. Home to the Wallace family for much of the 20th century, it has an exterior of Rowan granite, quarried from Whitney mines, and pink brick. Buerbaum's note simply states, "Above self explanatory."

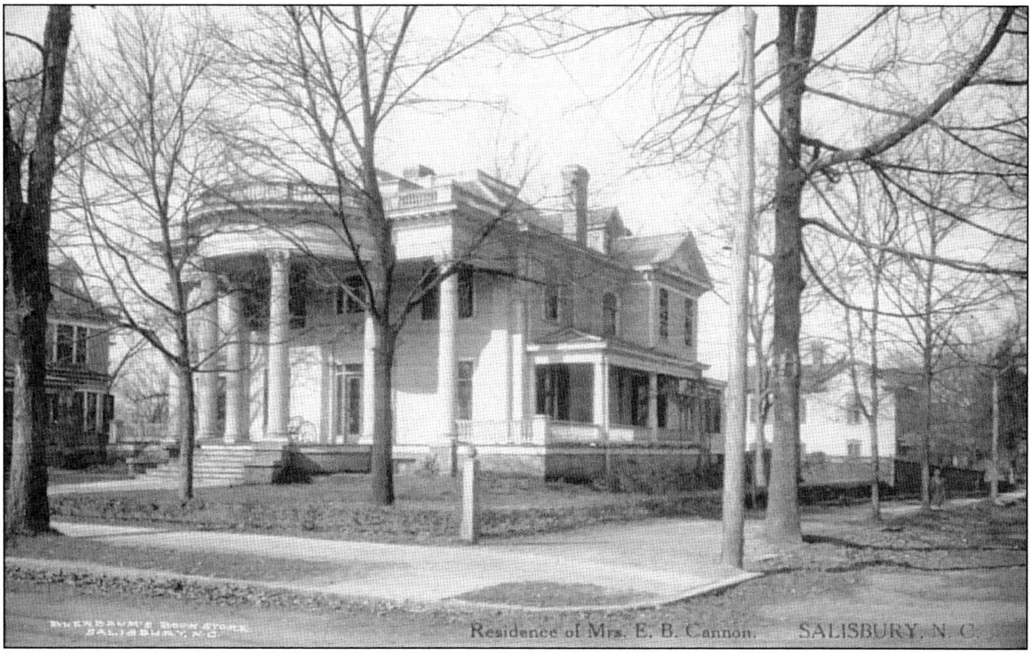

The Cannon-Guille home on Fulton Street was erected by Mrs. David Cannon on land her father, John Dixon Brown, purchased in 1855. Mr. A.R. Lazenby constructed the home in 1906. Mrs. Gettys Guille, the daughter of Mrs. Cannon and a force in local civic and cultural affairs, lived there until her death. (Card from Buerbaum.)

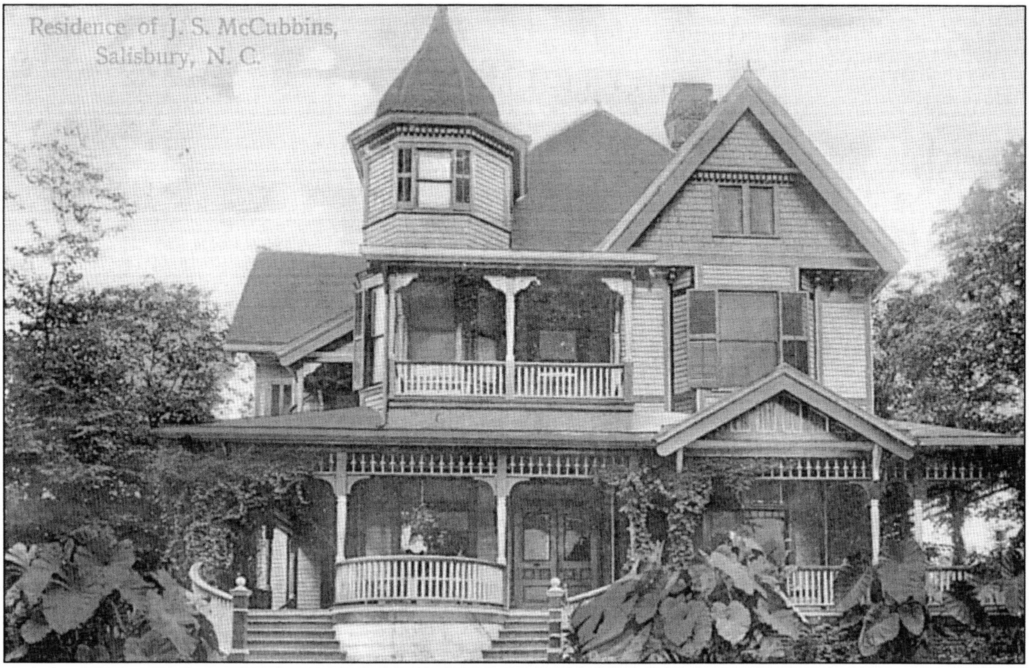

J. Samuel McCubbins, a real estate developer, lived in this home located at 514 South Main Street. He also owned Rowan Hardware and Machinery.

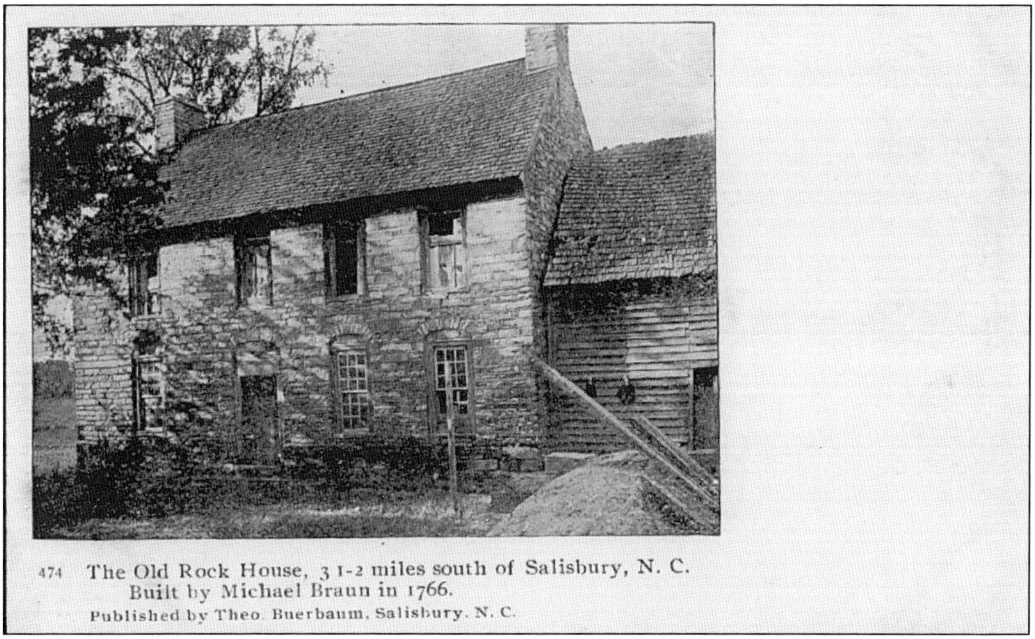

The only pre-Revolutionary house standing in Rowan County is the Michael Braun house, also known as the "Old Stone House," in Granite Quarry. It has been called the "noblest of N.C. Stone Houses." Built by a German immigrant who came down the great wagon road from Pennsylvania in the 1700s, the house has period furnishing and is open to the public as one of the Rowan Museum sites.

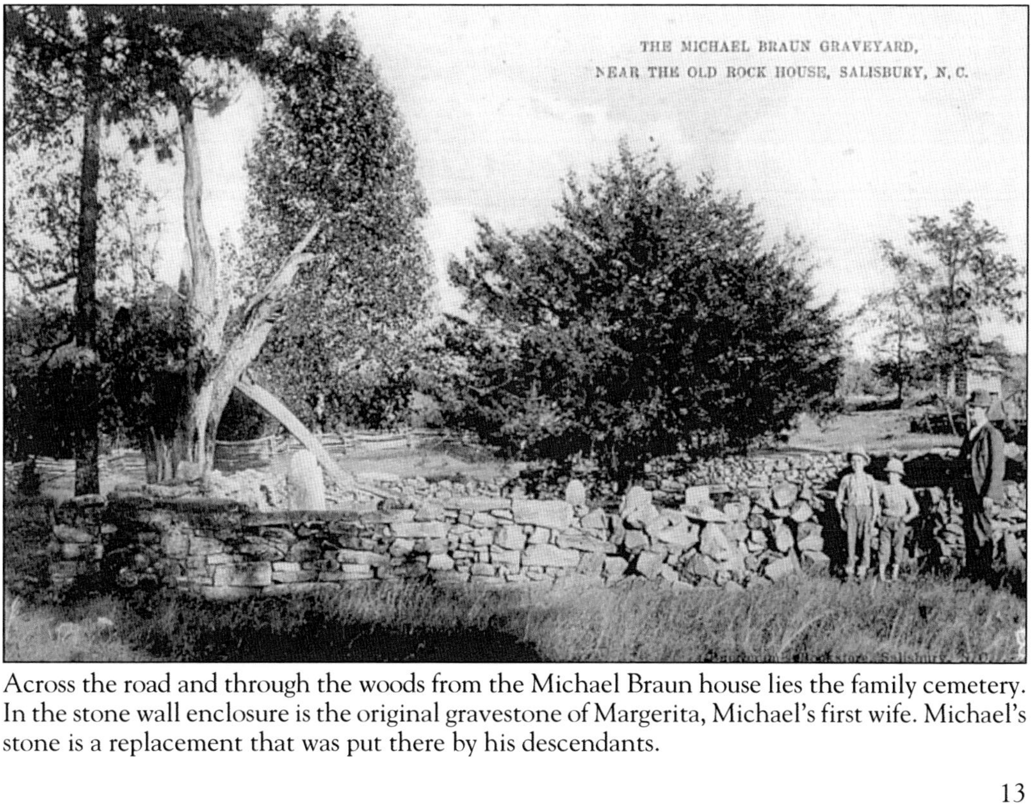

Across the road and through the woods from the Michael Braun house lies the family cemetery. In the stone wall enclosure is the original gravestone of Margerita, Michael's first wife. Michael's stone is a replacement that was put there by his descendants.

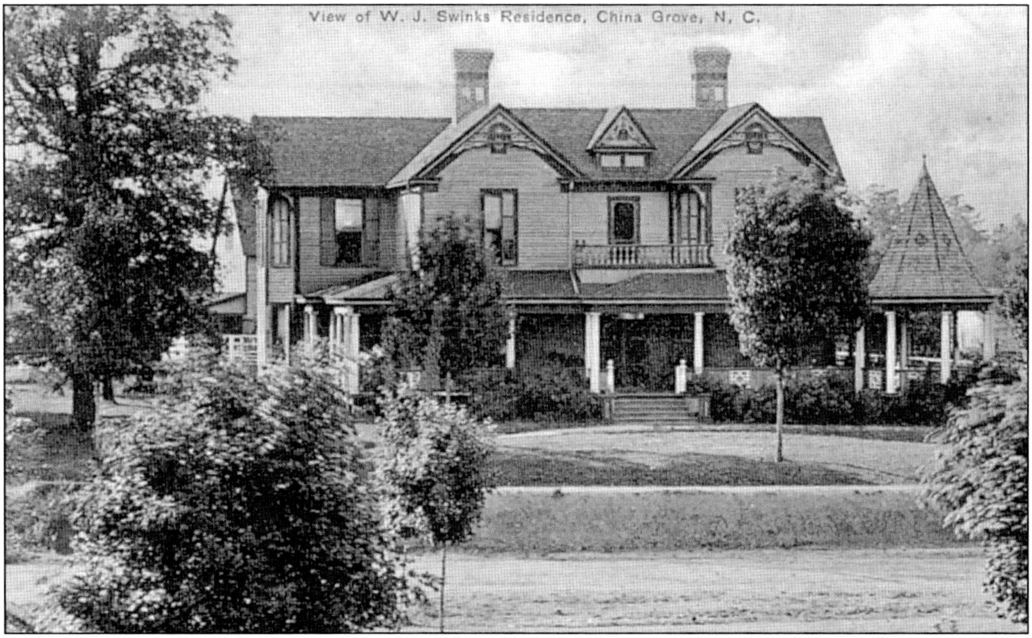

J.W. Swink served as alderman in China Grove for a number of years and started the campaign for the Farm Life School that was located there. Swink succeeded Frank Patterson as secretary-treasurer of Patterson Textile Mill.

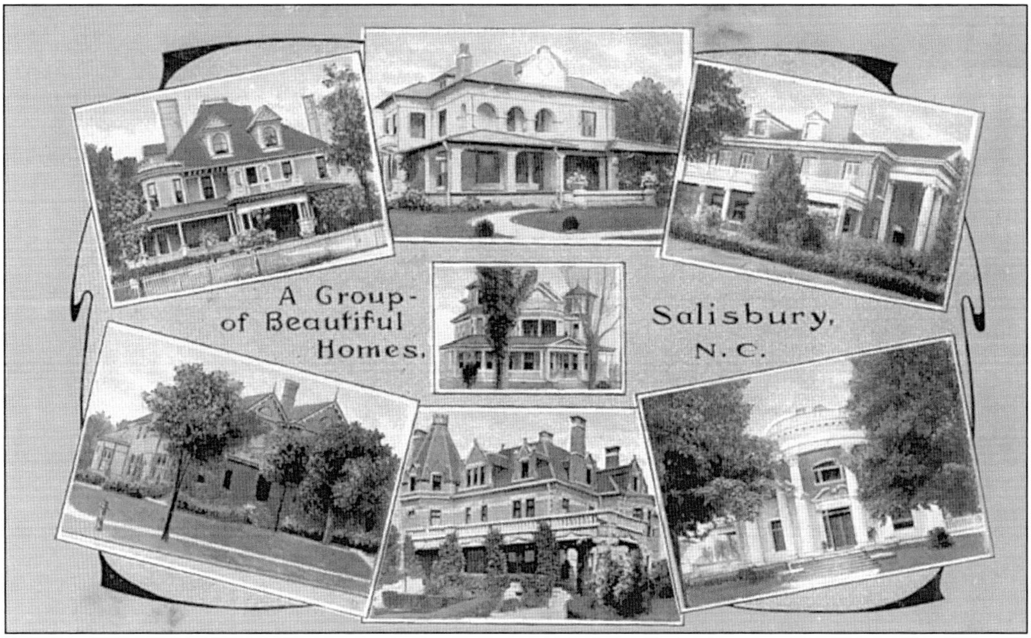

This group of homes is identified as Jerome House at 415 South Fulton Street (at center), and, from left to right, (bottom row) Senator Lee Overman Home on the corner of Innes and Ellis Streets, Hambley-Wallace Home at 508 South Fulton Street, and Cannon-Guille Home at 202 South Fulton Street; (top row) Louis H. Clement Home at 302 South Ellis Street, F.F. Smith Home at 201 South Fulton Street, and Davis and Wiley Bank on the corner of Main and Bank Streets (both bank and residence).

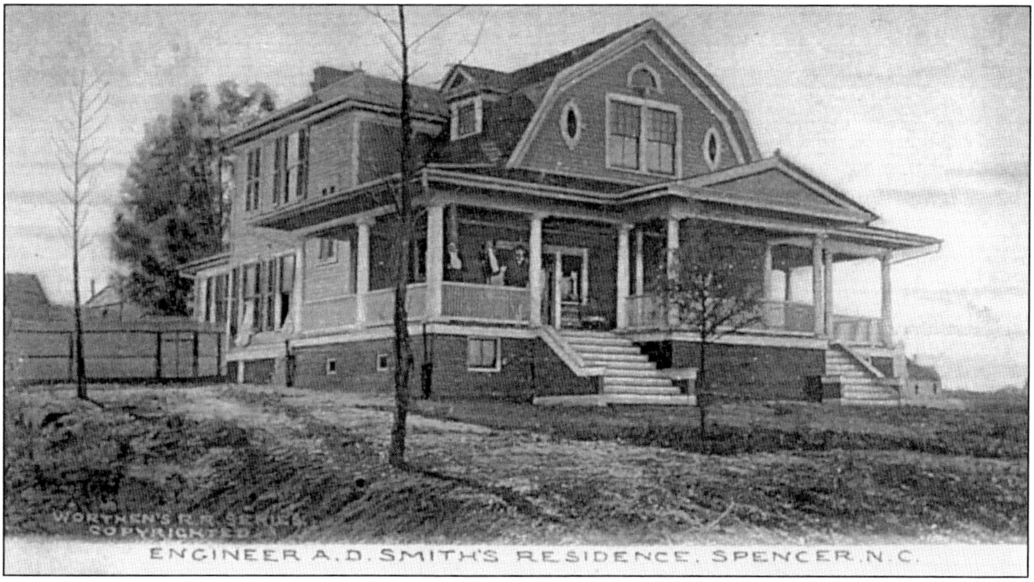

Erected c. 1904 of the "finest heart pine," Engineer A.D. Smith's residence is located at 207 North Salisbury Avenue in Spencer. Smith lived in this home near the Spencer Shops until about 1910 when Southern Railroad transferred him to Washington, D.C. The house was then sold to the Deal family, later turned into apartments, and has now been renovated back into a single-family residence. (Courtesy of the Durwood Barbour Collection.)

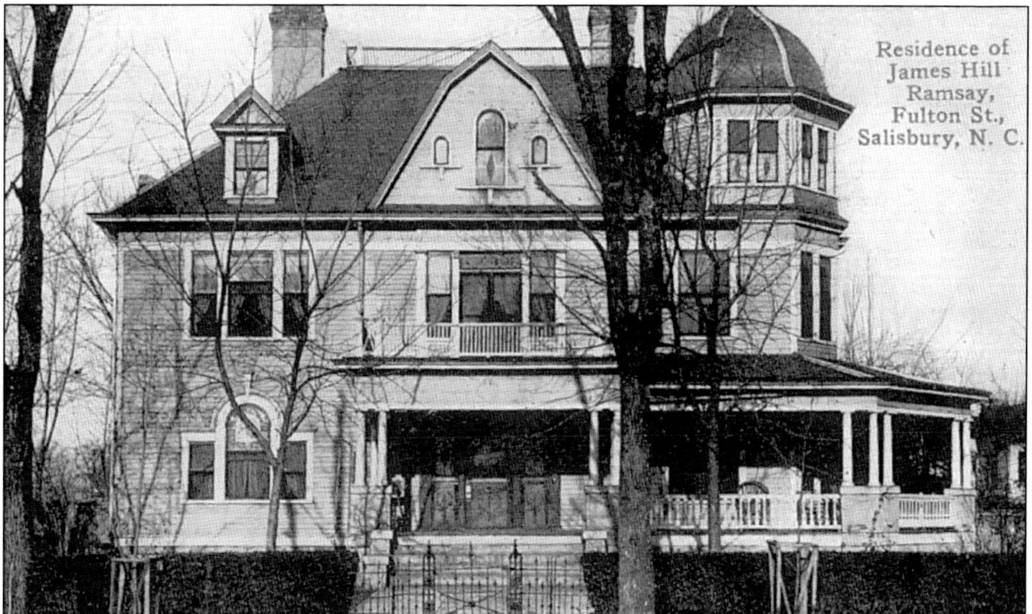

The residence of James Hill Ramsay was built in 1901 by Milton Brown. Ramsay served as postmaster under 13 presidents. The home, now a bed and breakfast called Rowan Oak, is located at 208 South Fulton Street. (Card from Buerbaum.)

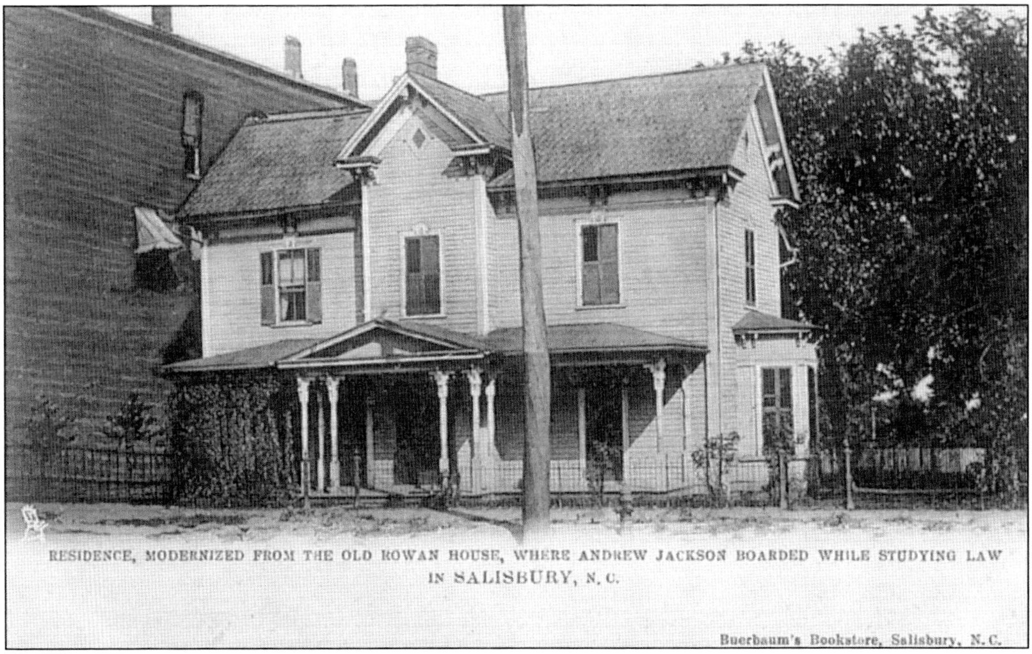

Andrew Jackson was granted a license to practice law by the justices of the Rowan County Court on November 6, 1787. He served as the seventh President of the United States. This site, located at 217 South Main Street, now holds the City of Salisbury offices.

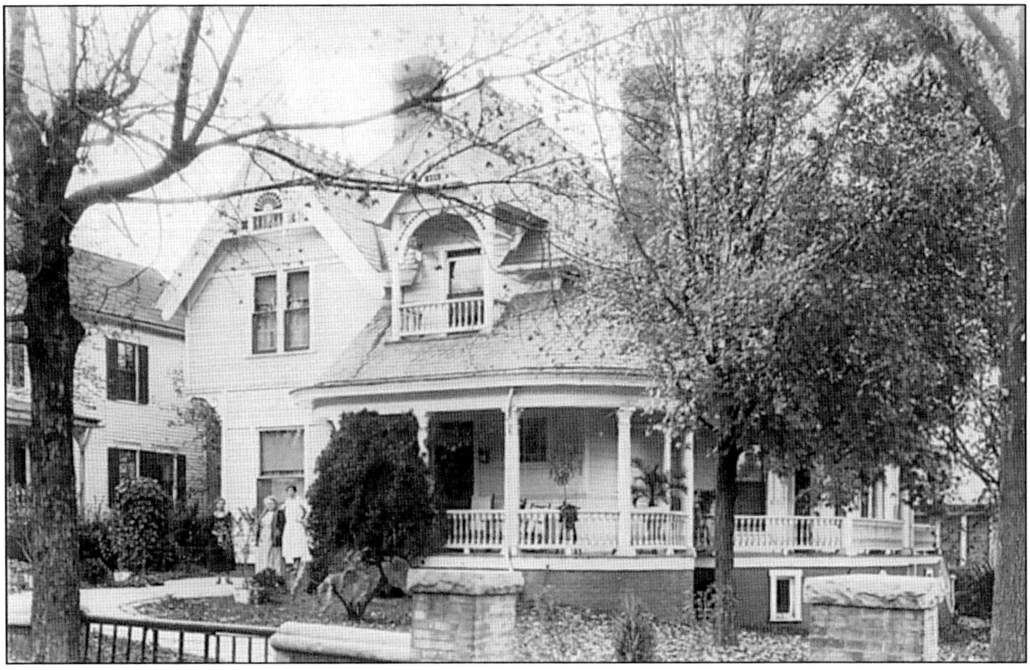

The Gaskill-Pierce house was erected in 1898 by David Gaskill and is now home to David and Eva Bernhardt Bingham. This Queen Anne–style home is located at 402 South Ellis Street. The iron gate is said to be from the fountain that was once on Salisbury's square. (Courtesy of Eva Bernhardt Bingham.)

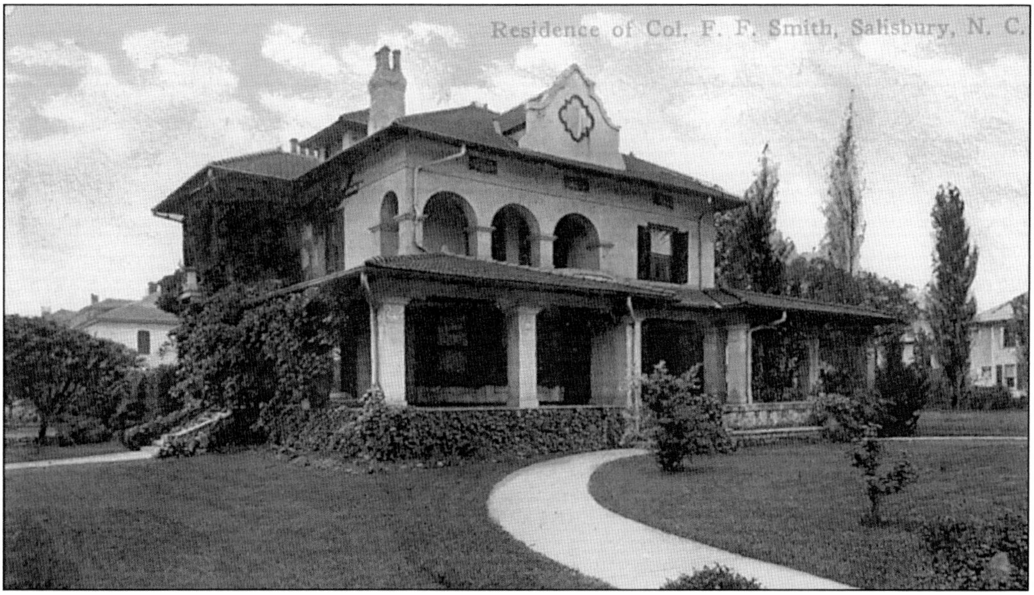

Col. Fletcher Franklin Smith was a leading businessman in Rowan County. He held an interest in Smith Drug Company, Peoples Drug Store, and Main Pharmacy and also organized the Salisbury Industrial Club. Smith's Spanish mission–style home was built *c.* 1910 and is located on Fulton Street.

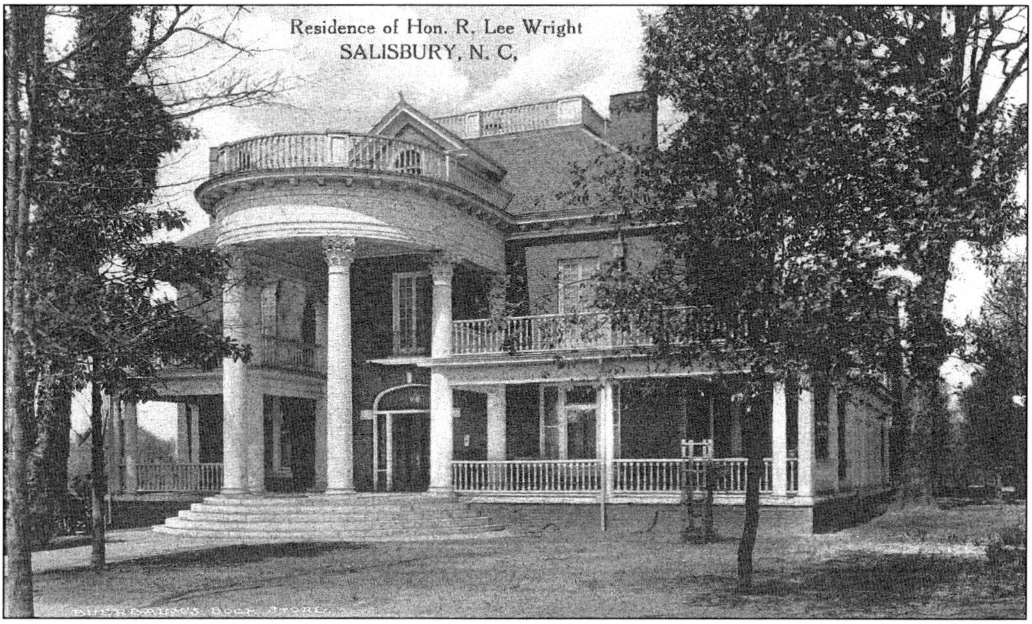

Judge R. Lee Wright's home, located at 302 South Fulton Street, was built in 1912 by architect Louis Asbury. Wright was an attorney in Salisbury from 1889 until his death in 1955. He represented Rowan County in the general assembly from 1901 to 1903 and in the state senate from 1905 to 1907 and from 1919 to 1920. Wright also served as a North Carolina Supreme Court justice from 1924 to 1927. His Chestnut Hill mausoleum is noted for its extensive notations, among them a citation regarding Wright and his wife's genealogy. (Courtesy of the Rowan Public Library.)

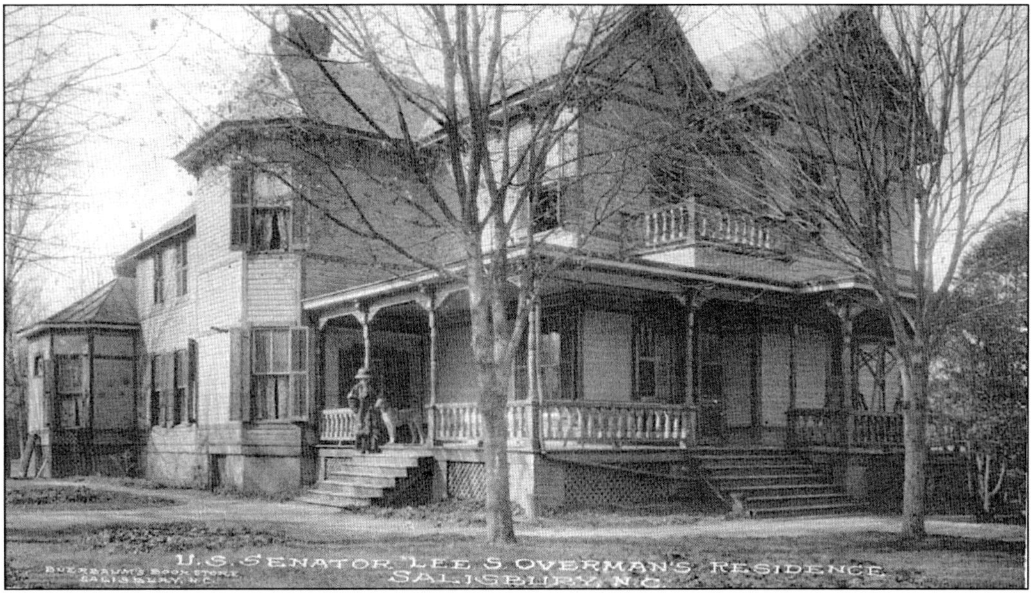

Salisbury native Lee Slater Overman opened a private law practice in 1880. He was married to Mary Paxton Merriman, the daughter of U.S. Senator A.S. Merriman. Overman served as a state legislator from 1883 to 1899, was elected president of the North Carolina Railroad in 1894, and served on the board of trustees of the University of North Carolina and Trinity College (now Duke University). Overman was elected to the U.S. Senate in 1902 and served until his death in 1930. His home was located at the corner of West Innes and South Ellis Streets. (Courtesy of the Rowan Public Library.)

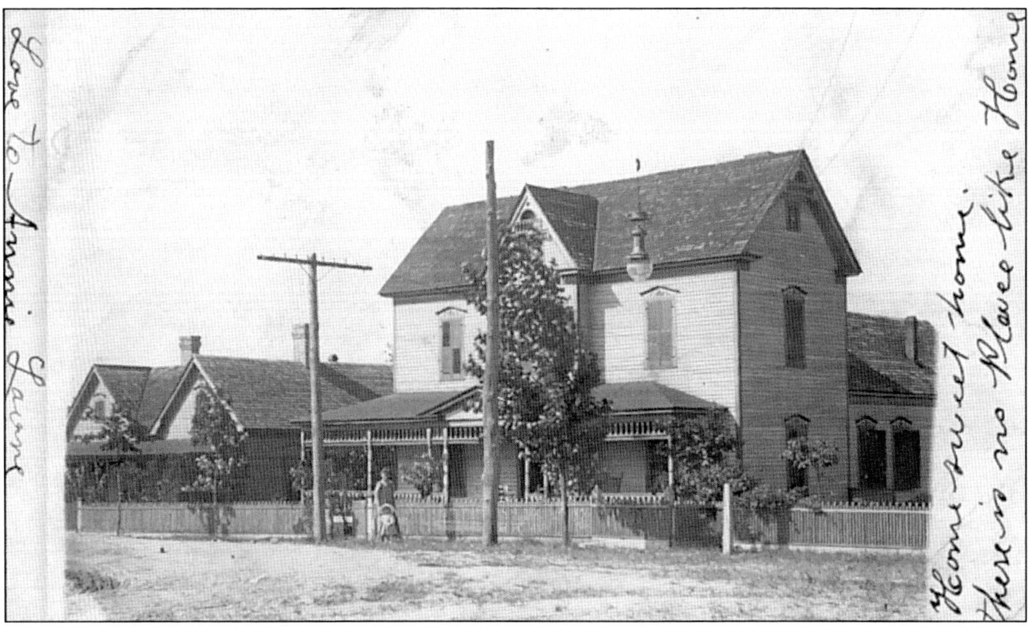

William M. Eagle was an engineer for Southern Railroad, and his home was located on Sixth Street in Spencer. Eagle later built a more substantial home for himself and also supplied the capital to construct many other homes in this area. Eagle was the father of Mrs. T.R. Burdette, the wife of the former Spencer mayor. (Courtesy of the Marian Harter Collection.)

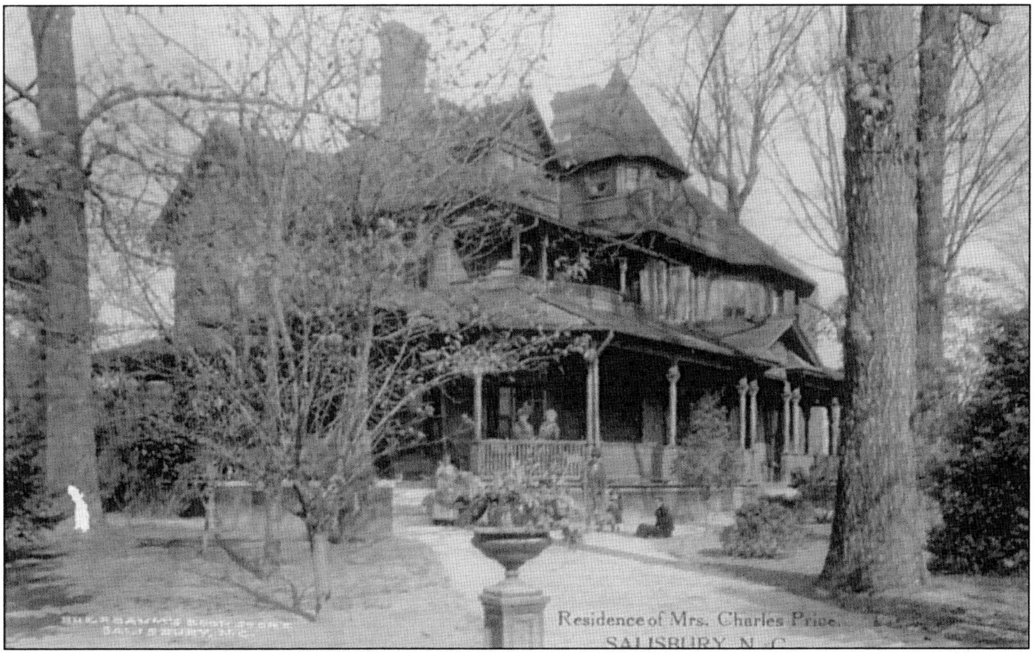

This home was erected for Capt. Charles Price, a prominent attorney and Republican leader in Salisbury. His home, fondly remembered for its ballroom, was razed for the Prince Charles Apartments at 300 North Fulton Street. (Courtesy of the Marian Harter Collection.)

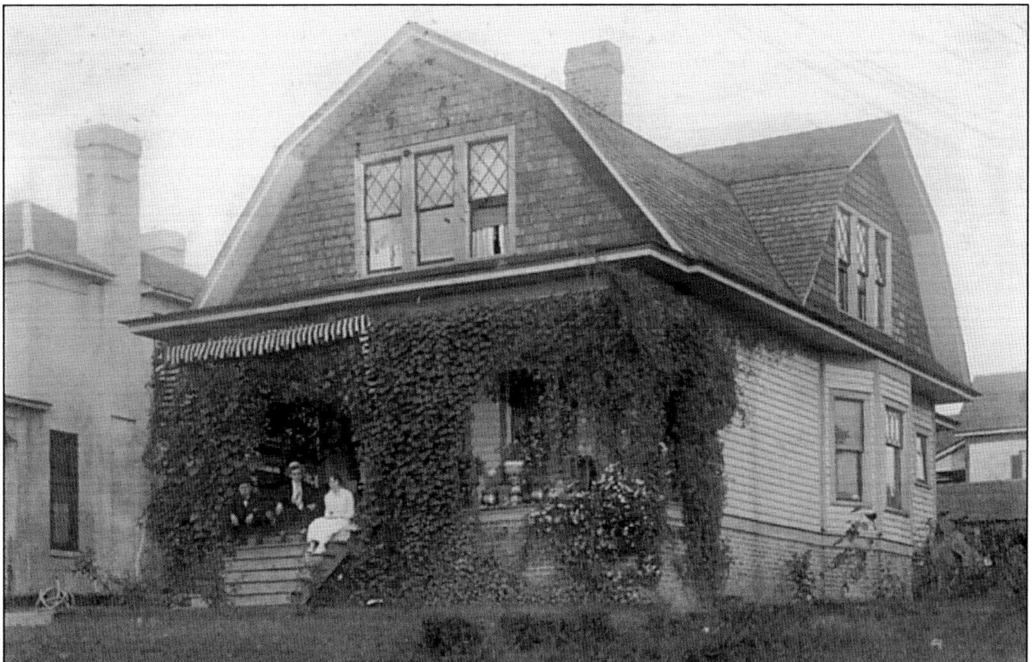

The James Lyons home at 801 North Main Street was erected c. 1912. Lyons was a Southern Railroad machinist and occupied this home until the 1940s. (Courtesy of the Marian Harter Collection.)

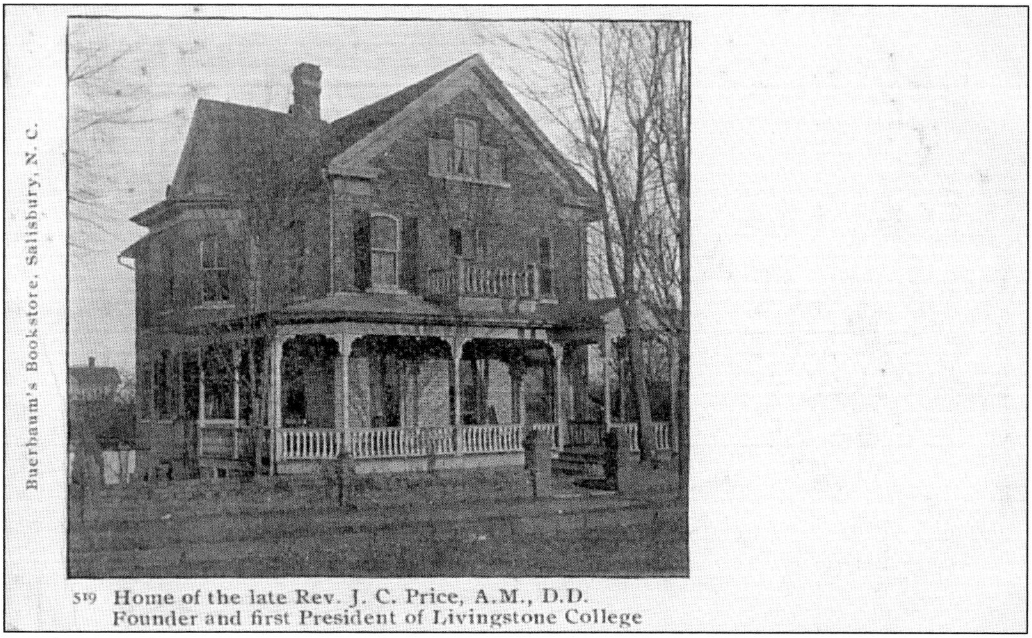

At the age of 28, Rev. J.C. Price became the president of the Zion Wesley Institute, which later became known as Livingstone College in honor of the British missionary and explorer David Livingstone. Livingstone's son died at the Salisbury Confederate Prison during the War Between the States. Reverend Price served as the president of the college from 1882 to 1893. (Courtesy of the Marian Harter Collection.)

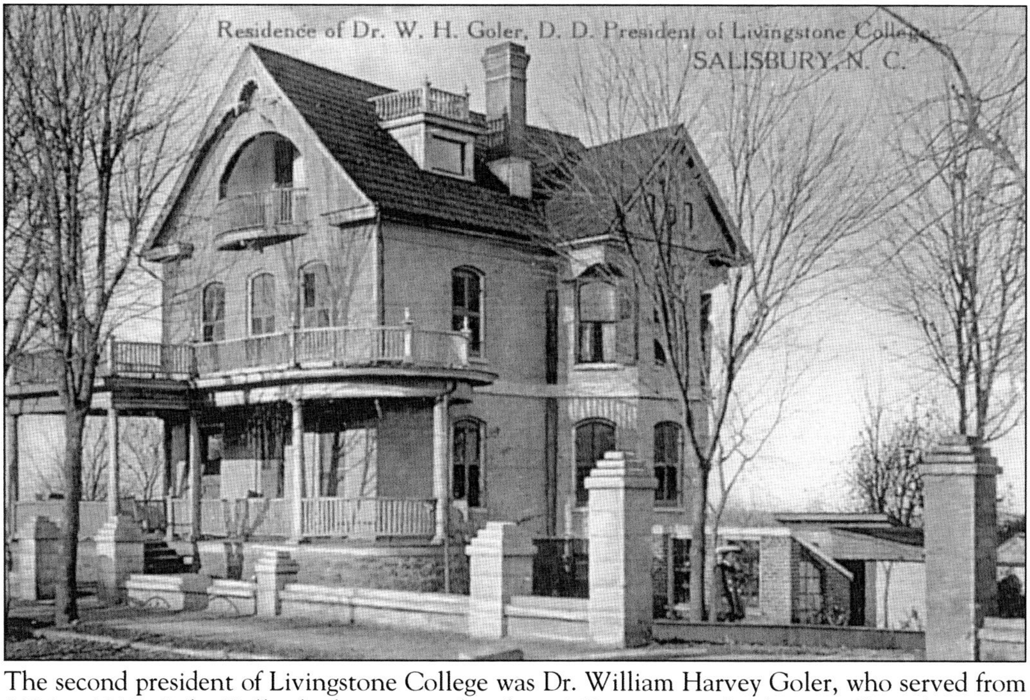

The second president of Livingstone College was Dr. William Harvey Goler, who served from 1894 to 1917. Goler Hall, which was completed in 1917, was named in honor of him. (Courtesy of the Marian Harter Collection.)

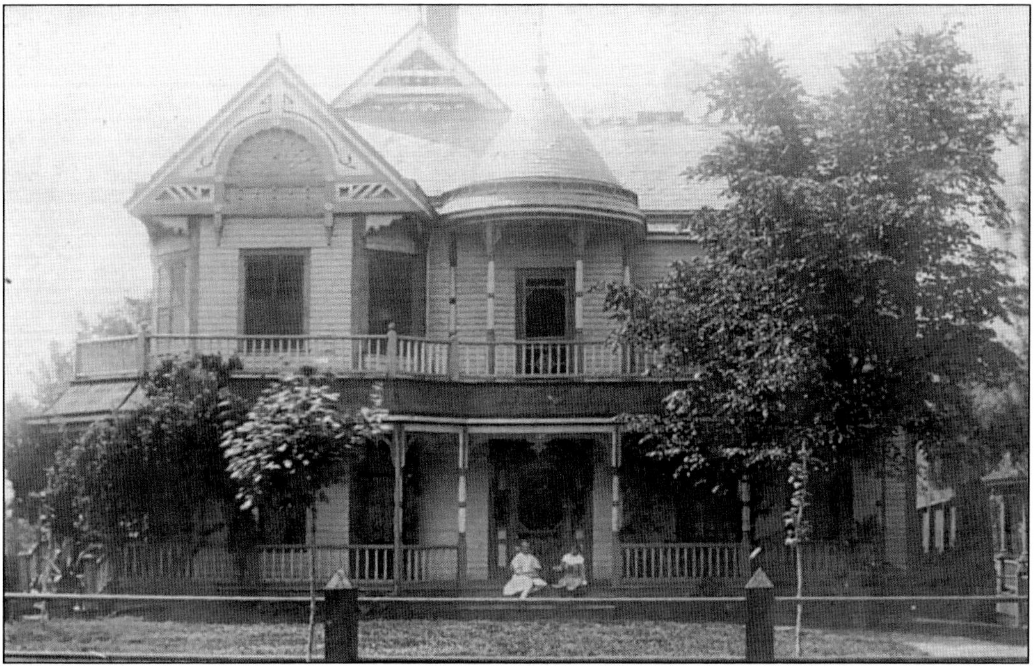

This beautiful home at 128 South Ellis Street is known as the Nicholson House after William Samuel Nicolson, a plumber and roofer who moved here from Lynchburg, Virginia. The 2-1/2-story, Queen Anne structure was built *c.* 1896. The home later became the home to Homer Lucas Sr. and later to Mr. and Mrs. Miles Smith Sr. (Courtesy of the Marian Harter Collection.)

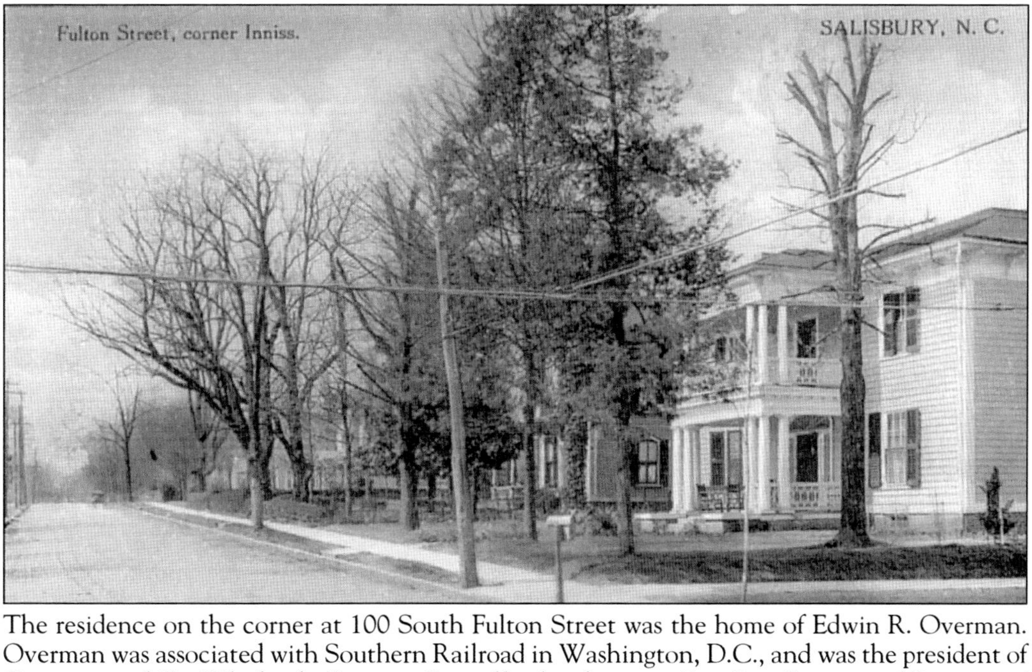

The residence on the corner at 100 South Fulton Street was the home of Edwin R. Overman. Overman was associated with Southern Railroad in Washington, D.C., and was the president of Overman and Co. Wholesale Grocers. One of his brothers was Sen. Lee Overman. (Courtesy of the Marian Harter Collection.)

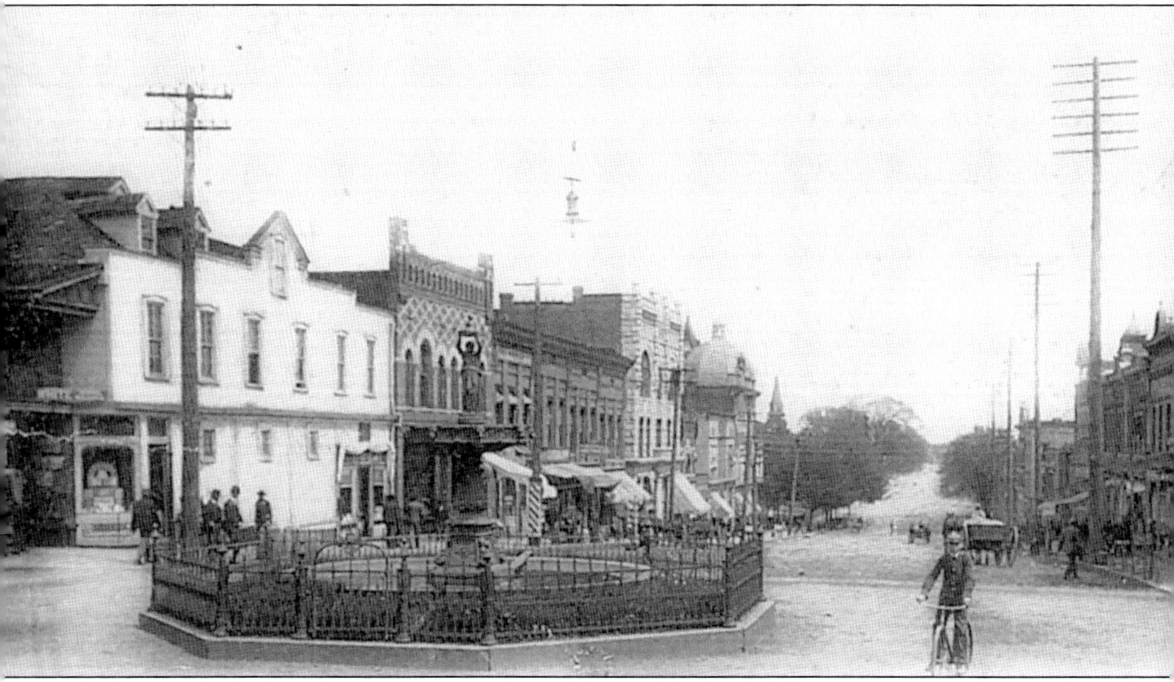

When the courthouse was removed from the square in 1855, a public well was built in its place. The central location insured a ready water supply in the event of a fire downtown. The beautiful fountain named "Rebecca of the Well" stood from 1888 until it had to be moved in 1905 to make way for the streetcar trolleys. The fountain was taken to Chestnut Hill Cemetery where it cracked during a storm and was sold for scrap metal during World War II. An exact duplicate was made from the original 1888 molds and installed at the intersection of Innes and Depot Streets. Buerbaum's note says, "Fountain is moved, instead we have street railway."

Two

Street Scenes and Businesses

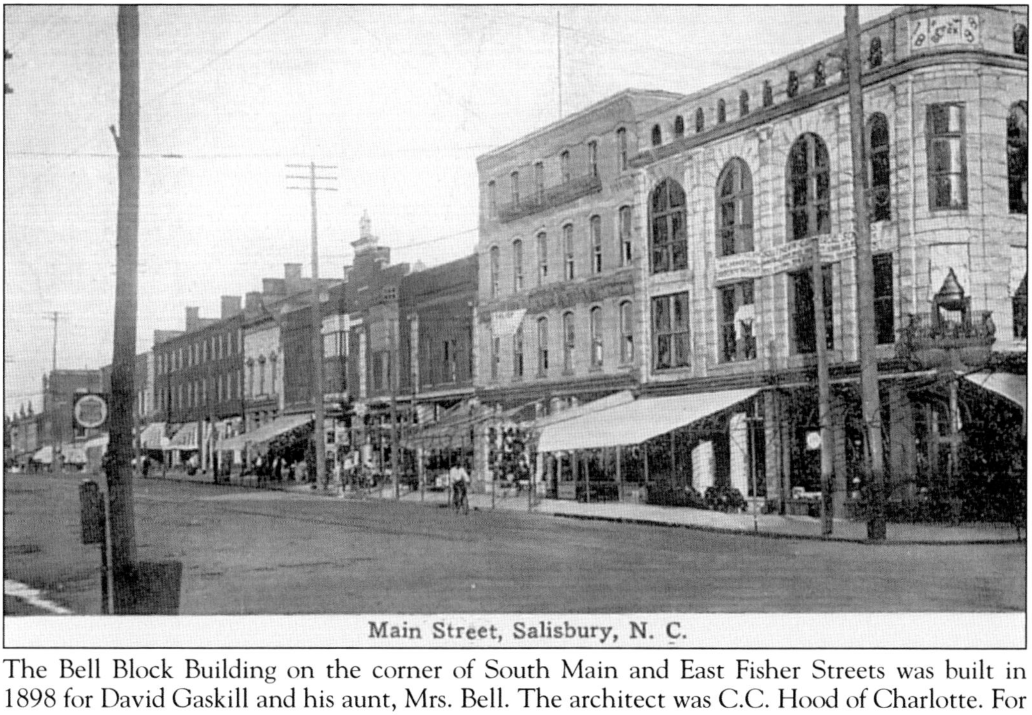

Main Street, Salisbury, N. C.

The Bell Block Building on the corner of South Main and East Fisher Streets was built in 1898 for David Gaskill and his aunt, Mrs. Bell. The architect was C.C. Hood of Charlotte. For years, the Belk Budget Shop housed the building. The banner across the front of the building advertises the Southern Commercial School.

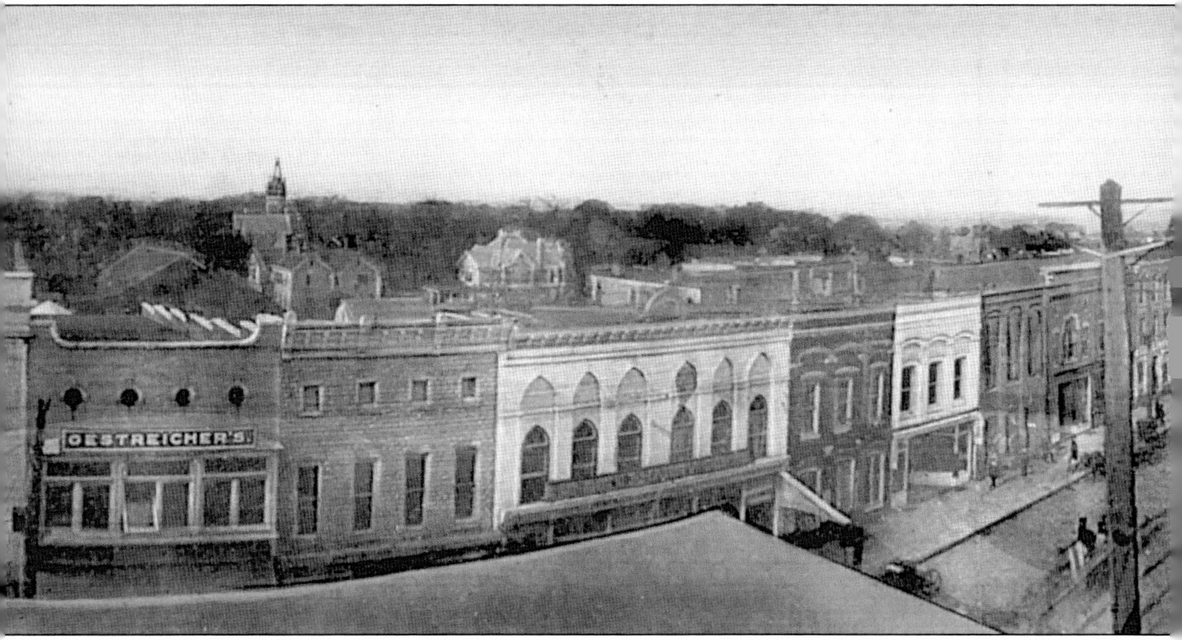

The exact date of this panoramic view is unknown. Streetcars were added to downtown in 1905. The town's well-known hotel, Mansion House, burned in 1907, and the Grubb Building was erected on that site in 1910. The Oestreicher name is clearly visible at 122 South Main Street. Just beyond was the Harry Store, which opened in 1892 at 116–118 South Main Street. The Harrys eventually joined

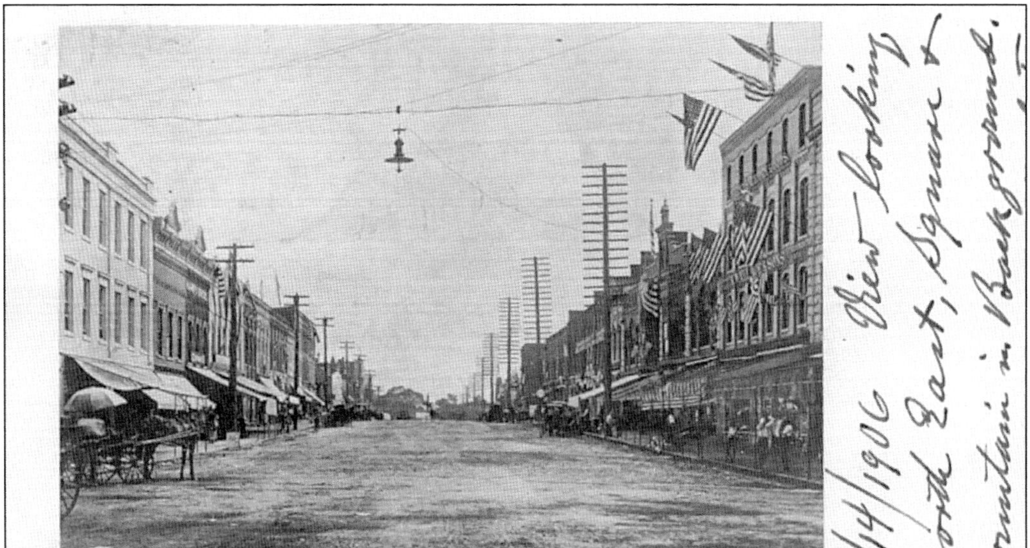

The building on the far right, decorated with flags, is V. Wallace and Sons. This company was established in 1885. In 1901, they expanded into the wholesale dry goods business, evolving into a real estate firm. Buerbaum's note states, "View looking North East, Square and fountain in background."

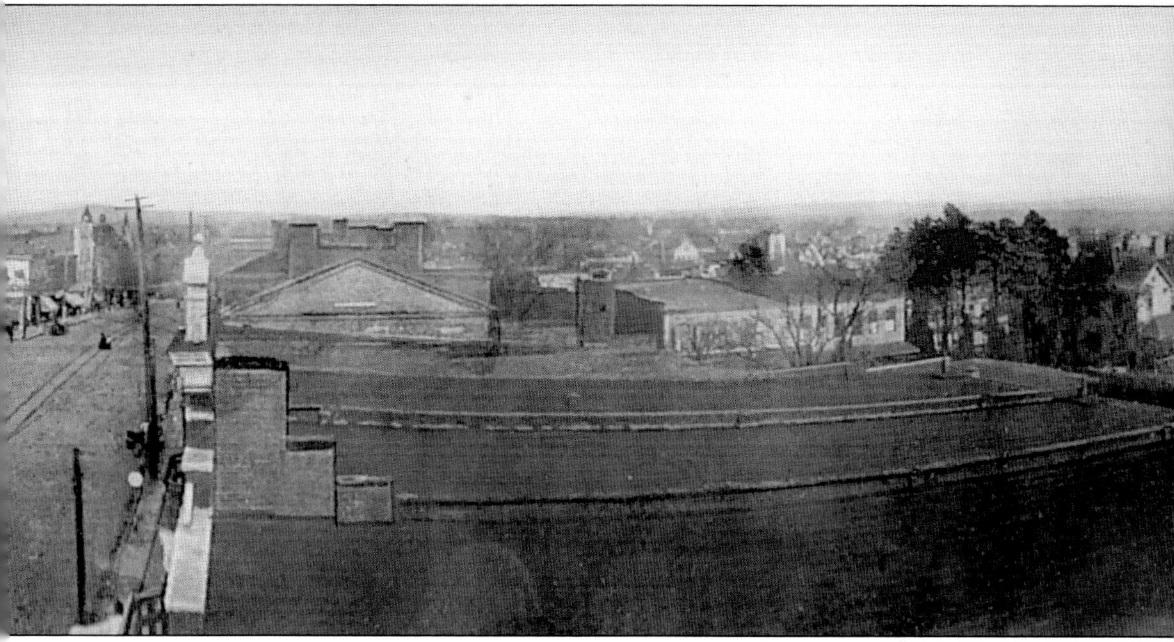

the Belks of Charlotte to form Belk-Harry of Salisbury. Other businesses on Main Street at that time included Purcell's Drug, Buerbaum's Books, Salisbury Hardware and Furniture, First National Bank, Salisbury Retail Merchant's Association, V. Wallace and Sons, R.W. Norman Furniture, St. John's Lutheran Church, T.F. Kluttz and Company-Druggists, and Salisbury Bakery.

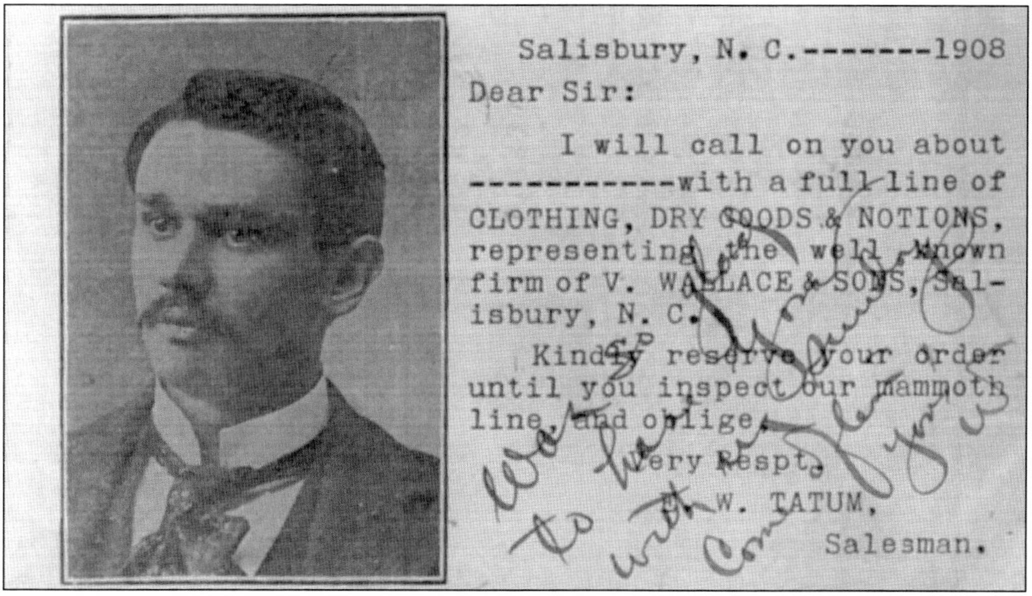

Ezra Walter Tatum was a traveling salesman for V. Wallace and Sons for many years and a one-time vice president of Salisbury Bank and Trust. Salisbury was perfect for a traveling salesman because of the railroad. Tatum was the grandfather of Walter Tatum of Salisbury. (Courtesy of the Durwood Barbour Collection.)

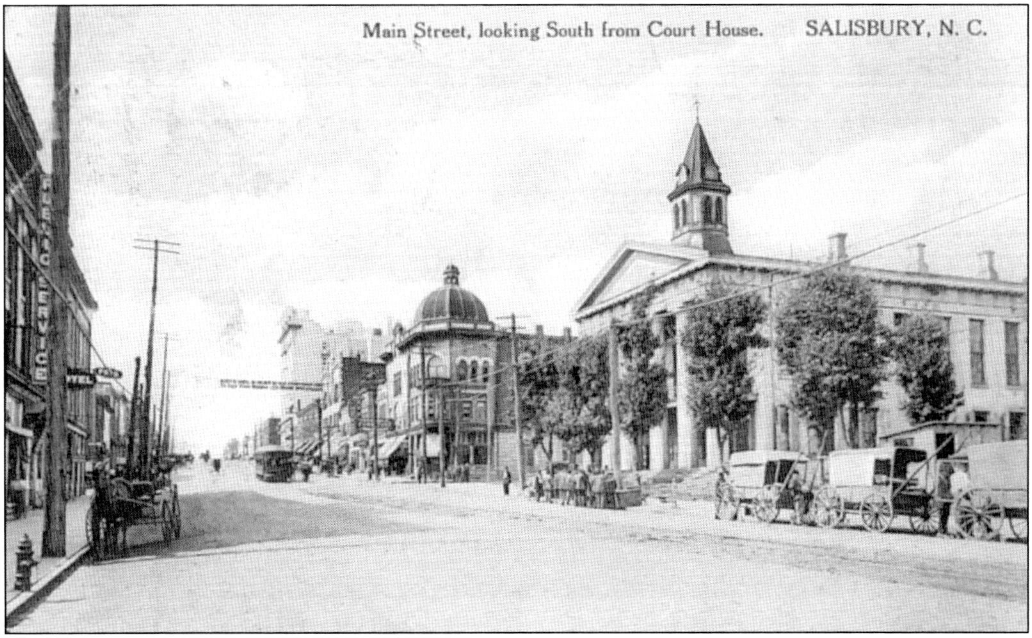

Why the covered wagons without horses are sitting on the right is a mystery. The crowd in front of the courthouse may be involved in an interesting court case.

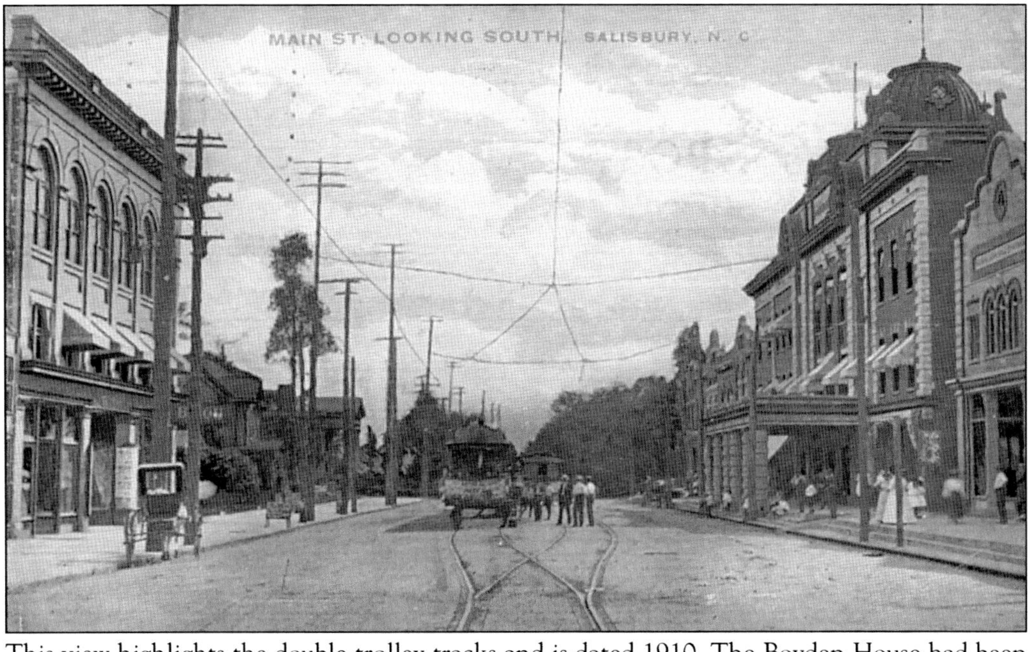

This view highlights the double trolley tracks and is dated 1910. The Boyden House had been remodeled into the Empire Hotel and had a balcony supported by brick posts.

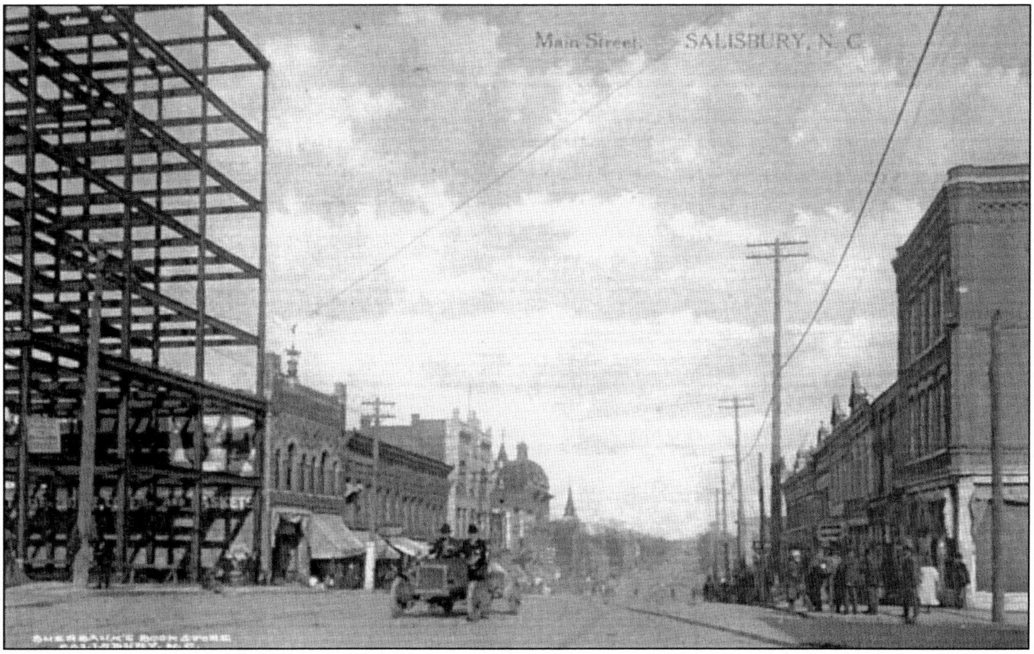

The Grubb-Wallace Building (now known as the Plaza) had an interesting beginning. Clay Grubb moved to Rowan County in 1903 when the Watts Law passed, which stated that whiskey making must be done in an incorporated town with not less than two policemen. In addition to his distillery, Grubb owned a wholesale liquor warehouse. He began construction on the seven-story skyscraper, but prohibition began to affect Salisbury and building had to be halted until Grubb received some financial help. In 1913, Clay Grubb, who had earlier killed his brother-in-law in self-defense, was killed by his wife. She alleged that her drunken husband had beaten her, and she was cleared of all charges. (Top image: courtesy of the Durwood Barbour Collection; right: courtesy of the Rowan Public Library.)

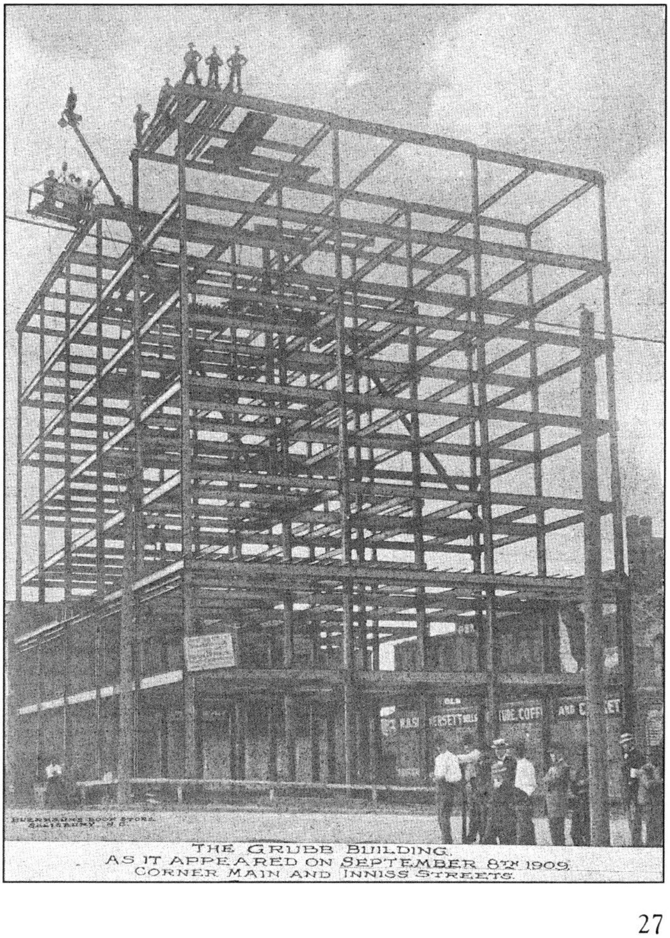

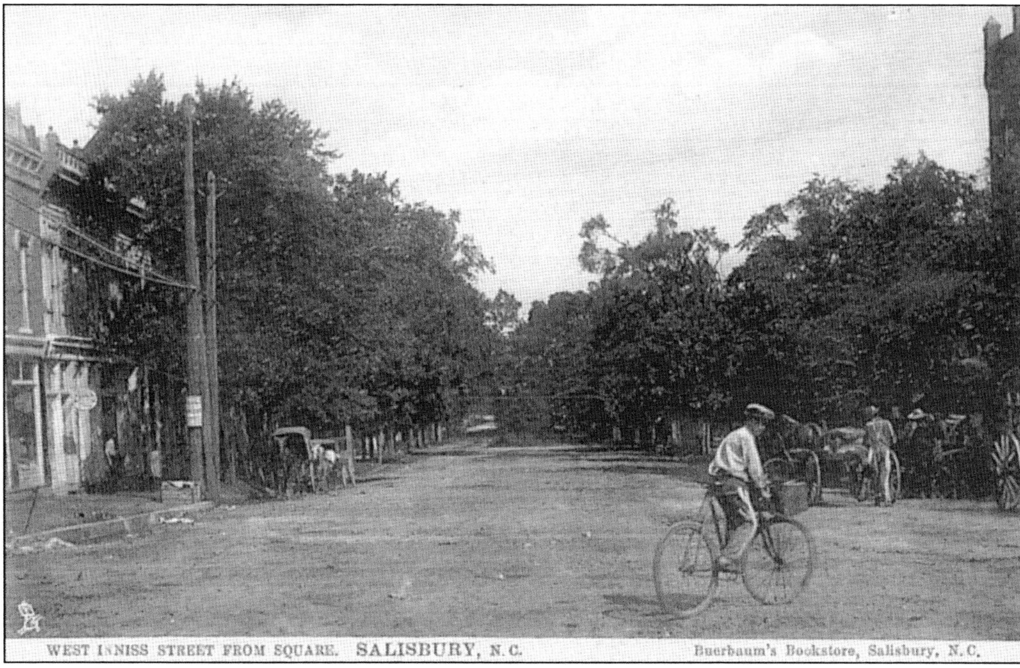

This view of Salisbury's West Innes Street from the square shows no post office, no Confederate Monument, no paved sidewalks, and no cars! The tree-lined road gives a glimpse of 1907 Salisbury. (Courtesy of the Marian Harter Collection.)

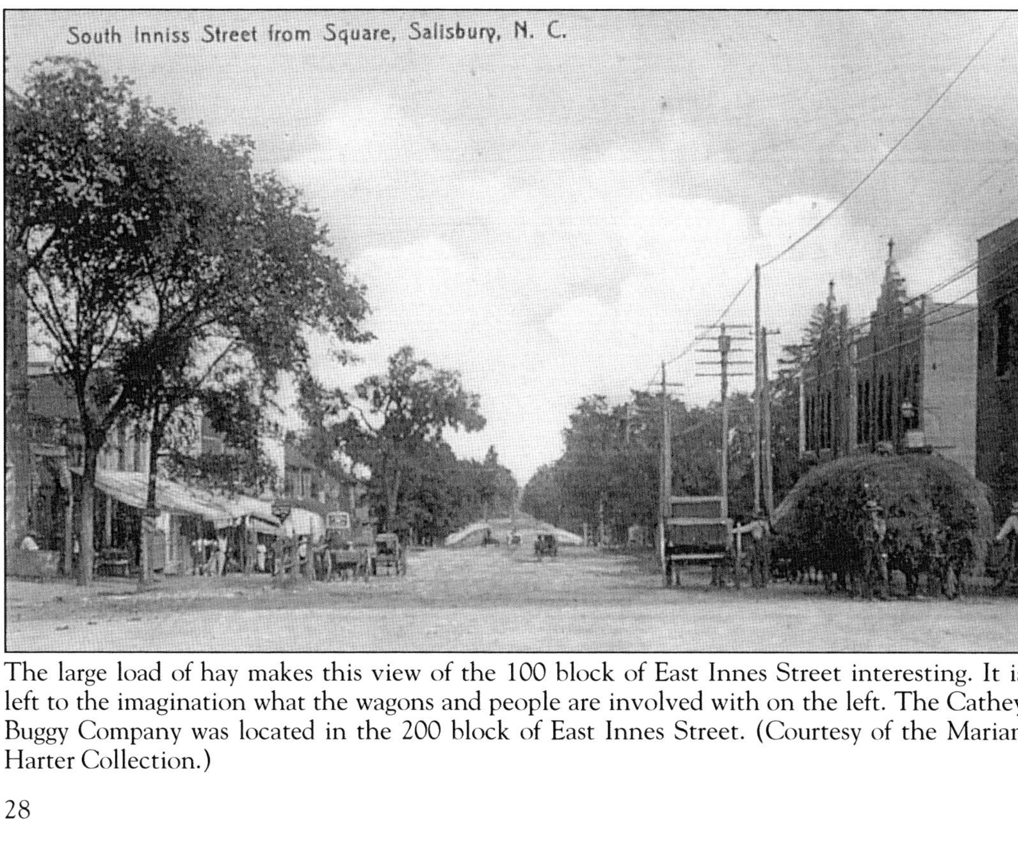

The large load of hay makes this view of the 100 block of East Innes Street interesting. It is left to the imagination what the wagons and people are involved with on the left. The Cathey Buggy Company was located in the 200 block of East Innes Street. (Courtesy of the Marian Harter Collection.)

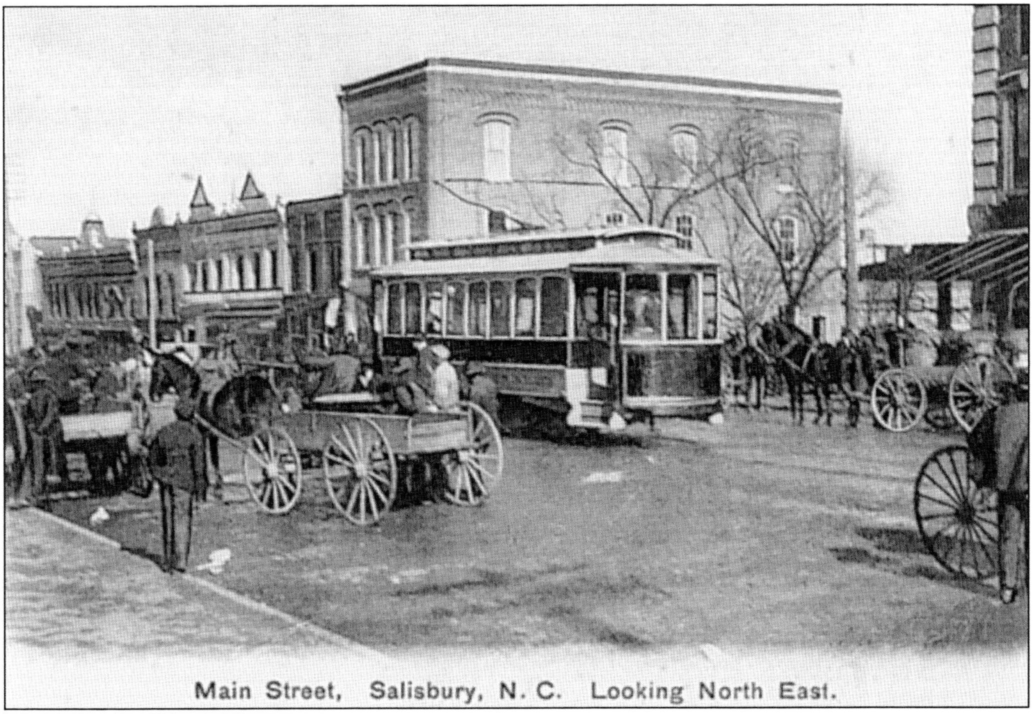

This spectacular view shows a busy day in downtown Salisbury in the early 1900s. The trolley car seems almost planted in the midst of a community of horses and wagons. Changes are under way!

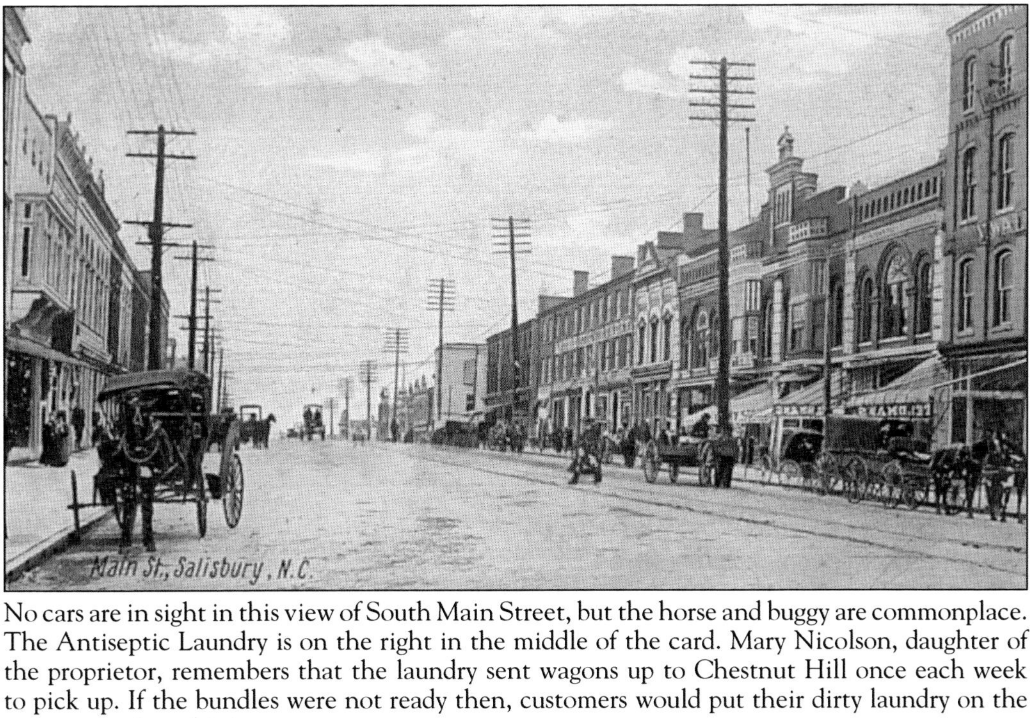

No cars are in sight in this view of South Main Street, but the horse and buggy are commonplace. The Antiseptic Laundry is on the right in the middle of the card. Mary Nicolson, daughter of the proprietor, remembers that the laundry sent wagons up to Chestnut Hill once each week to pick up. If the bundles were not ready then, customers would put their dirty laundry on the streetcar and send it into town.

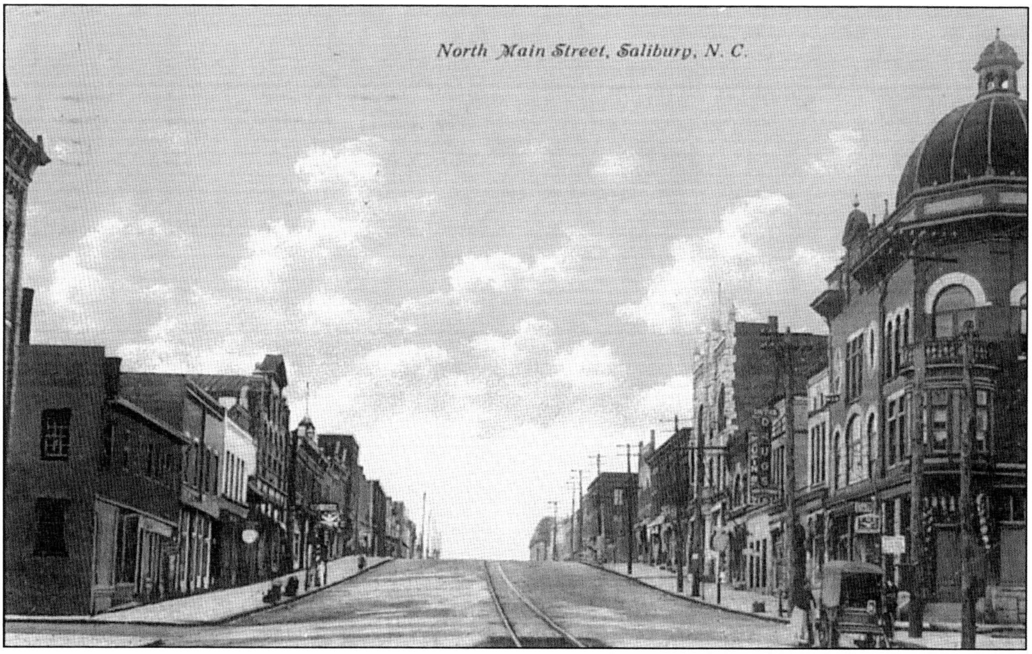

Salisbury has sidewalks in this view. Smith's Drugs and Maupin Brothers, a real estate and general insurance firm, are identified in signs on the right. The building with the onion dome was the Salisbury Savings Bank.

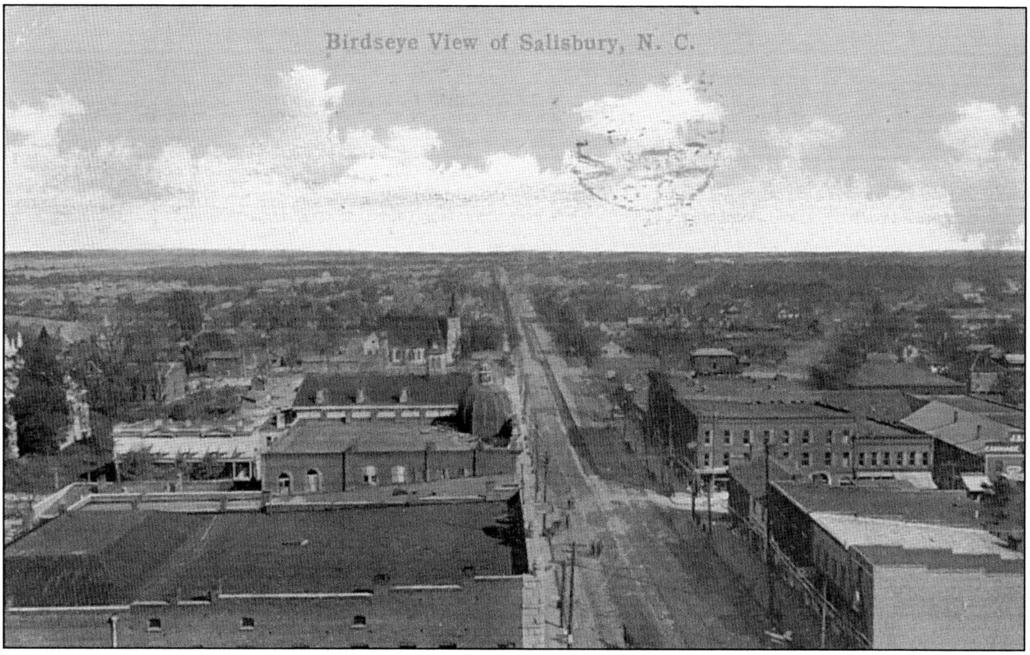

On October 14, 1927, Col. Charles Lindbergh was making a cross-country tour in his famous monoplane, *Spirit of St. Louis*, and was scheduled to fly over Salisbury. Many people were atop the Wallace Building, and the streets were filled. A view much like this one must have met the famous aviator as he circled low, tilted his plane to a side angle, and dropped greetings.

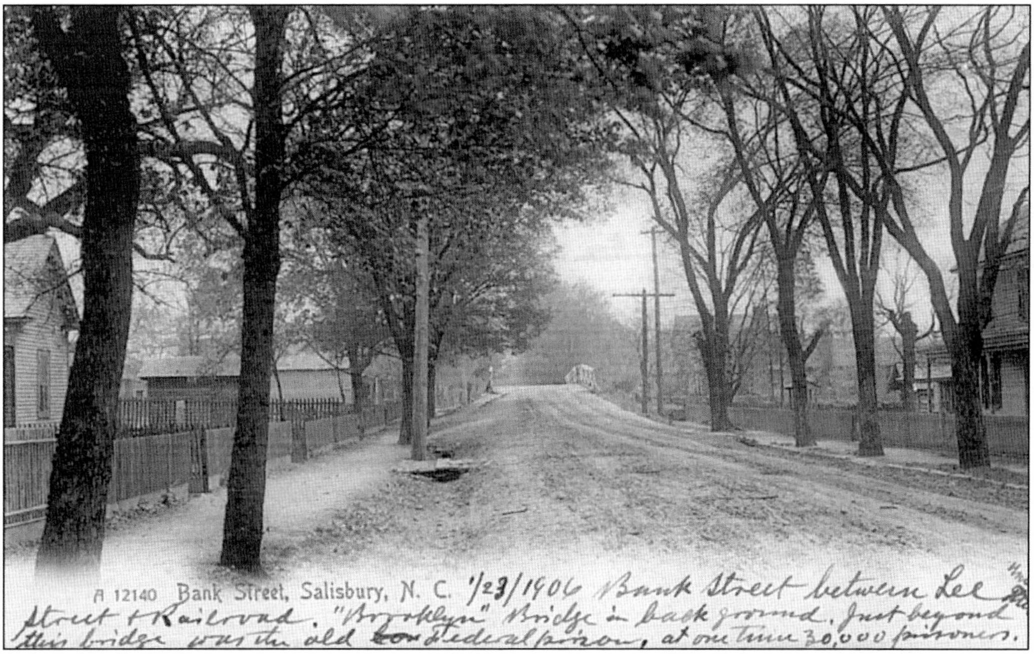

This card shows the homes built on the site of the Confederate Prison; Buerbaum's note says, "Bank Street between Lee Street and Railroad. 'Brooklyn Bridge' in background. Just beyond this bridge was the old Federal prison, at one time 30,000 prisoners."

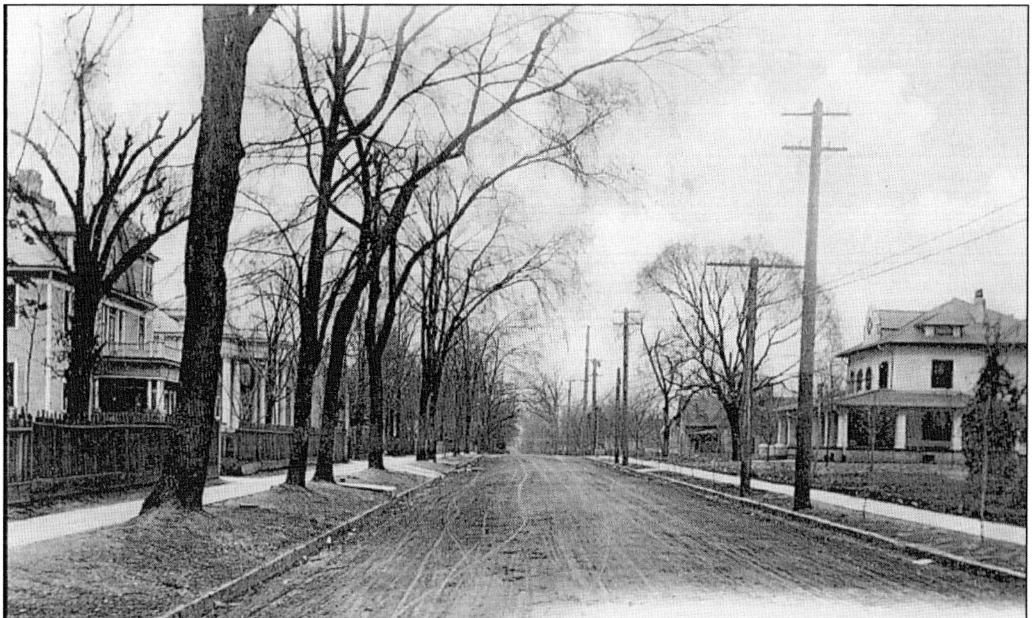

Fulton Street was named for John Fulton. He finished a boardinghouse for students of the Salisbury Academy in 1821. Actor Sidney Blackmer later lived in this home. The homes on the left are the Ramsey home and the Cannon-Guille home, and on the right is the home of Col. F.F. Smith.

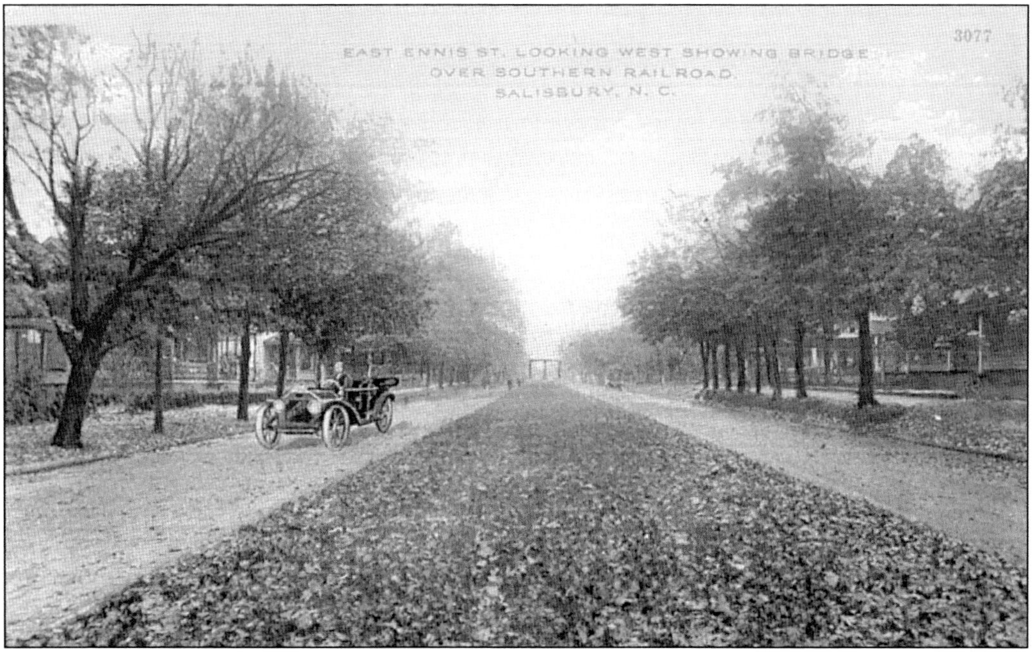

It seems impossible to imagine Salisbury's East Innes Street, now home to chain restaurants and other businesses, as a tree-lined residential area. The message on the reverse of this card says, "Apples are plentiful here and scuppernong grapes are ripe. We're going for a ramble this afternoon and hope to find some!"

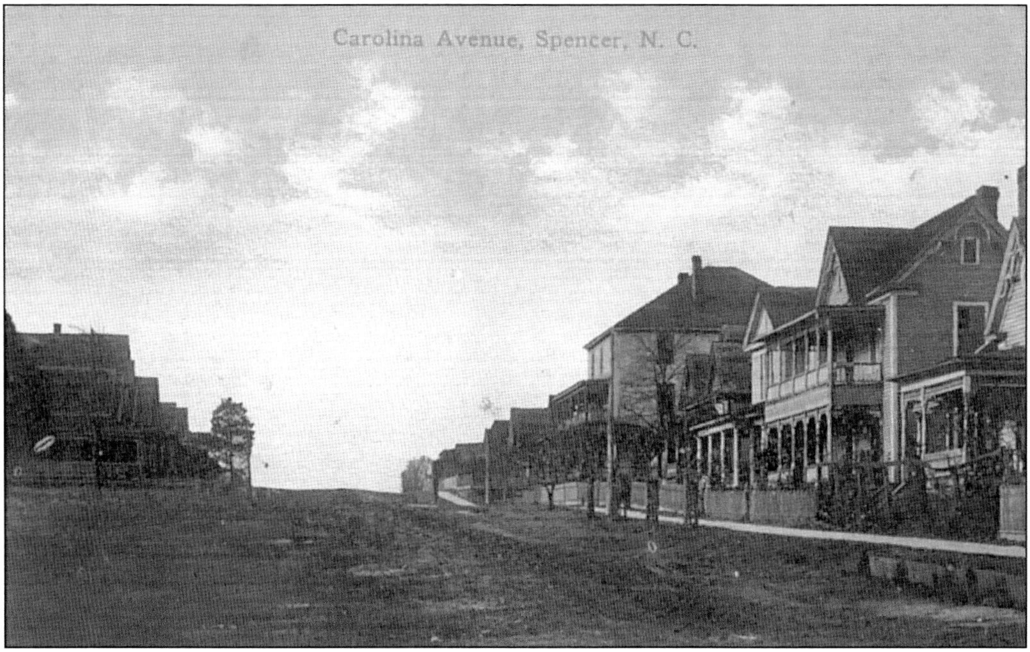

Carolina Avenue in Spencer was a residential area. The street appears to be strictly grass and dirt in this *c.* 1910 view.

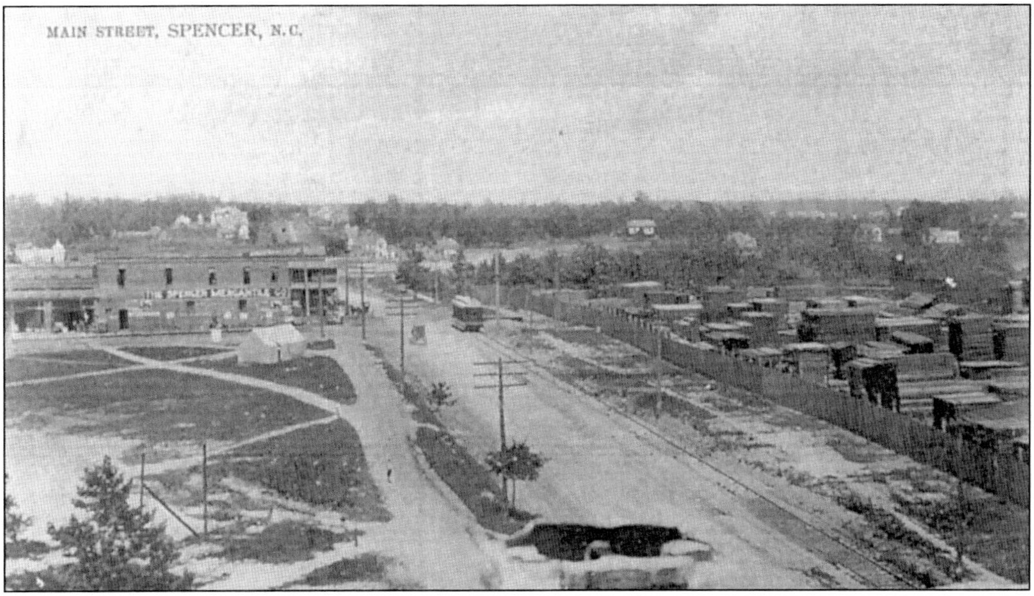

Spencer had a trolley that followed Main Street all the way to Salisbury. The Spencer Mercantile Company, shown on the card, supplied the community with a wide variety of items. The railroad brought many changes to this community through the years. Hundreds of people came to Spencer to work on the railroad, which in turn brought new residences and businesses to this area. (Courtesy of the Durwood Barbour Collection.)

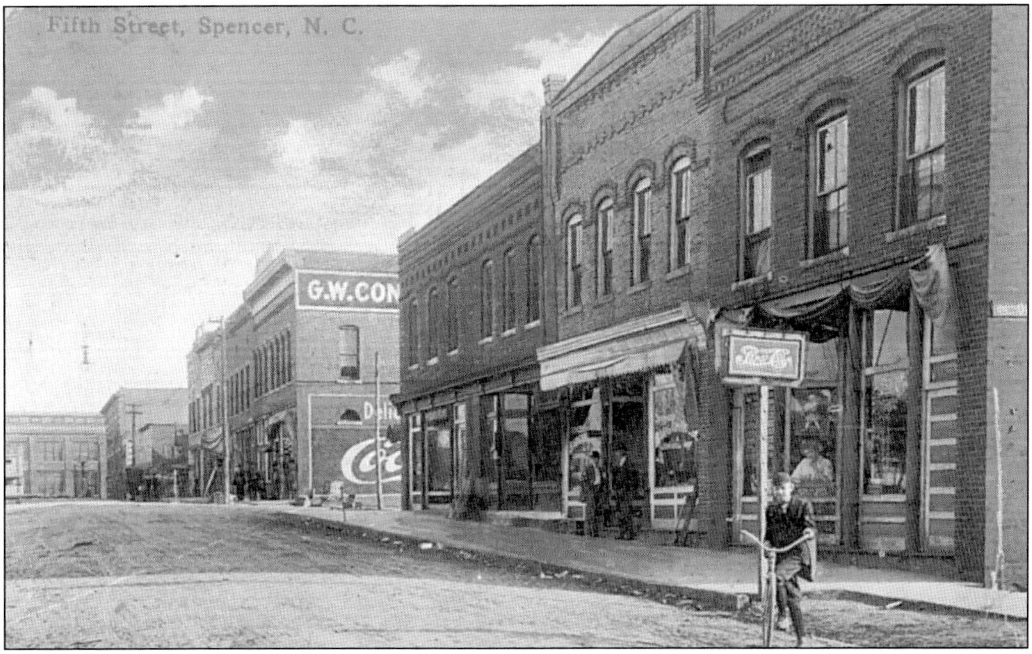

In 1910, Fifth Street in Spencer had a jeweler, a druggist, a physician, a baker, a clothing store, and a hardware store. In 1924, Dr. Tom Stanback and his brother Fred began the promotion of Stanback headache powder. Their first business was located in the 200 block of Fifth Street in Spencer. The company is now located on South Main Street in Salisbury. (Courtesy of the Marian Harter Collection.)

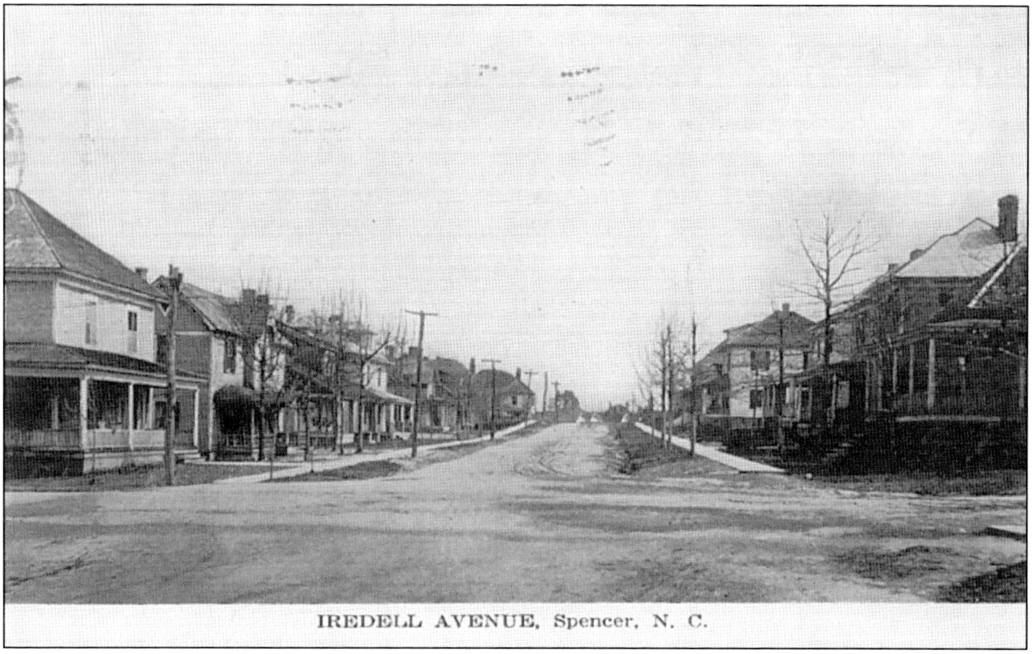

A view of Iredell Avenue in Spencer, *c.* 1910, shows the beautiful large residences on unpaved streets. Notice the power lines. (Courtesy of the Marian Harter Collection.)

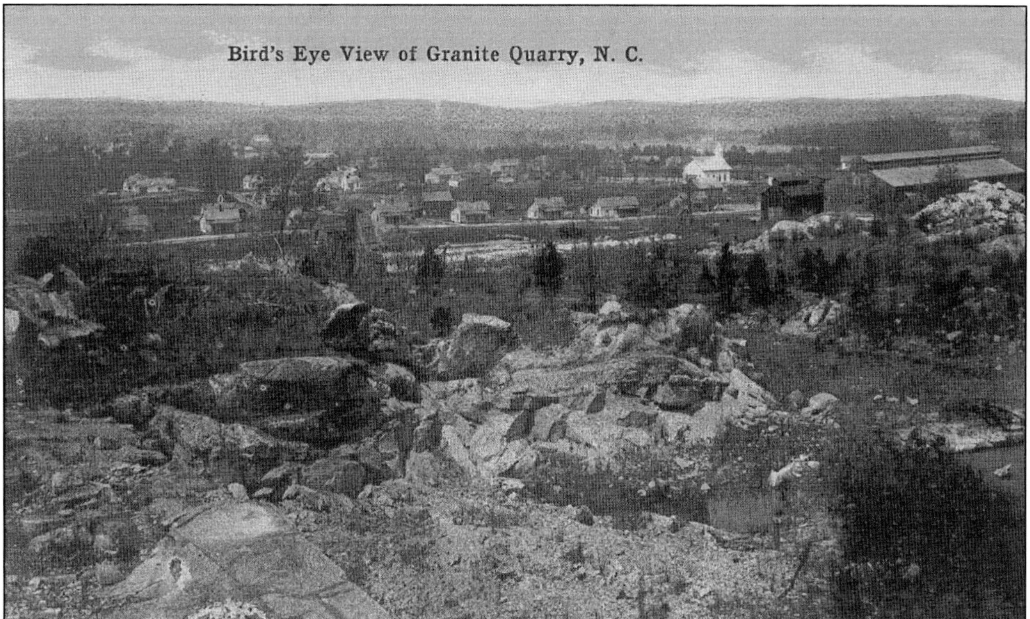

This view of Granite Quarry shows the small houses used by the stonecutters employed by the local quarries. The old Shiloh Methodist Church can be seen beyond Rowan Quarry's warehouse. (Courtesy of the Rowan Public Library.)

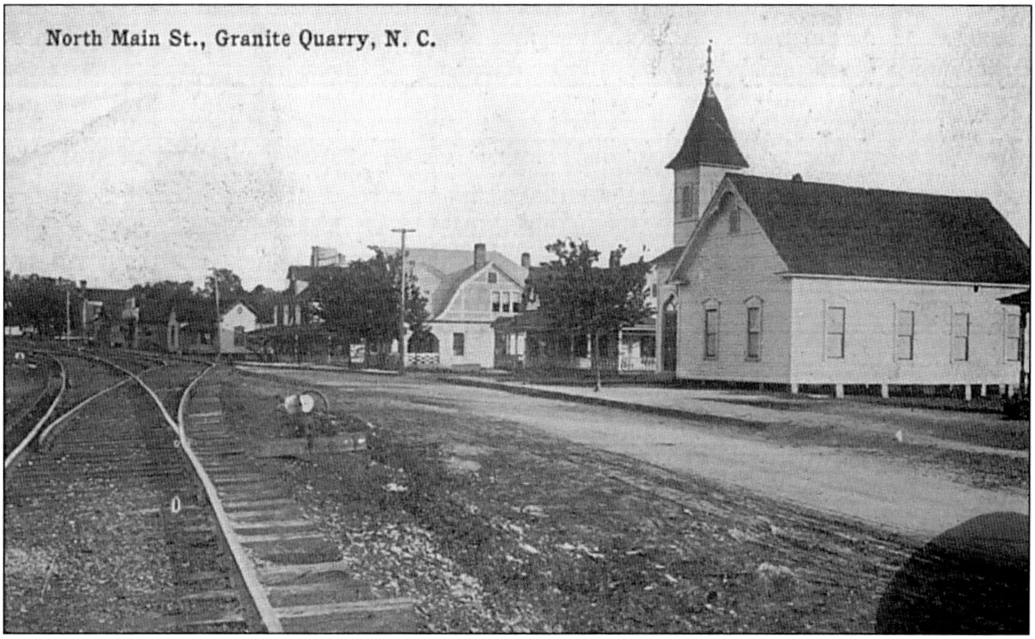

Granite Quarry was incorporated in 1901. Earlier known as Woodside, after the Wood family, the town changed its name in 1905 because of the volume of granite quarries in the vicinity. This view shows J.H.A. Lyerly's store, several residences, and the old Wittenburg Church, which burned in the 1940s.

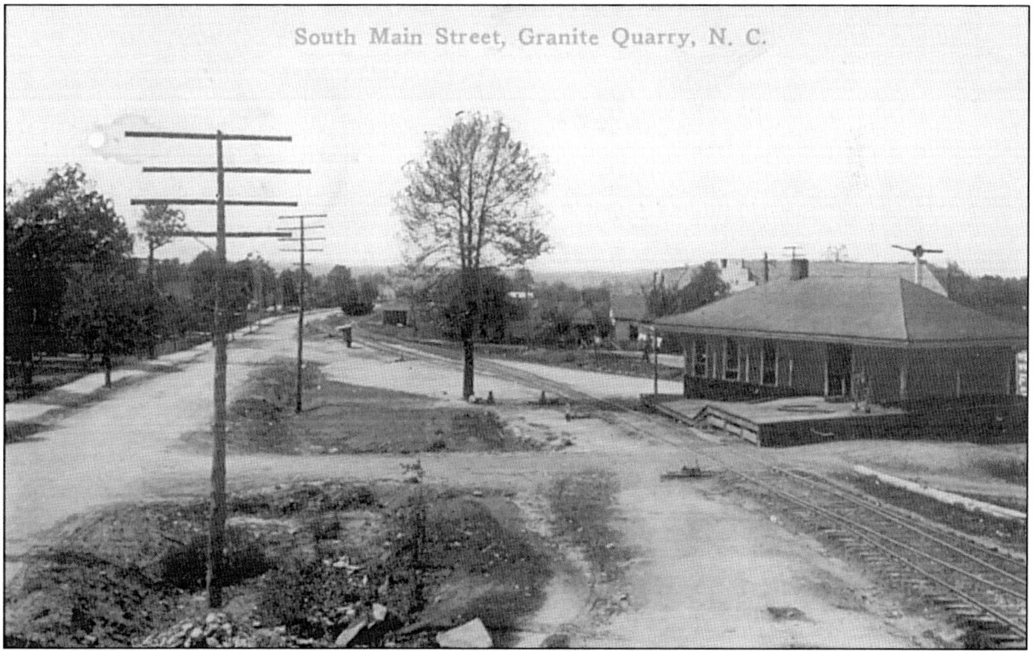

The railroad dominates this South Main Street Granite Quarry view. Streets are dirt, but power lines have been installed.

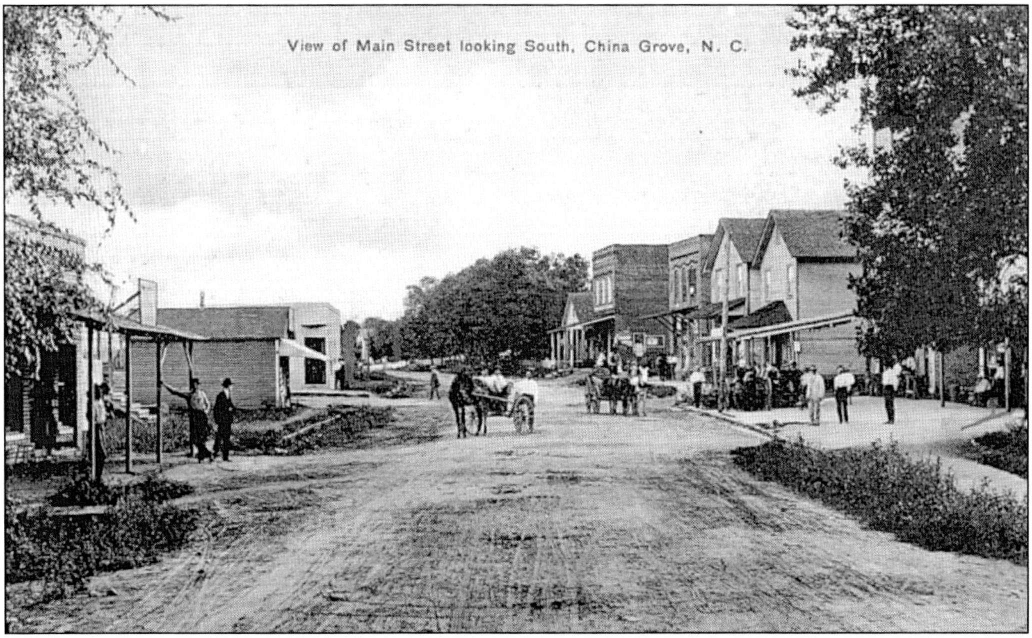

China Grove was so named because of the abundance of Chinaberry trees in this area. This Main Street view is dated 1908.

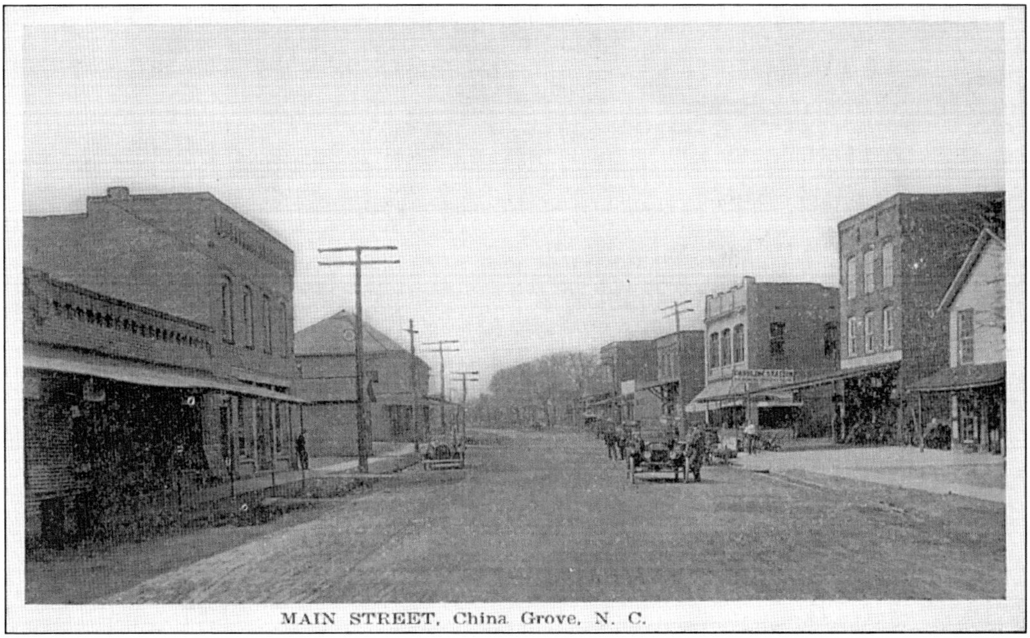

The town of China Grove has the distinction of being the first town in North Carolina and the second in the nation to have Rural Free Mail Delivery. (Courtesy of the Sarah Manning Pope Collection.)

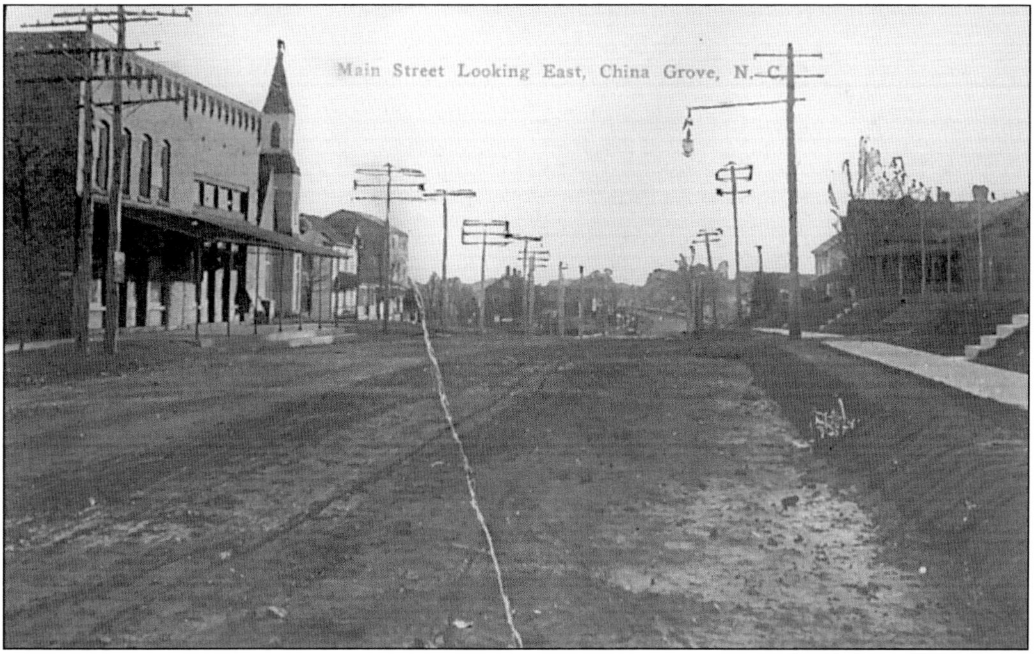

Paved sidewalks began to be installed in 1917 in China Grove. Notice that the sidewalks are higher than the unpaved road. The first St. Mark's Lutheran Church is shown on the left.

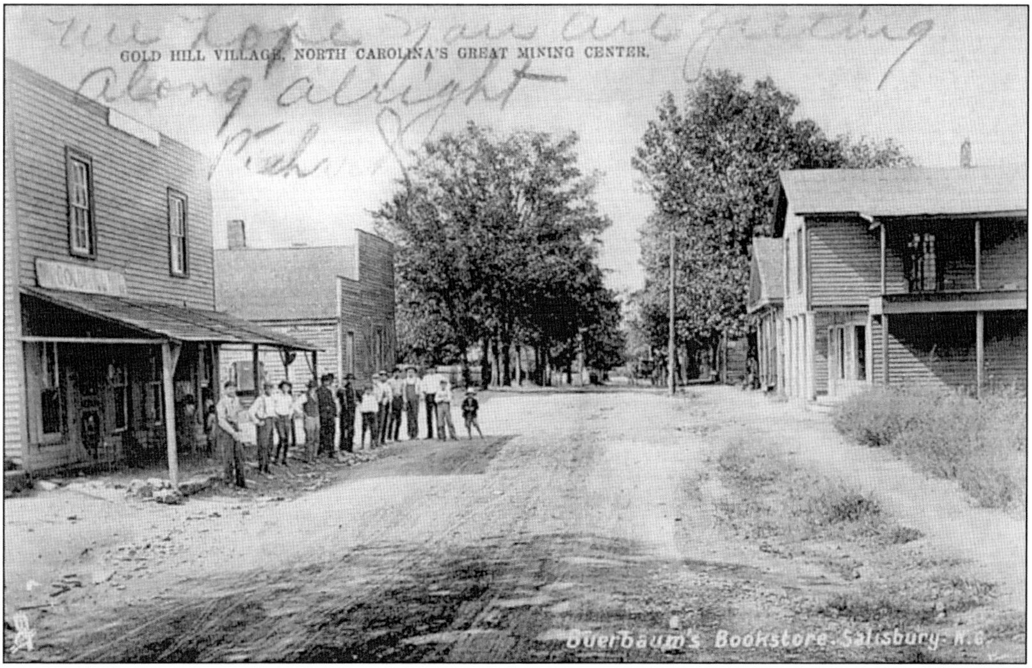

This view of Gold Hill resembles an old western scene. Mining operations were plentiful in Gold Hill from 1842 to the early 1900s, and both gold and copper were mined in this area. (Courtesy of the Wayne R. Chapman Collection.)

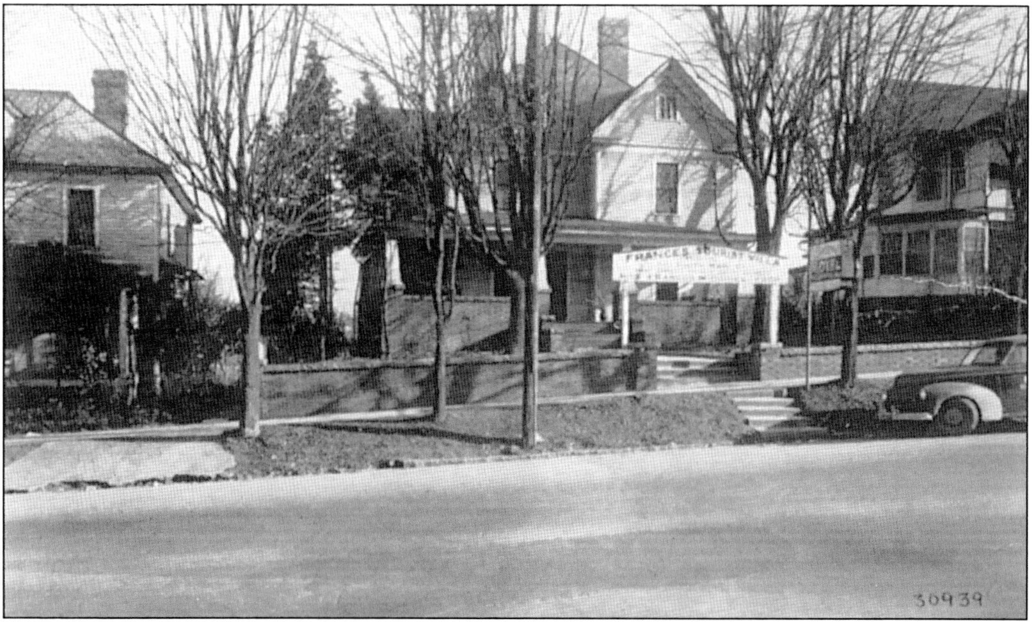

The Frances Tourist Villa was owned by Joseph and Frances McDaniel and was located at 721 South Main Street in Salisbury.

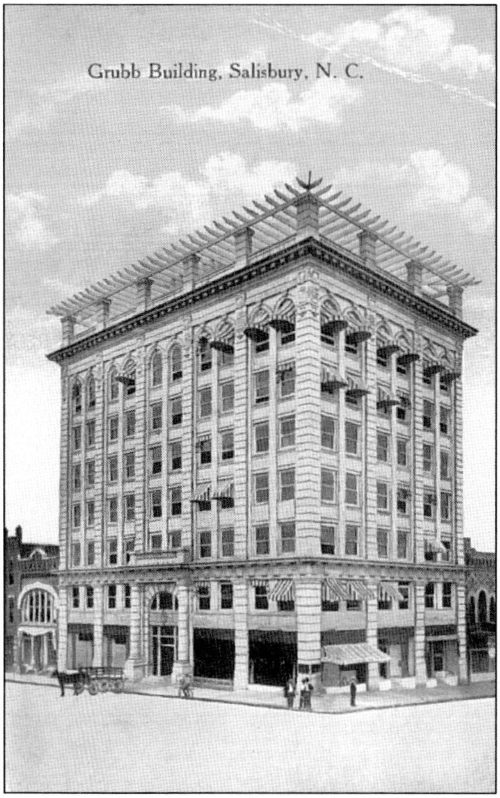

The Grubb Building, completed in 1910, was bought by Jake and Leo Wallace in 1914 and renamed the Wallace Building. Anne and Ralph Ketner purchased the building and, in conjunction with the City of Salisbury, completely renovated the structure. In 1991, the Ketners gave the Plaza to the City of Salisbury.

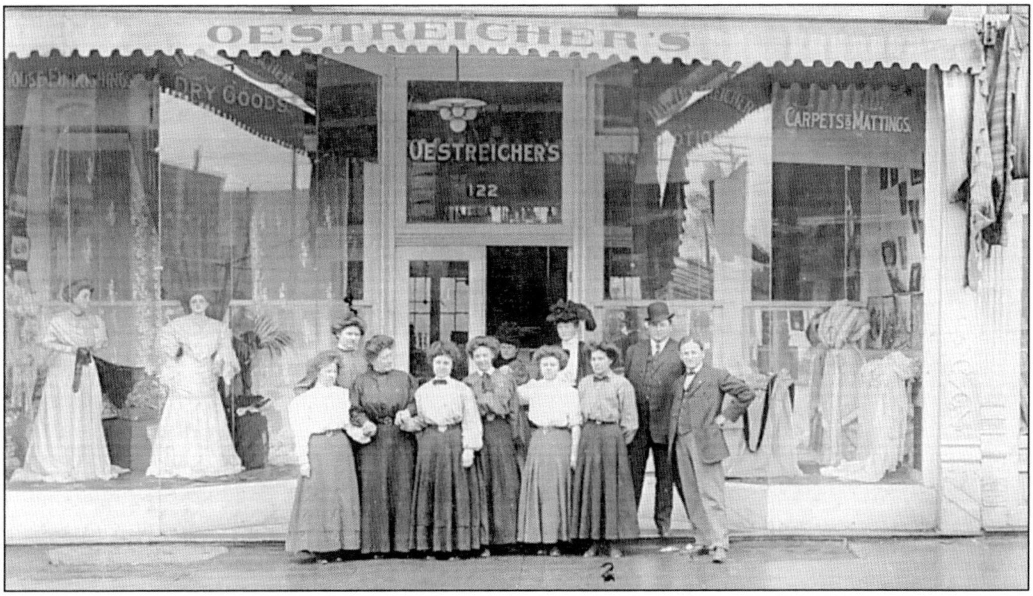

David Oestreicher, on the far right, had a tremendous impact on Rowan County. In fact, Theo Buerbaum moved to Salisbury because of their friendship! Located at 122 South Main Street, Oestreicher's store sold a variety of goods ranging from the beautiful bustle dresses on the left to matting from China, which was used as floor coverings. The tall lady in the second row on the left is believed to be America Aaron Weinbrum, who married Carl Weinbrum. The couple met at Oestreicher's and both worked there approximately 50 years. Oestreicher's, under David and his son Irvin, was for many years one of Salisbury's "fancy stores." (Courtesy of Rachel Oestreicher Bernheim.)

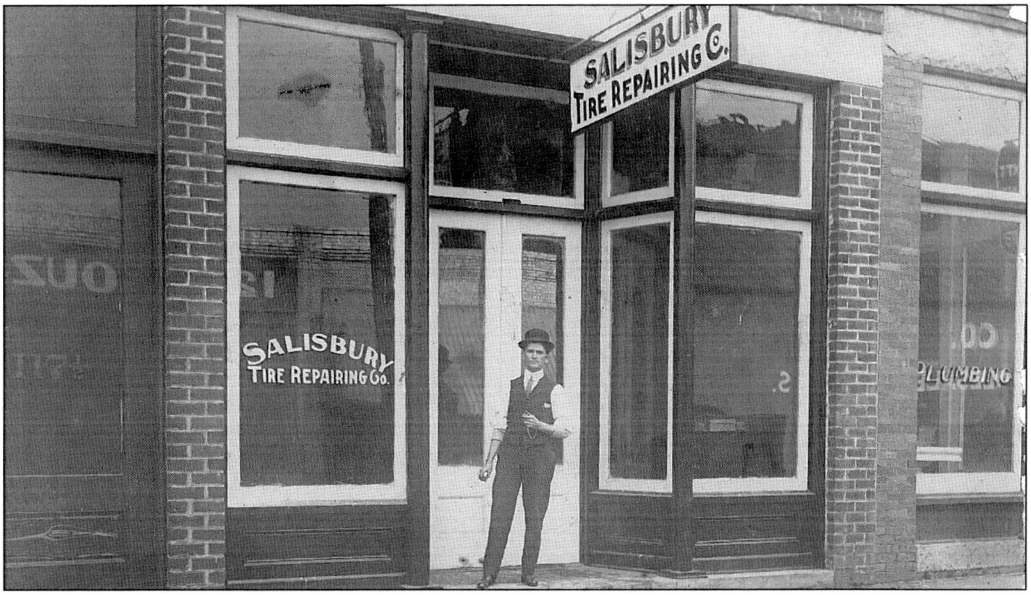

Salisbury Tire Repairing Company was located at 117 1/2 North Main Street. The owner John N. Haden was known as "Hurry Up Haden." He later moved to 217–219 North Main Street and then again to the 300 block of North Main at the site of the Crawford Professional Building. (Courtesy of the Rowan Public Library.)

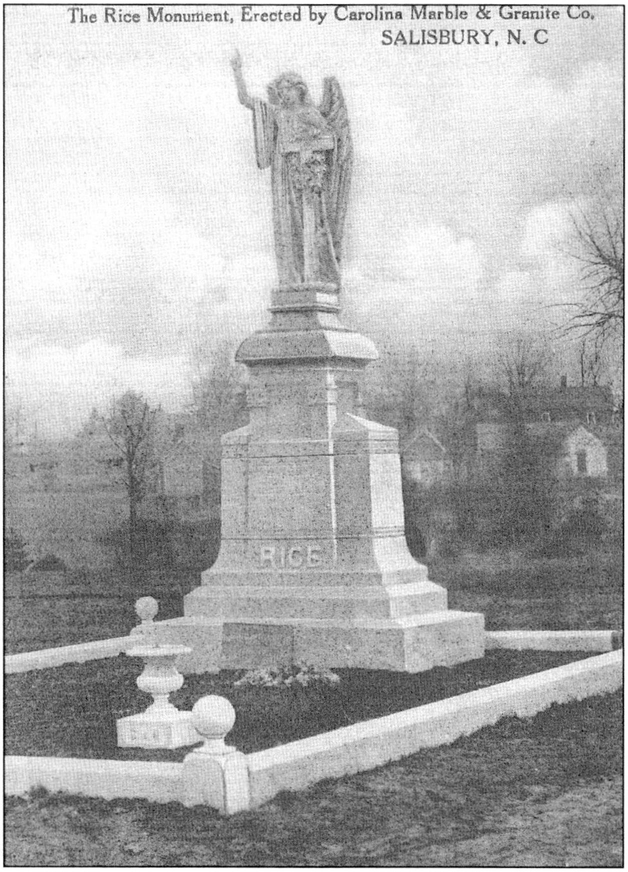

The impressive Rice monument, erected by Carolina Marble and Granite, is located in Chestnut Hill Cemetery. Cathew Albert Rice and his wife are buried at the foot of this monument. (Courtesy of the Rowan Public Library.)

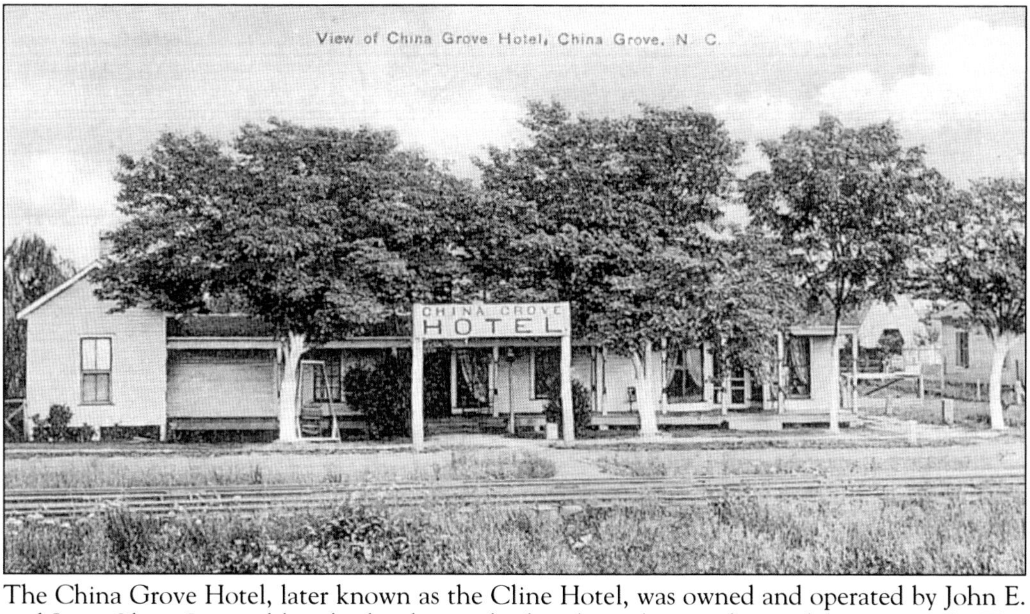

The China Grove Hotel, later known as the Cline Hotel, was owned and operated by John E. and Josie Cline. Located beside the depot, the hotel was known for its delicious meals. The building was demolished to make way for offices. (Courtesy of the Marian Harter Collection.)

The Washington Building at 118–120 North Main Street was built in 1902 on the site of the Yarborough House where Pres. George Washington allegedly spent the night in 1791. At the time this card was made, the building housed Rowan Hardware on the left and Rogers Clothing Company on the right. (Card from Buerbaum.)

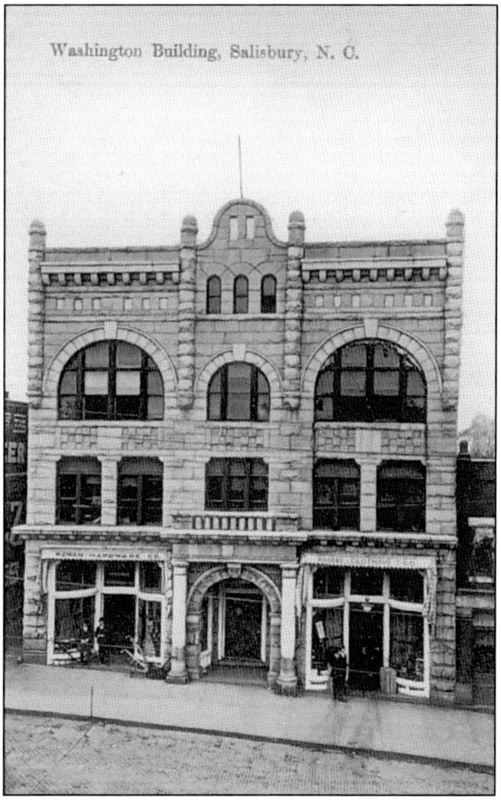

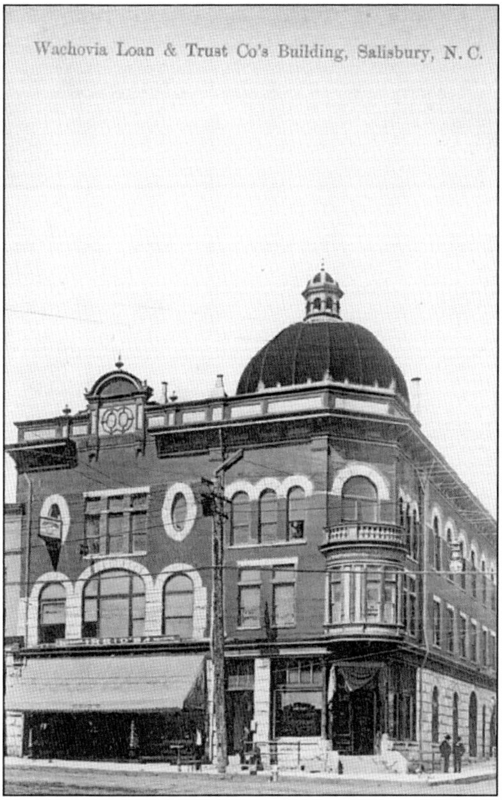

The Salisbury Savings Bank was erected on the corner of Council and Main Streets in 1900. The bank merged with Wachovia Loan Company of Winston-Salem in 1903. The old bank building was razed in 1926, and a new building, which would eventually house the city government, was built. (Card from Buerbaum.)

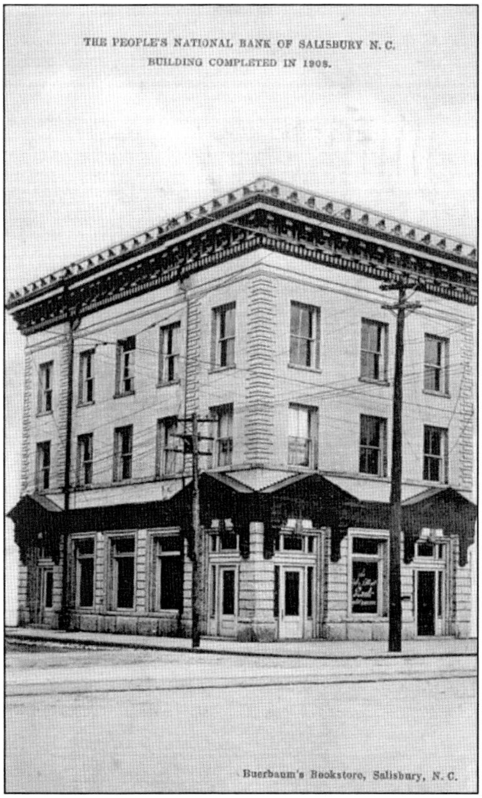

The Peoples National Bank was organized in October 1905. Subscribers were R. Lee Wright, N.B. McCanless, J.D. Norwood, D.R. Julian, John S. Henderson, and T.M. Kerns. The bank closed in August 1923. Its failure was attributed to the connection the bank had with the Mecklenburg Mills, which went into bankruptcy. Following long litigation, depositors were finally paid approximately 57 percent of the money they had on deposit when the bank ceased operation.

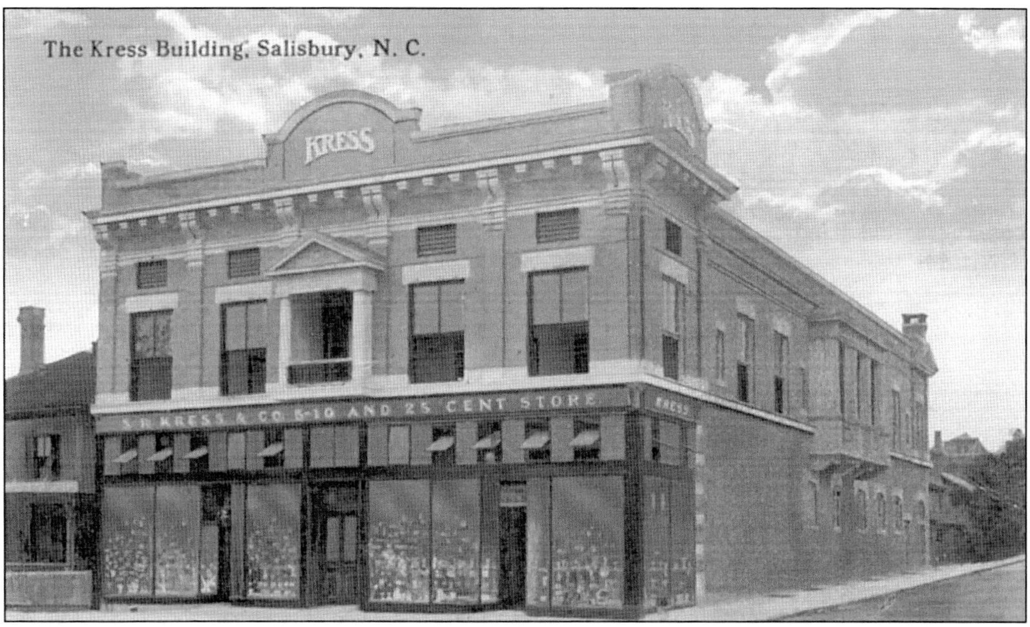

In March 1907, S.H. Kress purchased property on the corner of Main and Bank Streets on which to erect a store. Kress opened in 1910 as a variety store, employing 40 people, and came to be called a "five and dime" store. The first concert of the Salisbury Cornet Band, one in a long and distinguished line of Salisbury brass bands, was played at the Kress opening.

The Meroney Theatre, which opened in 1905, welcomed to its stage such well-known talents as Sarah Bernhardt, Lillian Russell, John Philip Sousa, and William Howard Taft. The Old Hickory Club, a gentleman's social club in Salisbury, and the Masons shared this building with the theatre. (Card from Buerbaum.)

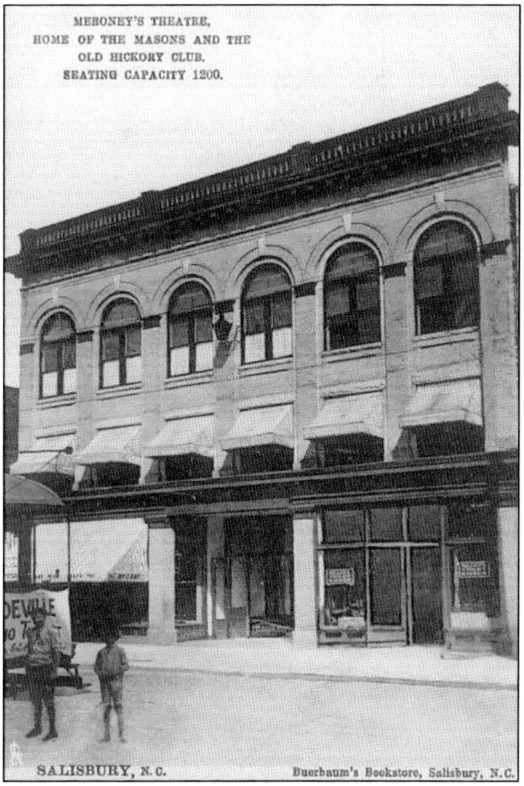

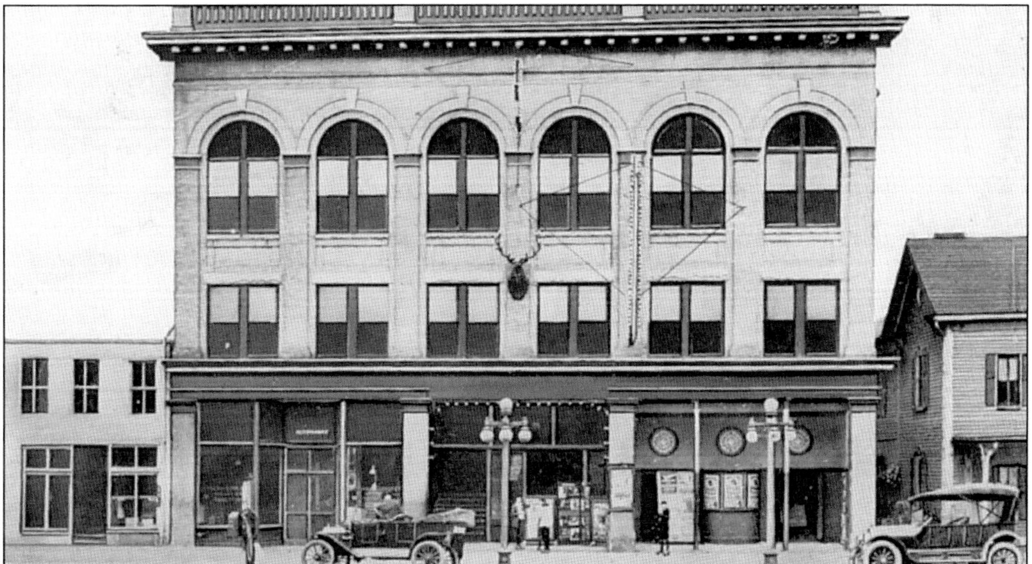

This view illustrates some of the changes the Meroney has undergone. Called the Colonial Theatre at the time this view was made, the Masons and the Elks (notice the Elk head on the building) claimed it as home. The Meroney Theatre was restored and reopened in 1995 as home to the Piedmont Players. (Courtesy of the Marian Harter Collection.)

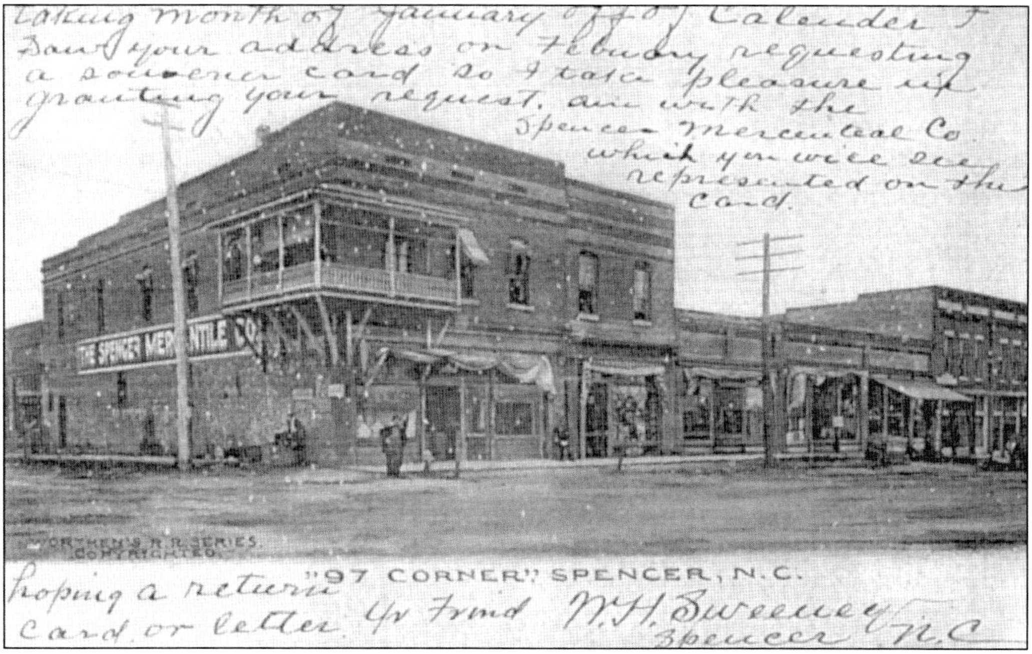

Spencer Mercantile on the corner of Fourth Street and Salisbury Avenue was a two-story, three-section building with a double-tier porch. The building held a general store, Bryan Drug, and the Bank of Spencer. Calling this "97 Corner" may be referring to the mail train "The Old 97" that traveled from Monroe, Virginia, to Spencer and wrecked, killing 11 people. The incident was immortalized in a famous ballad. (Courtesy of the Durwood Barbour Collection.)

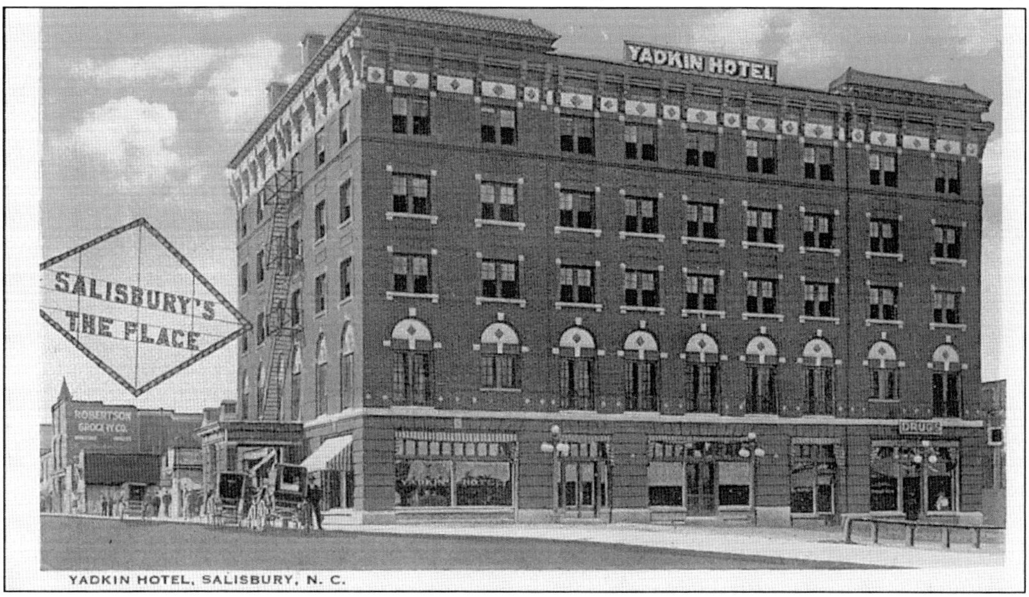

The Yadkin Hotel, built in 1912, was designed by the Charlotte firm of Wheeler and Sterne. Located across Salisbury's Depot Street from the Southern Railroad Station, the hotel was often crowded with overnight guests waiting for their trains. In 1913, the Industrial Club erected the largest electric sign in the state at the hotel, proclaiming "Salisbury's The Place." Sixty additional rooms were added to the hotel in 1922.

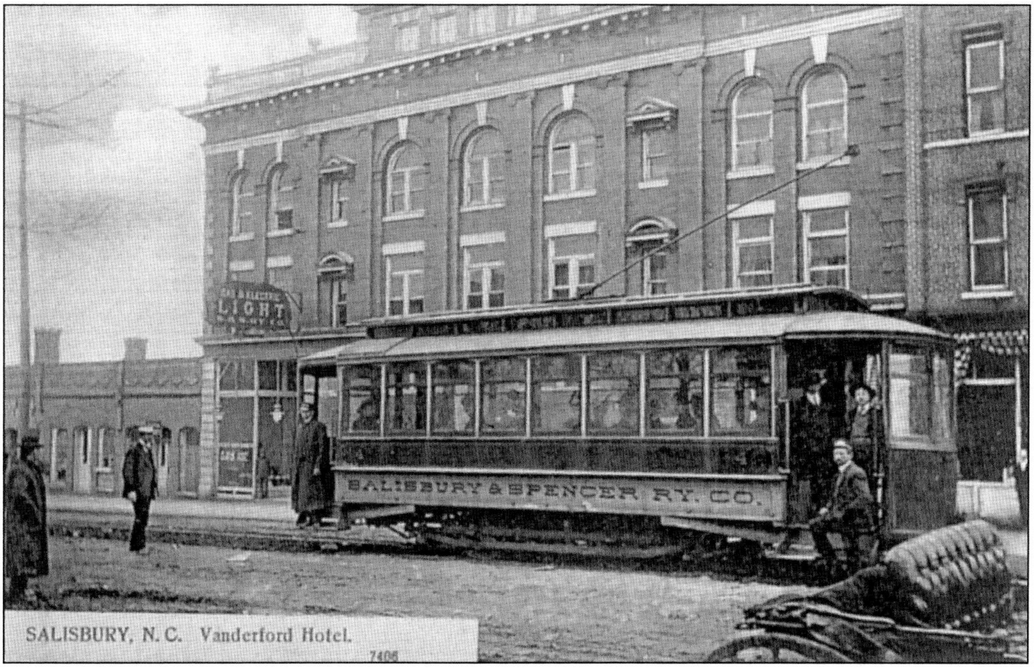

The Vanderford Hotel, later known as the Ford Hotel, was located on the northeast corner of Council and Main Streets. The first floor was Salisbury's Post Office. The second and third floors were the hotel. The Ford Hotel and Cafeteria also became known as the Earl, the Milner, and the Bates Hotel. Late in its life, this fine old hotel fell into disrepute, and the building was demolished in 1979–1980. (Courtesy of the Durwood Barbour Collection.)

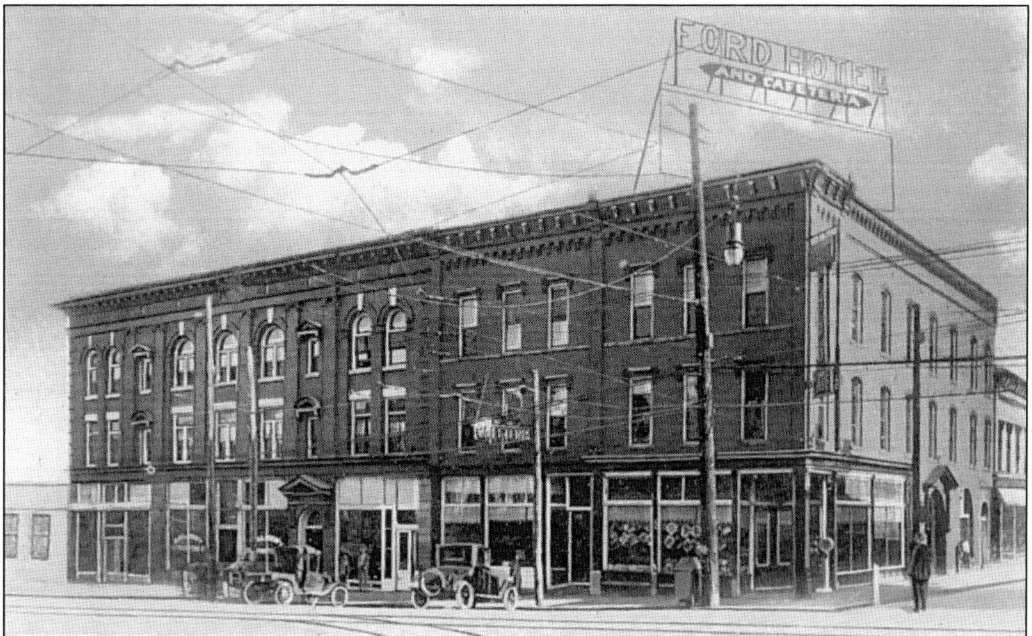

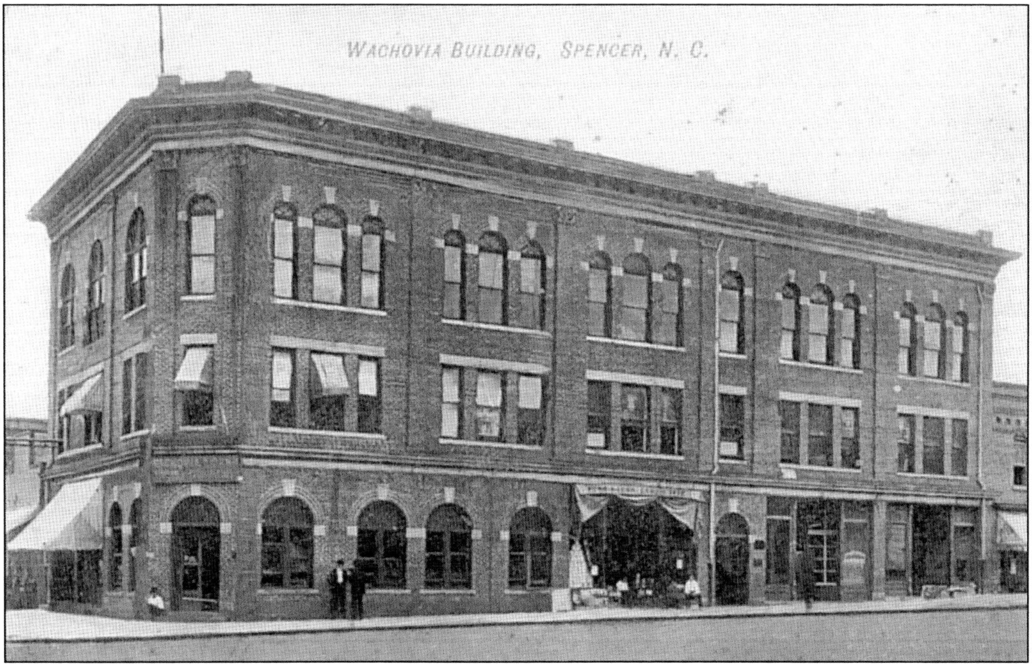

The Wachovia-First National Bank Building in Spencer was built in 1904 at Salisbury Avenue and Fifth Street. It later became First National Bank and, in 1923, Fidelity Bank. It was condemned and torn down in the 1970s.

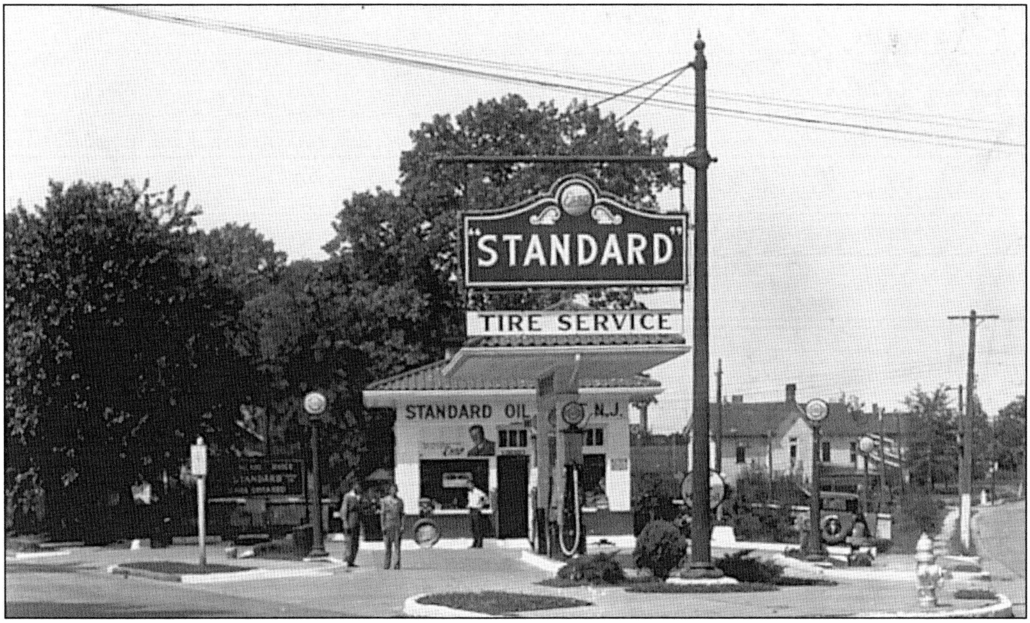

Rodgers Exxon located in the triangle bordered by Fulton, Lincolnton, and Harrison Streets started as "Buck" Rodgers Esso. On this card, C.L. "Buck" Rodgers is on the left. A.W. Fisher is on the right, and the man in the white shirt is not identified. This scene is dated approximately 1929. The Caleb Nussman home once stood at the location but was later moved and then torn down.

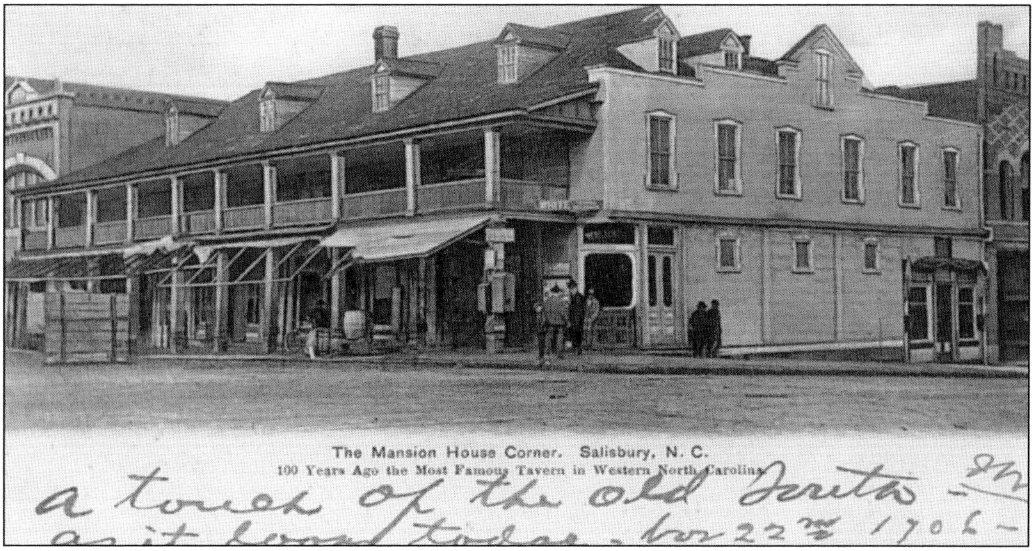

Salisbury's famous Mansion House stood on the square facing Innes Street on the site that would later hold the Grubb-Wallace Building. The tavern and inn attracted many visitors from the nearby train station. Stagecoaches and livery stables used the lot behind the inn. There were four stores facing Innes Street and two facing Main Street, which at one time included a barroom, a grocery store, a bakery, a jewelry store, and a barber shop. Fire destroyed the Mansion House in 1907.

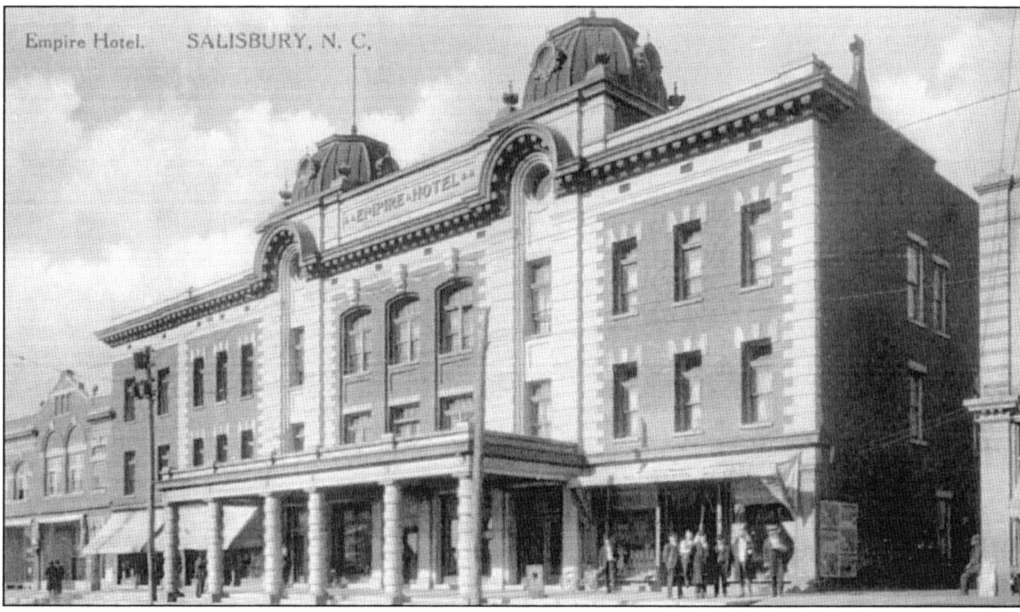

Originally built in 1855 by Nathaniel Boyden, this hotel was known as the Boyden House. Major renovations were made in 1907 by architect Frank Milburn, and the hotel's name was changed to the Central Hotel. It later became the Empire Hotel. The Empire advertised 75 rooms, including 25 with private baths. Among its famous guests were an ailing Robert E. Lee just before his death and Charlie Chaplin. In 1917, Chaplin came here to help with the Liberty Loan drive to sell war bonds. A crowd met him at the depot and followed him to the Empire Hotel. The Bond Drive went over the top in Salisbury. The hotel closed in 1959.

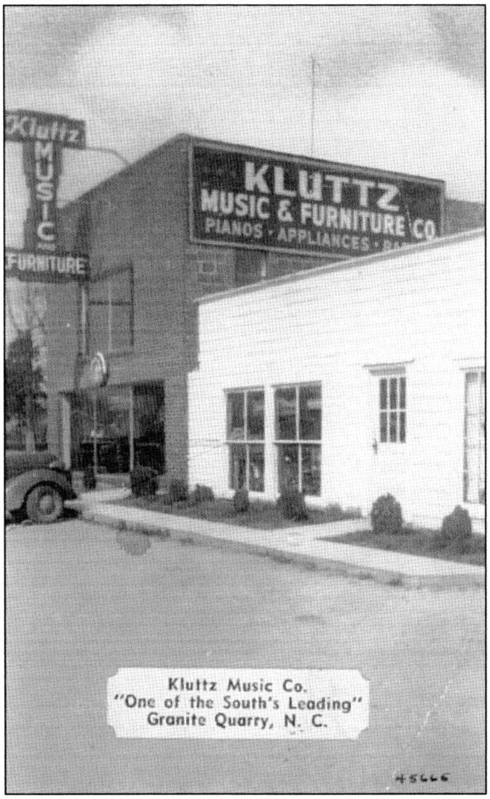

Granite Quarry's Kluttz Music and Furniture Company was organized in 1931 and was owned by George Lee Kluttz and Elbert Walker Kluttz. The company sold furniture, appliances, and musical instruments. The original brick building burned in the early 1950s. After the fire, only the piano business remained in operation. (Courtesy of the Marian Harter Collection.)

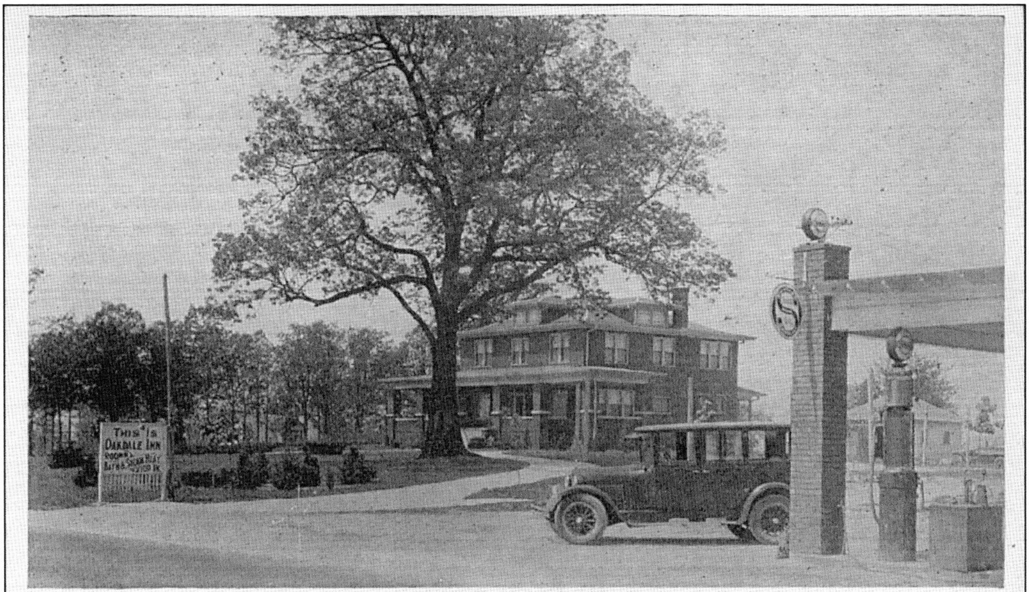

The Oakdale Inn, which advertised rooms, bath, and steam heat, was located in the 700 block of North Salisbury Avenue and Hudson Street in Spencer. The service station shown is long gone, but the inn is still standing and is now a private residence. (Courtesy of the Marian Harter Collection.)

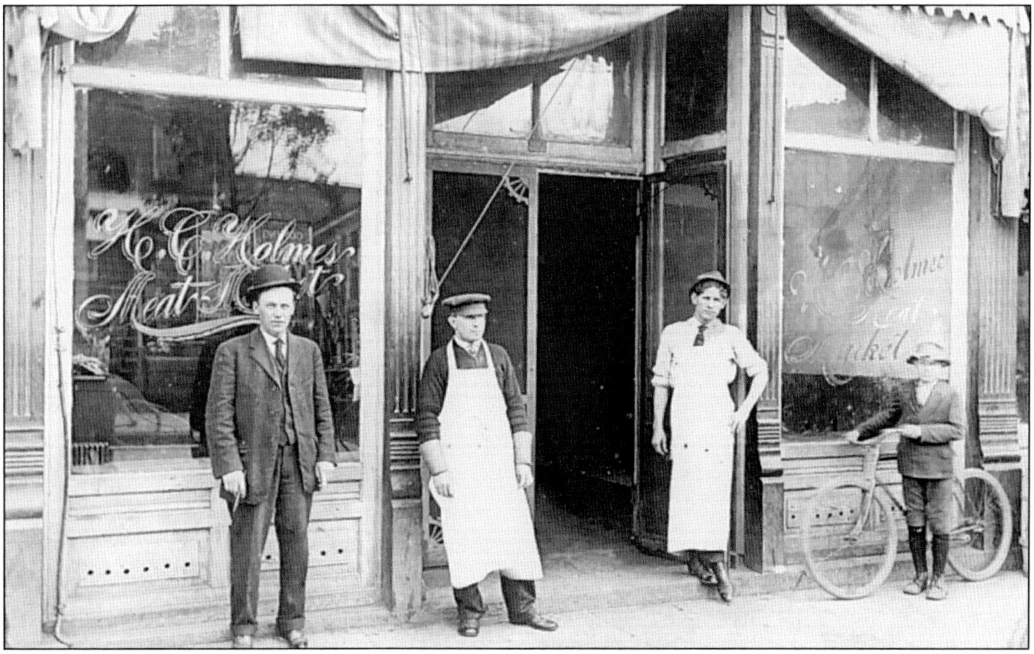

The H.C. Holmes Meat Market was owned by Haden Charles Holmes (pictured on the left), who bought the market from his father in 1904. Holmes served as city manager in Salisbury and died while in office. He was the driving force behind the creation of the City Lake and Park. Holmes was the grandfather of Jim and Gordon Hurley and the late Haden Hurley, Salisbury's prominent newspaper family.

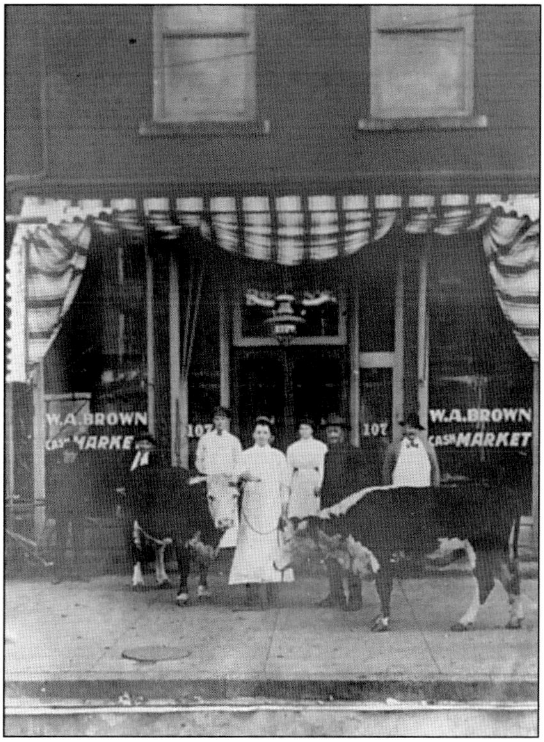

The W.A. Brown Cash Market was at 107 Main Street. This 1910 view shows western longhorn cows, which would be fattened with grain and slaughtered. The beef would be sold at the store. The market closed in the early 1930s. (Courtesy of Jack and Peg Swicegood.)

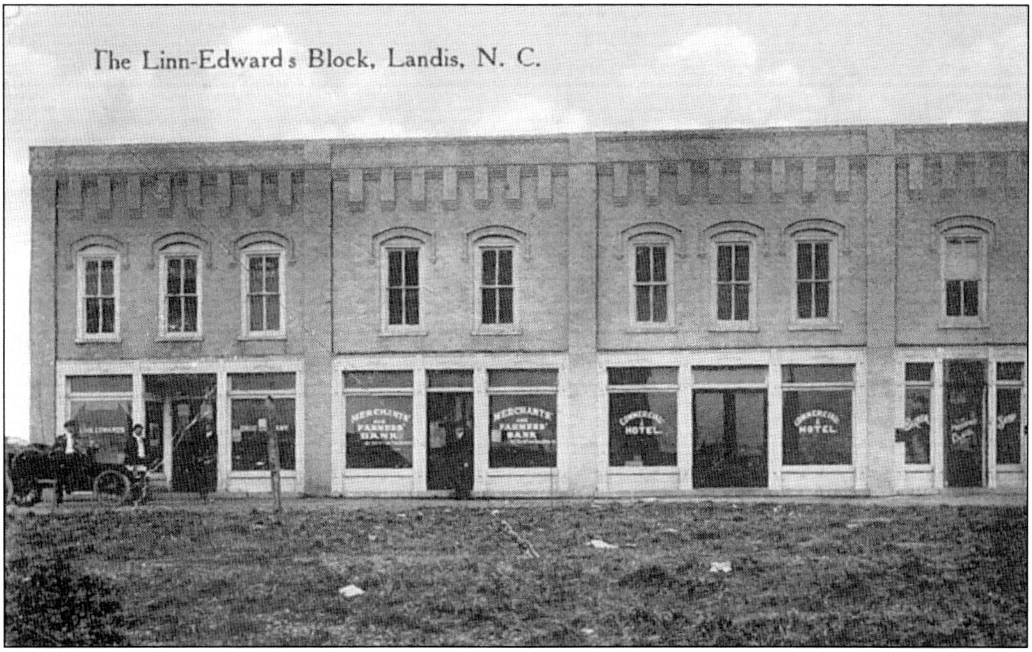

At the time of this image, the Linn-Edwards block in Landis housed, from left to right, the Linn-Edwards Drug Company, organized in 1911; the Merchants and Farmers Bank, organized in 1911; the Commercial Hotel; and a barber shop. The Merchants and Farmers Bank closed for one day during the Depression of the 1930s and reopened after the deposits were given a personal guarantee from Lotan Corriher. (Courtesy of the Marian Harter Collection.)

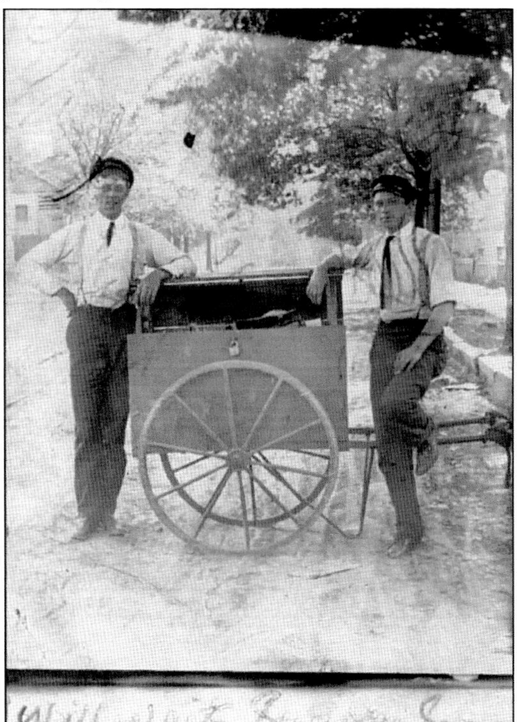

The trailer shown was the telephone service cart used to install phones in Salisbury. The man on the left is unidentified. On the right is Mr. W.A. Carter Sr. (the father of Don Carter), who became the manager of the telephone company here. This scene is dated 1907. (Courtesy of Don Carter.)

Three

Industry

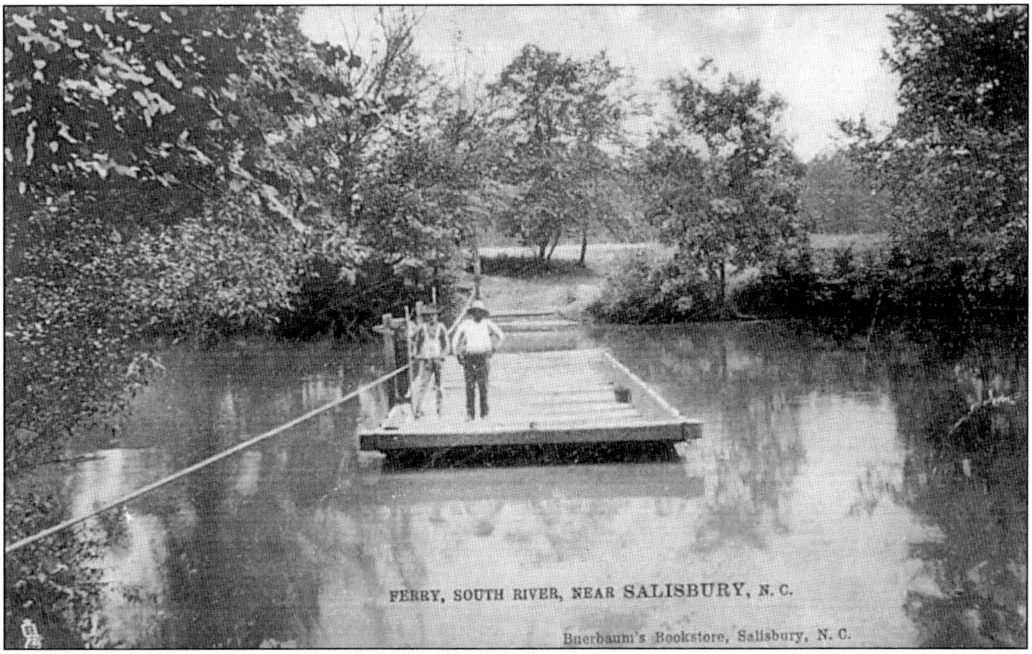

Ferries were built long enough and wide enough to accommodate two wagons with teams. Some ferrymen used an overhead cable that was attached to the ferry to keep it on course while other ferrymen used long poles or long oars to power the boat across the Yadkin River. The ferries, although long gone, are remembered in Salisbury's road names: Bringle Ferry, Long Ferry, and Stokes Ferry.

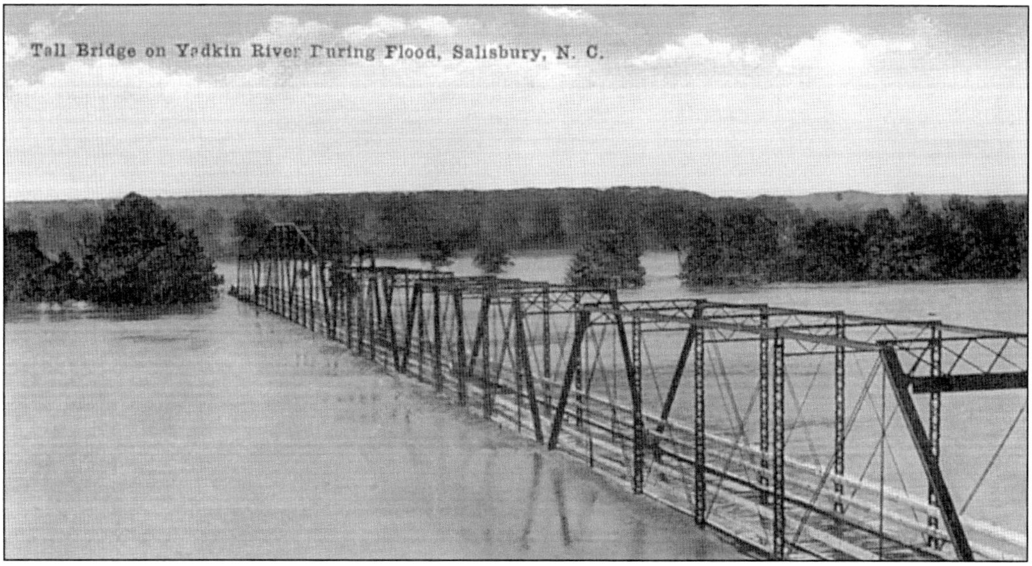

In July 1916, a hurricane hit Charleston, South Carolina, and moved into the North Carolina mountains. The result in Salisbury was 22 inches of rain that caused the Yadkin to rise higher than it ever had. Trees were uprooted, and logs, telephone poles, a cow, and a horse were all reported to be floating downstream. The water did cross over the bridge but somehow it managed to hold. Several thousand people gathered to see the raging waters. Traffic was discontinued by Bridge Keeper Yarborough. The toll bridge was operational until 1926 when it was replaced by a free bridge.

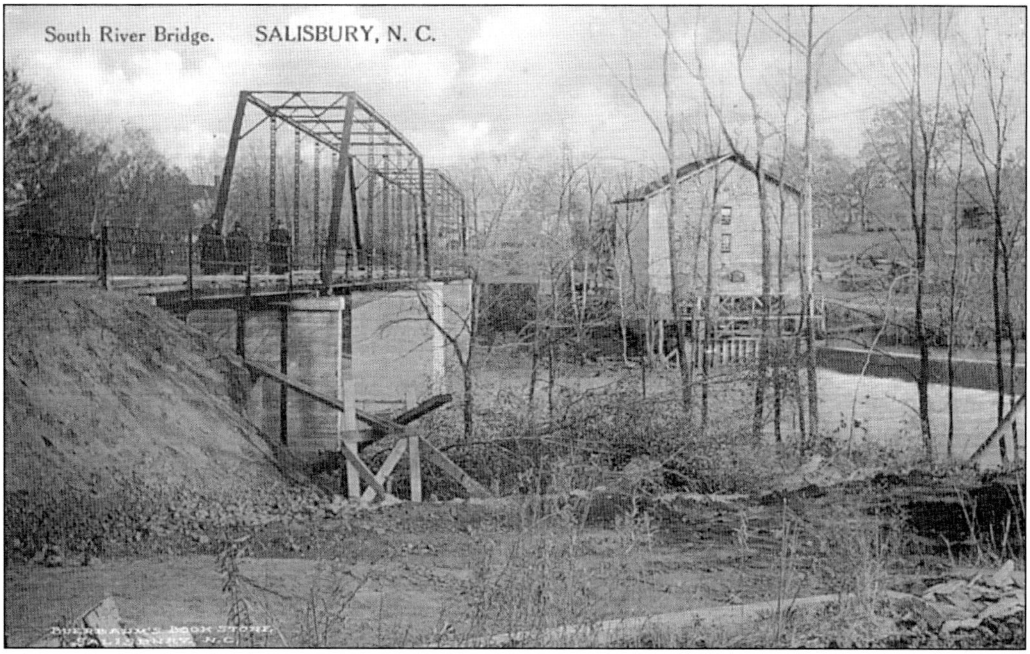

This was the first bridge erected to replace the ferry on the South River on Highway 601 at the Davie County line. The three men on the bridge are P.B. Beard, P.A. Hartman, and C.G. Bailey, all members of the bridge committee. The building visible is the Lindsay-Foard Grist Mill.

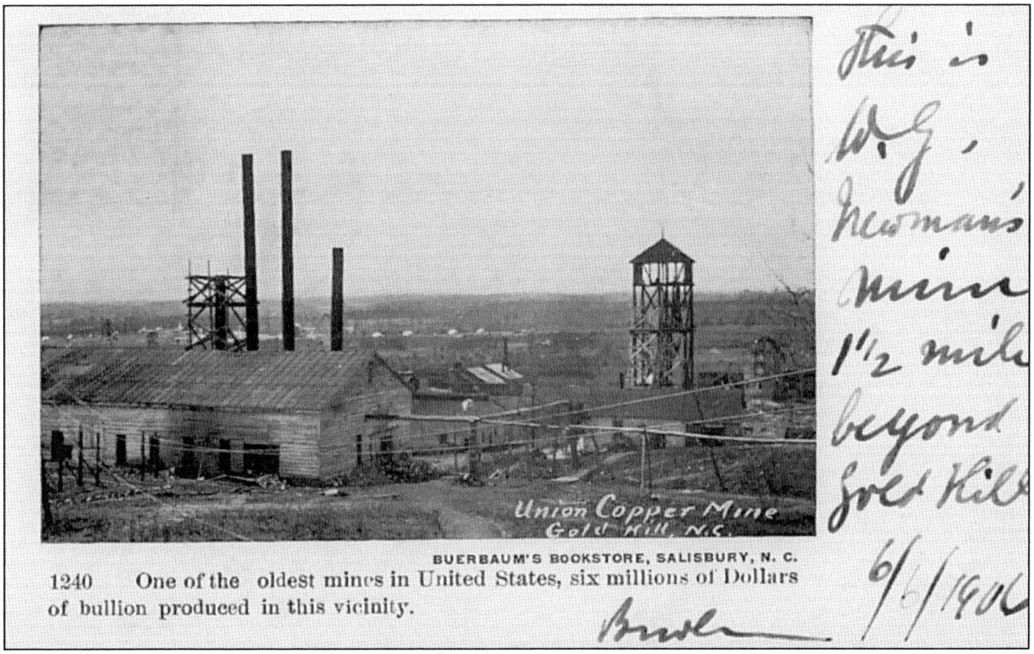

Walter George Newman, one of Rowan County's most colorful individuals, loved publicity. As electricity was in its infancy, copper was the metal of the future. As the gold mines played out, much attention was given to copper, which was also found in Rowan County. Newman's business propositions included gold and copper mines; however, he made most of his fortune selling stock in his ventures, eventually leaving his investors to lick their financial wounds. Buerbaum's note states, "This is W.G. Newman's mine 1 1/2 mile from Gold Hill."

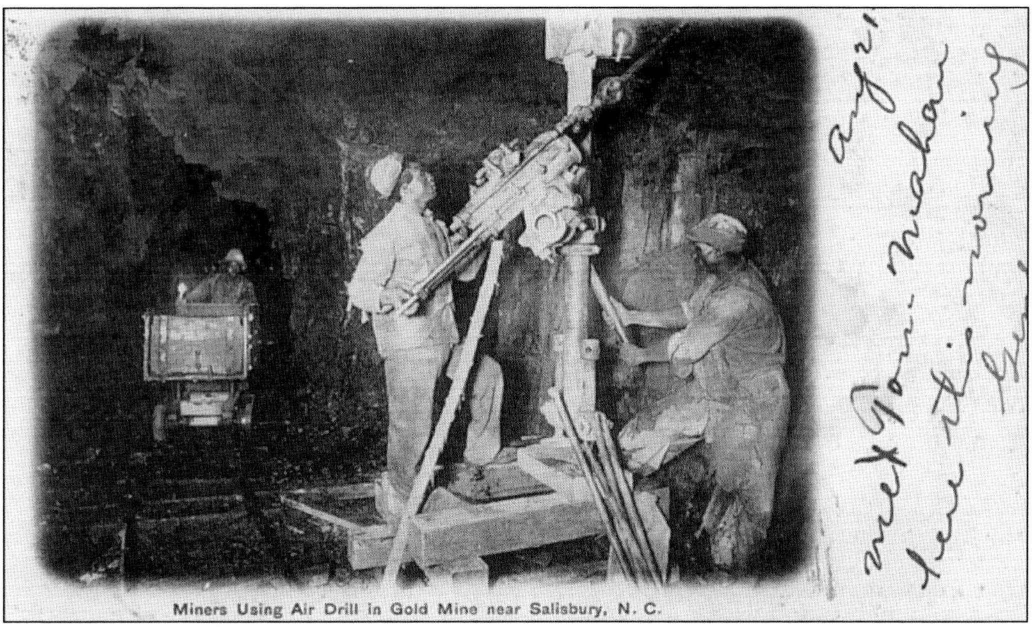

This picture was taken underground in an unidentified mine. This is possibly one of Walter George Newman's mines, as there were close to 1,000 shafts dug around Gold Hill. This view shows the most modern technology used during this time.

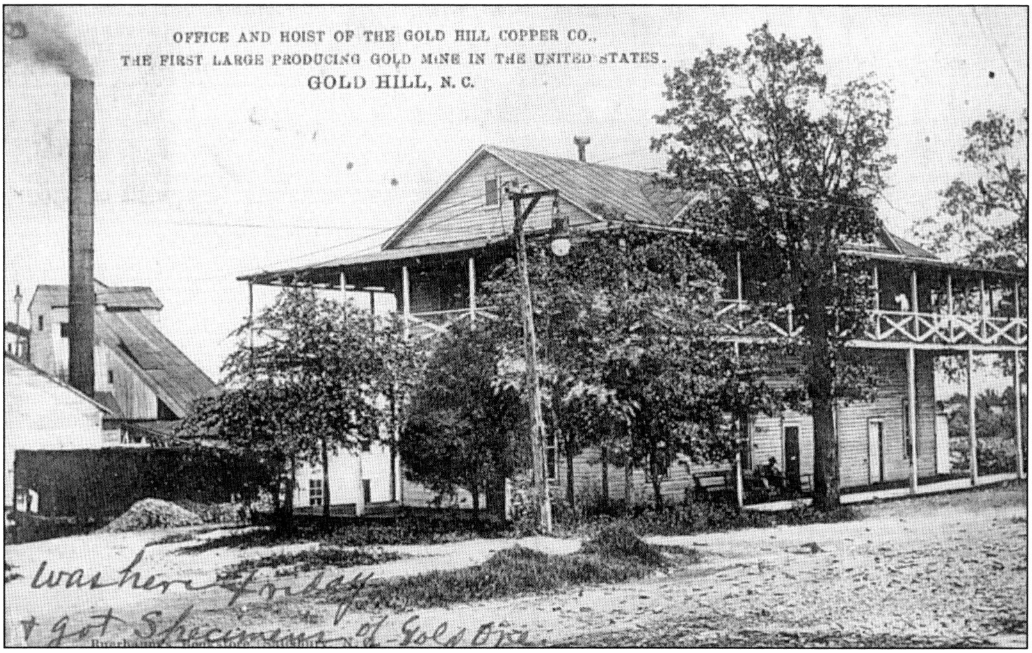

This mining office was directly in front of the Randolph shaft. It burned in the late 1960s, killing Claude Robert Hayes, the last of the Gold Hill miners. The hoist house in the background was directly over the Randolph shaft, which was 830 feet deep. This was, at one time, the richest of all North Carolina gold mines. The photographer was standing on St. Stephen's Church Road.

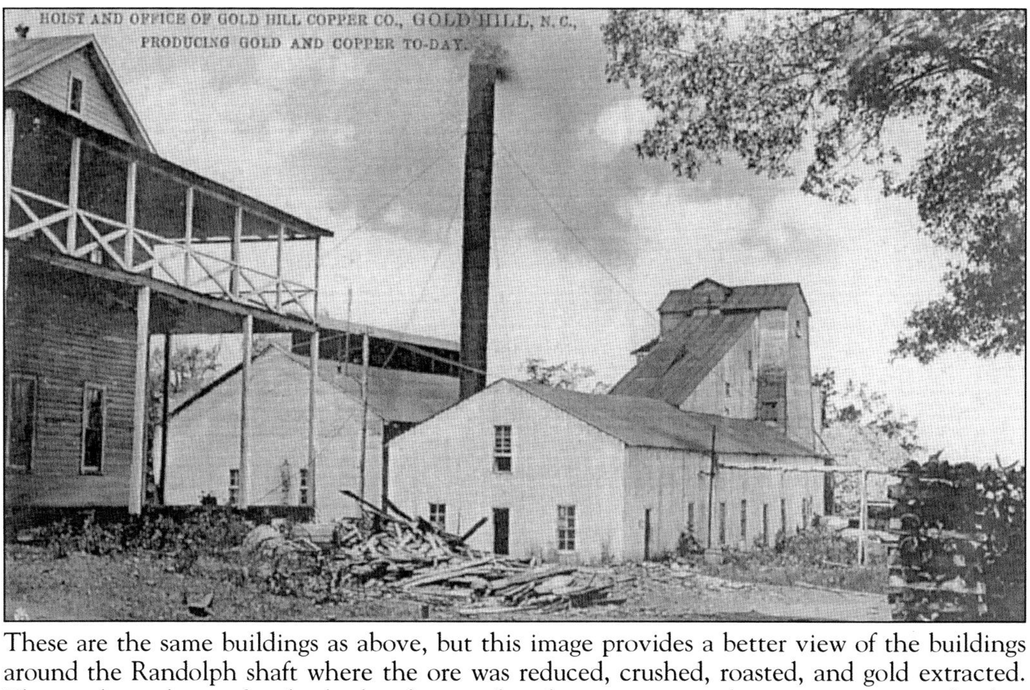

These are the same buildings as above, but this image provides a better view of the buildings around the Randolph shaft where the ore was reduced, crushed, roasted, and gold extracted. The smokestack was for the boiler that produced steam to run the water pumps and other machinery to work the ore. (Courtesy of the Durwood Barbour Collection.)

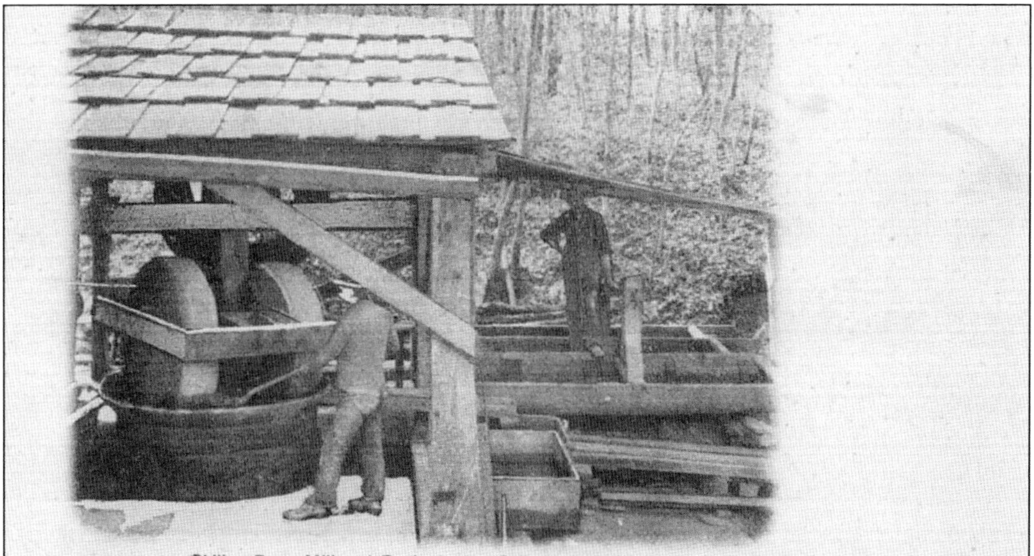

Chilian Drag-Mill and Rockers near Salisbury, N. C.

The Chilean Mills consisted of two large granite millstones attached side by side that rotated by horsepower on their ends inside a "bedstone." There are many broken bedstones in Gold Hill park today. The gold containing quartz was shoveled into the bedstone where the rotating millstones would crush it into a fine paste. This paste was then put into the log rockers with water to extract the gold. (Courtesy of the Rowan Public Library.)

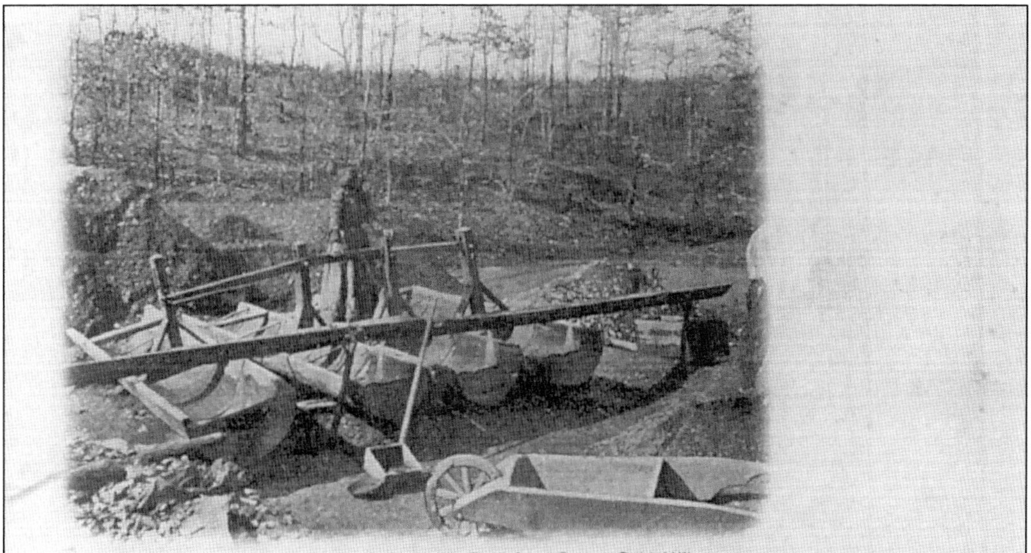

The Old Log Rocker Method of Extracting Gold from Ore at Gold Hill.

In the log-rocker method of gold extraction, the four logs were tied together, usually by young people. In the bottom of the log rockers was a deep groove where mercury was placed. As the rocking slowly moved the gold (being the heaviest) down into the mercury, they actually blend together in a process called amalgamation. After the rocking was complete, the amalgam was collected and put on a hotplate and heated. The mercury would evaporate leaving the gold behind. Although this process is one of the oldest, it proved to be the most efficient in gold recovery. This method was used from the 1840s through the early 1900s. (Courtesy of the Durwood Barbour Collection.)

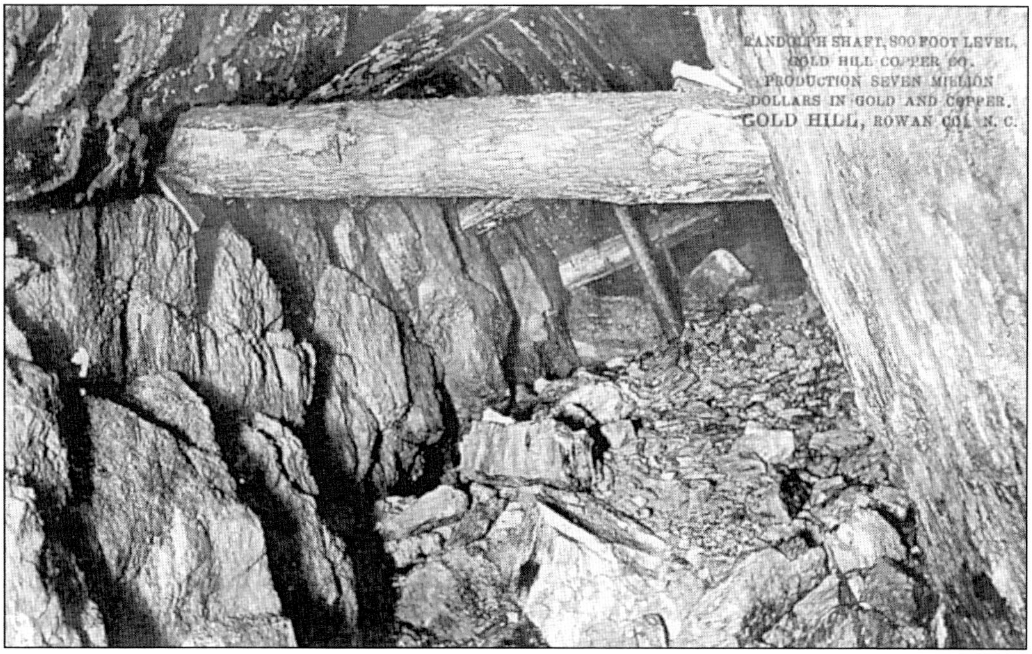

This image shows Gold Hill's Randolph shaft at the 800-foot level showing a "stoped" area where ore has been removed. Stoping was when miners would open up a vein of gold-bearing ore (usually quartz) by digging upward then carrying out the ore. This left a void or cavern inside the mine. (Courtesy of the Durwood Barbour Collection.)

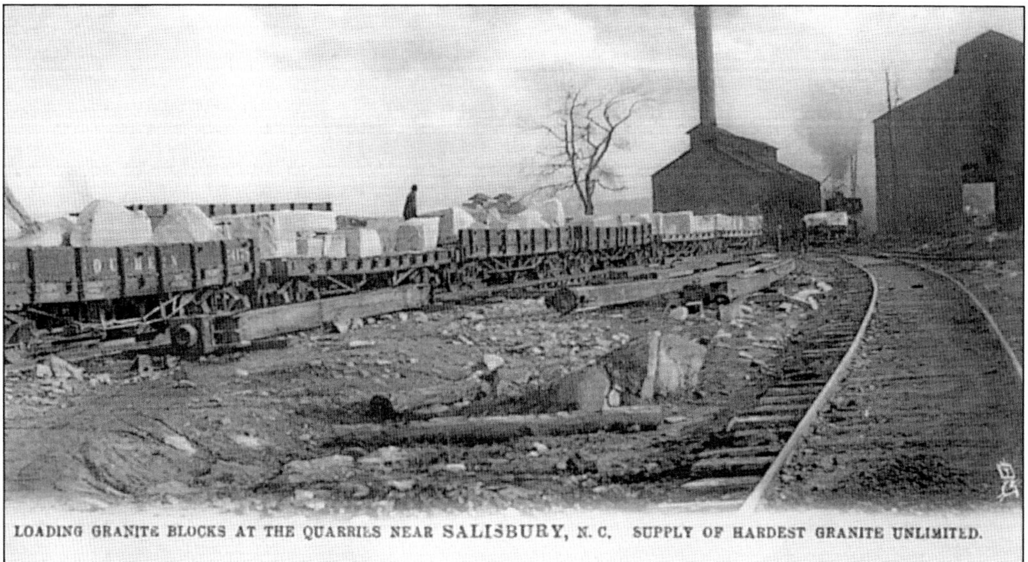

Southern Railroad was essential in shipping granite from the quarries. The granite could not have moved any distance with a horse and buggy due to the size and weight. (Courtesy of the Marian Harter Collection.)

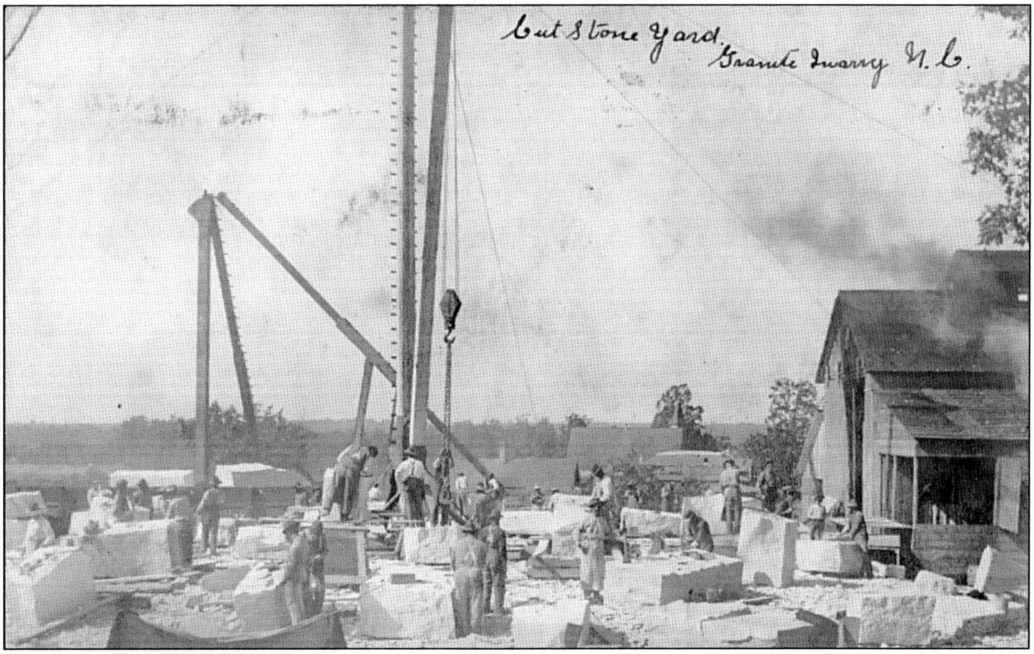

Over one-third of the granite produced in North Carolina in 1903 was used for building and monument purposes. Rowan County, with ten operators, was second in the state in the value of its granite production. (Courtesy of the Sarah Manning Pope Collection.)

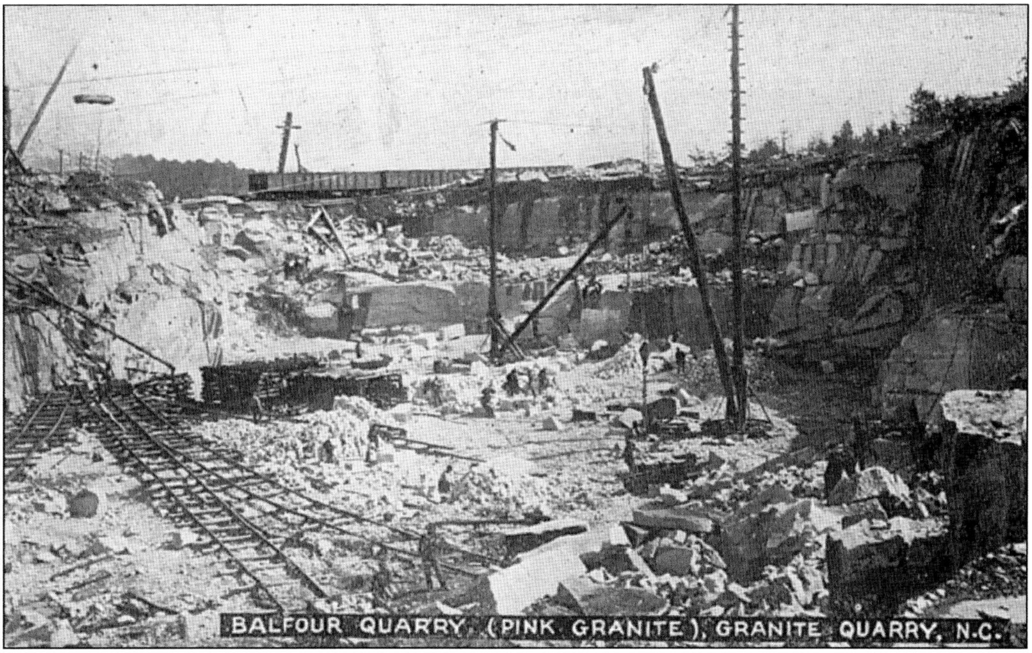

The Balfour Quarry was most notable for its pink granite, which was caused by the pink-coloring material in the feldspar of the stone. J.T. Wyatt, Rowan's beloved newspaper correspondent, known as the "Venus of faith," quarried for a time at Balfour. Prior to World War II, the quarry had more than 160 employees. The granite was used for monuments, curbstones, building blocks, rubble, and grinding stones.

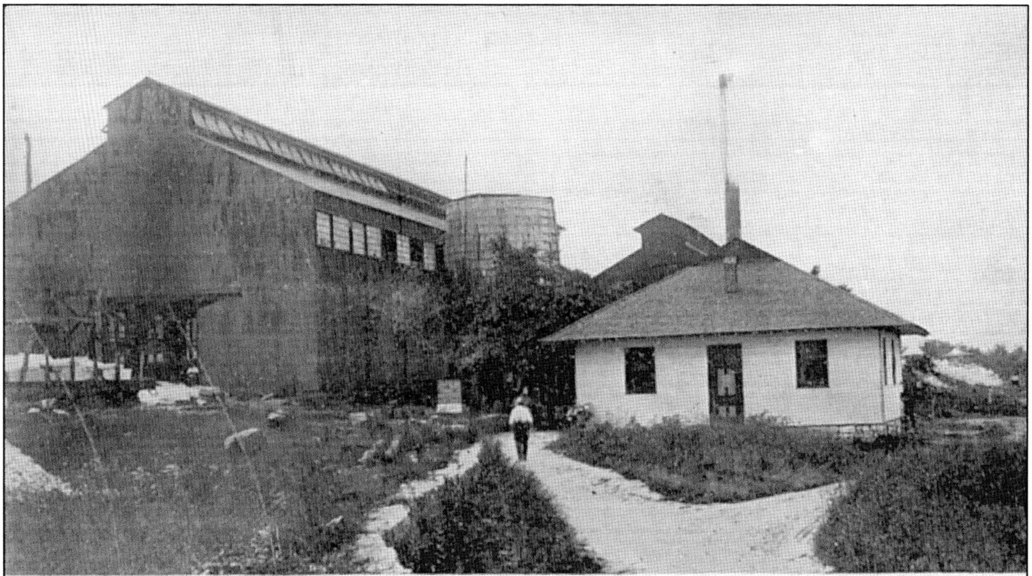

Rowan Granite Co. Stone Shed and office, Granite Quarry, N. C.

The Rowan Granite Company quarries were located near the Granite Quarry Station on the Yadkin Railroad. Some of the stones quarried weighed 70 to 100 tons each. (Courtesy of the Sarah Manning Pope Collection.)

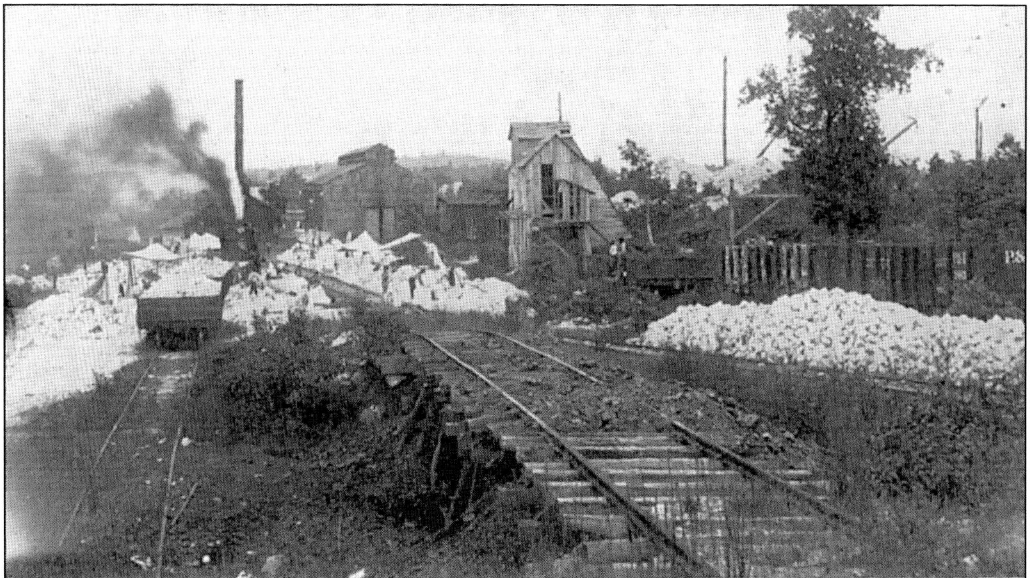

West End Rowan Granite Co. Crusher and Paving Yard, Granite Quarry, N. C.

Most stone quarried in Rowan was light-gray granite with small specks of pink and was used as a general building stone for curbs and blocks on streets and some monuments. Some of the quarry waste was used for ballast and macadam for roads. This is an excellent view of the crushed granite ready to be shipped.

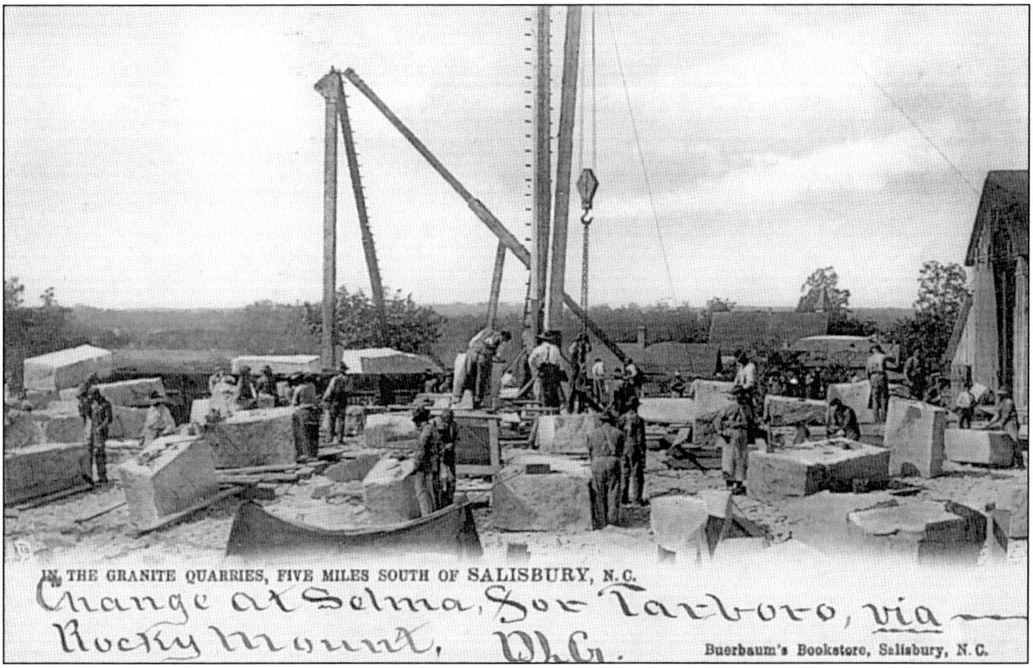

These quarry views, which are not identified by company name, represent a very important part of Rowan County's history. The Harris Granite Company completed a large plant in 1915, holding 20 cutting machines for making Durax blocks. Durax, small irregular cubical blocks, was used for paving streets. This plant was the only one of its kind in the South. Among the Harris Granite Company's large orders was one in 1915 for 636,000 tons of granite for the Cape Lookout sea wall.

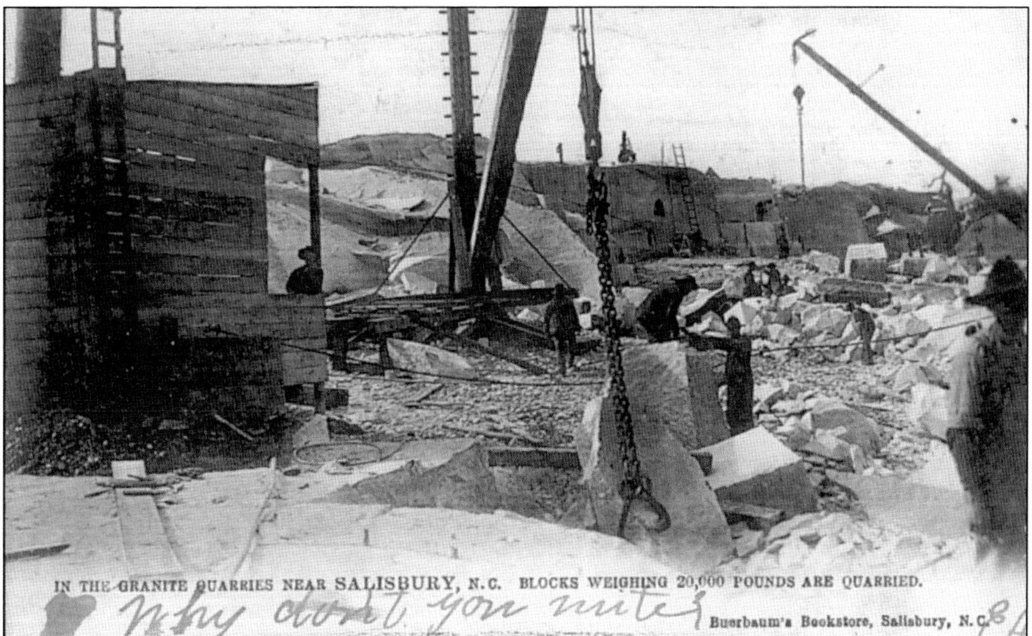

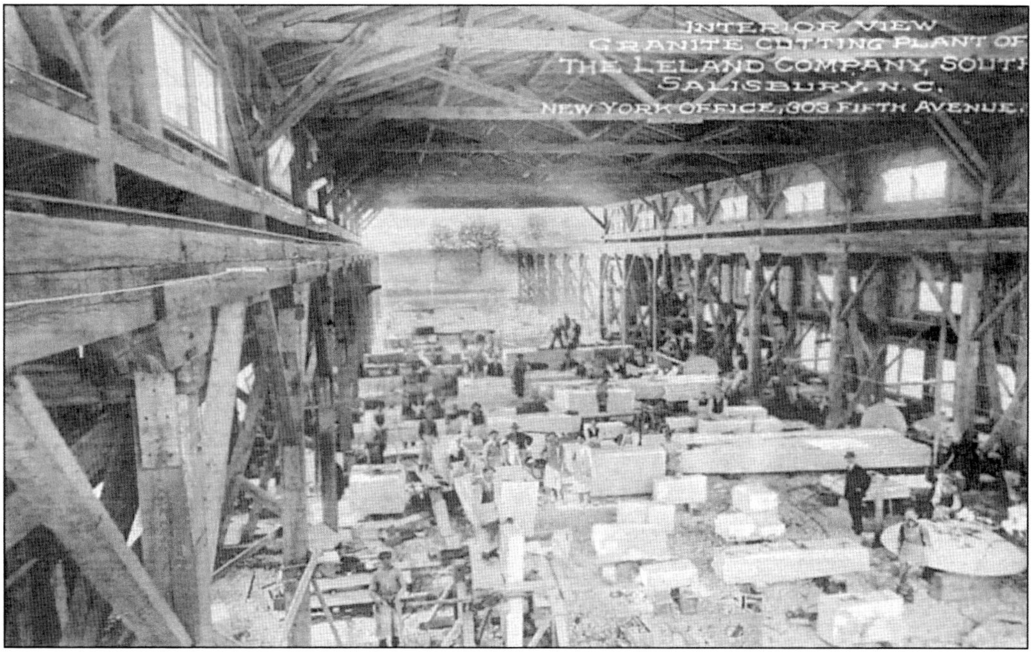

The Leland Company was one of Rowan's many quarrying companies at the turn of the century. This company was bought by the Harris Company in 1911. In this view, their official office is listed as Fifth Avenue, New York.

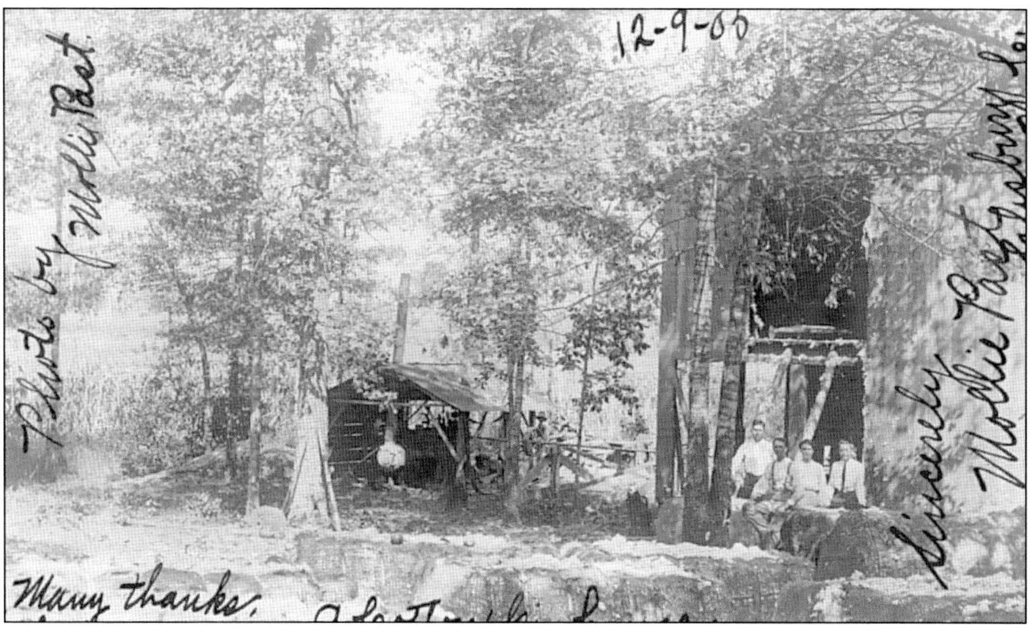

The exact location of this Salisbury cotton-gin house is unknown. The cotton gin separates seeds, hulls, and foreign material from cotton. The bales of cotton in front would later be sent to a cotton mill. (Courtesy of the Marian Harter Collection.)

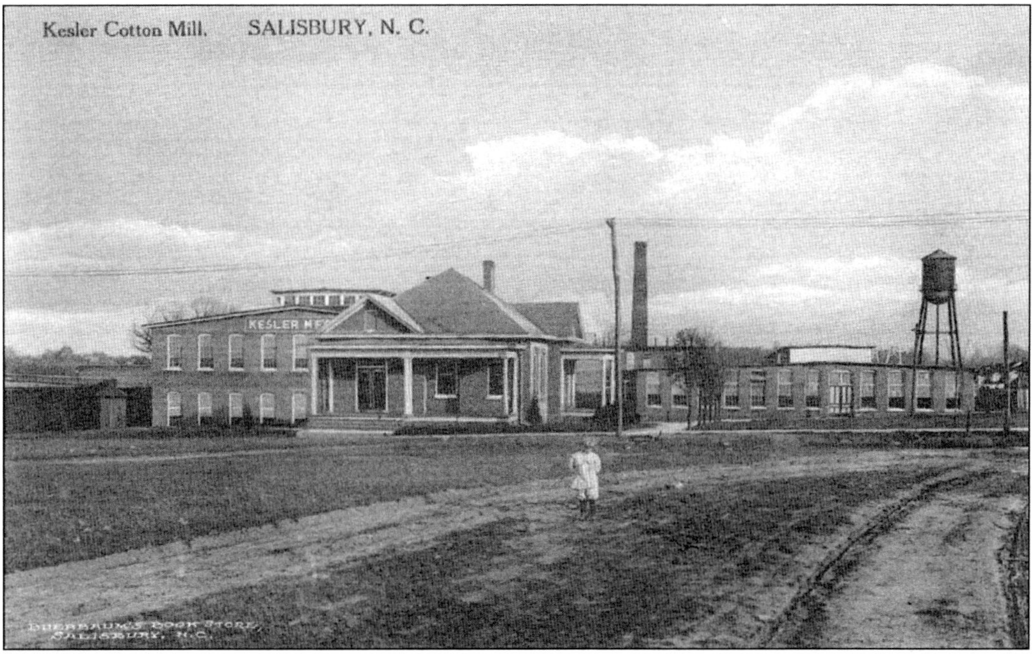

The Kesler Cotton Mill was organized in 1895. It was named for Tobias Kesler, a Rowan County farmer and the mill's largest stockholder. When a robbery in the countryside convinced the frugal farmer to deposit his savings, a local banker, amazed at the sum, suggested he become an industrialist. This mill became Cannon Mill #9 after consolidation in 1928. (Courtesy of the Rowan Public Library.)

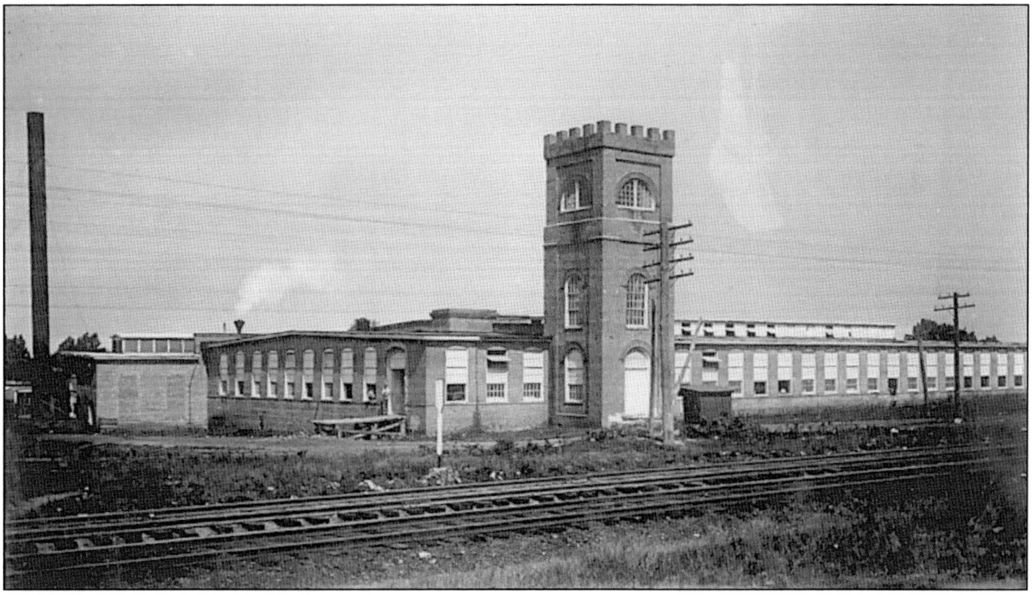

The Linn Mill in Landis was organized in April 1900. The founders of the mill included Columbus Linn, Linn's sons, Lotan Corriher, Dr. C.W. Corriher, Calvin Deal, and George Lipe. In 1909, the Corriher Mill was organized. Later, the two mills combined to become Linn-Corriher Mills. The mill tower burned *c.* 1950. (Courtesy of the Marian Harter Collection.)

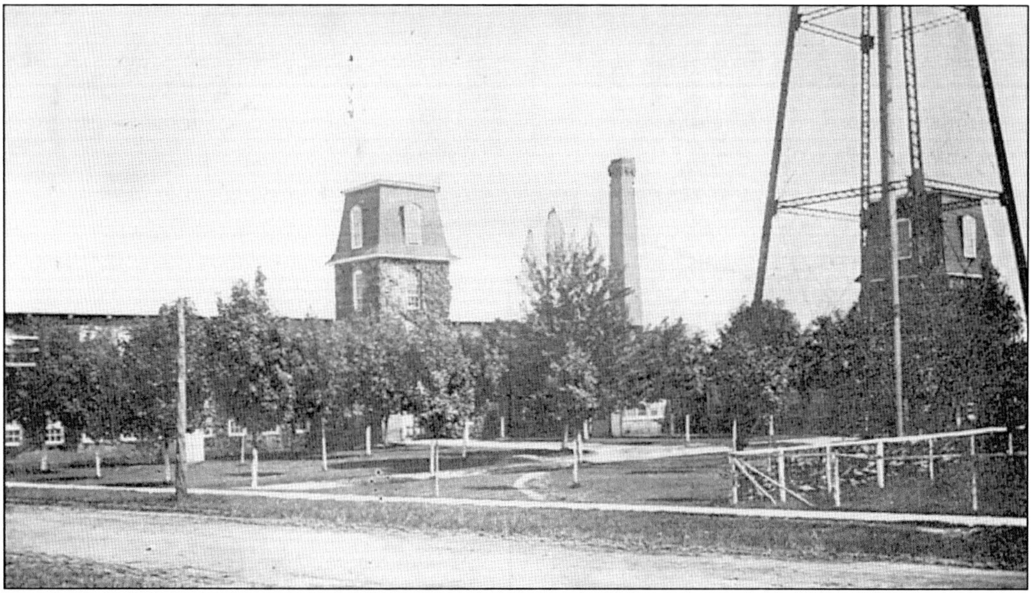

The Patterson Manufacturing Company was organized in 1893 on North Main Street in China Grove. I. Frank Patterson was secretary-treasurer. This plant eventually became Plant #8 of Cannon Mills in 1928. (Courtesy of the Sarah Manning Pope Collection.)

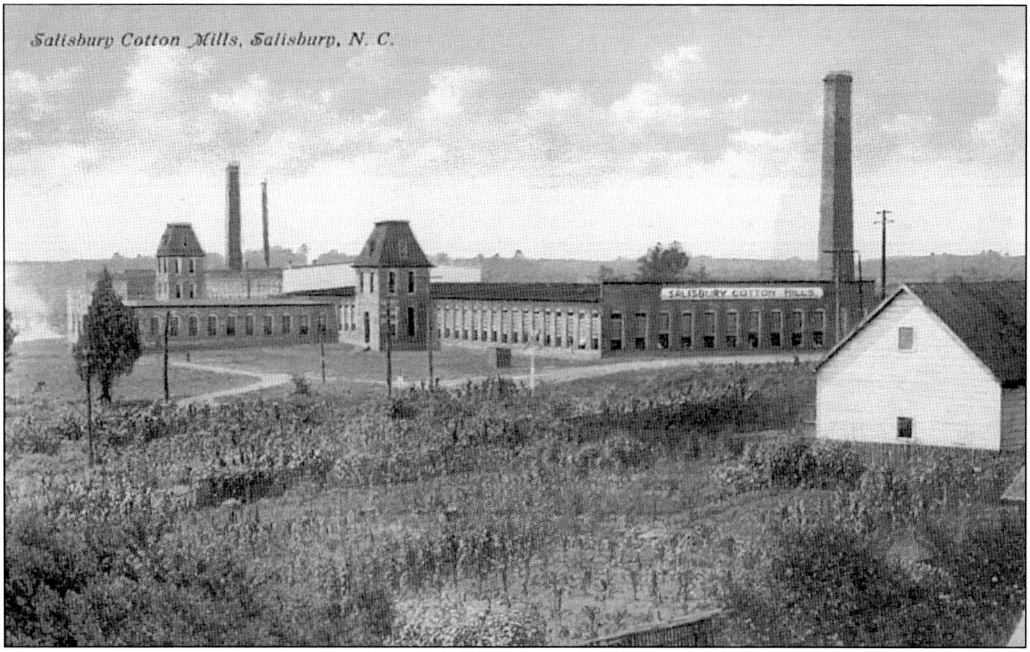

The Salisbury Cotton Mill was built in 1888 as the result of a successful revival. When a traveling evangelist challenged local businessmen to put idle hands to work, they met his challenge. Salisbury's Episcopal priest, Francis Murdoch, was one of the driving forces behind the mill. Eventually, Cone Mills took over the plant. After 110 years of continuous operation in the same location, the mill closed in 1999.

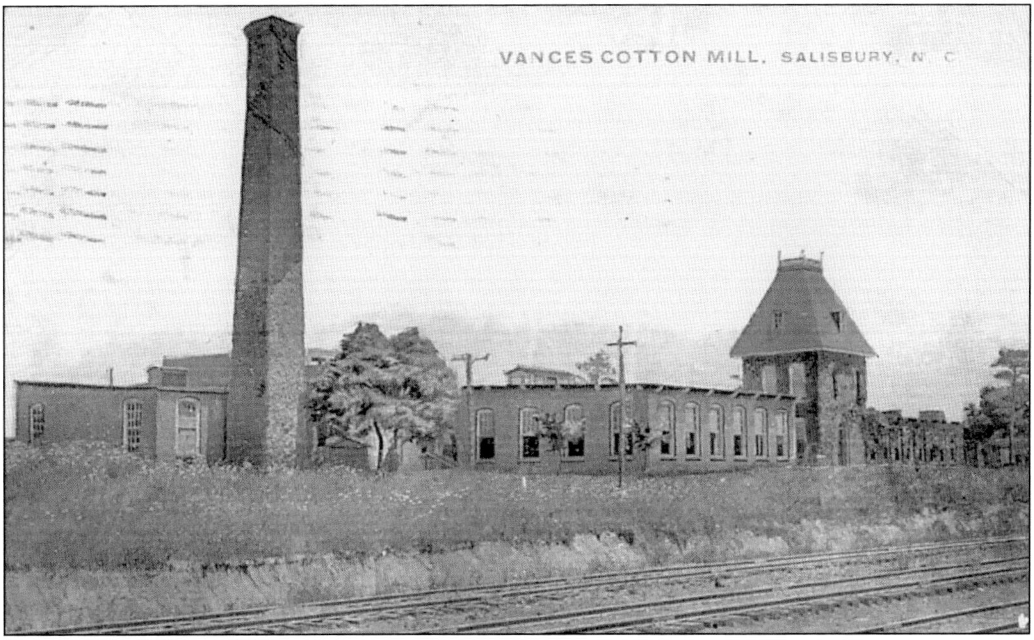

The Vance Cotton Mill was named for Gov. Zebulon B. Vance. The first president was Rev. F.J. Murdoch, and he was succeeded by A.C. Lineberger. The mill was acquired by Carl Rudisell in 1931, and its name was changed to Cartex.

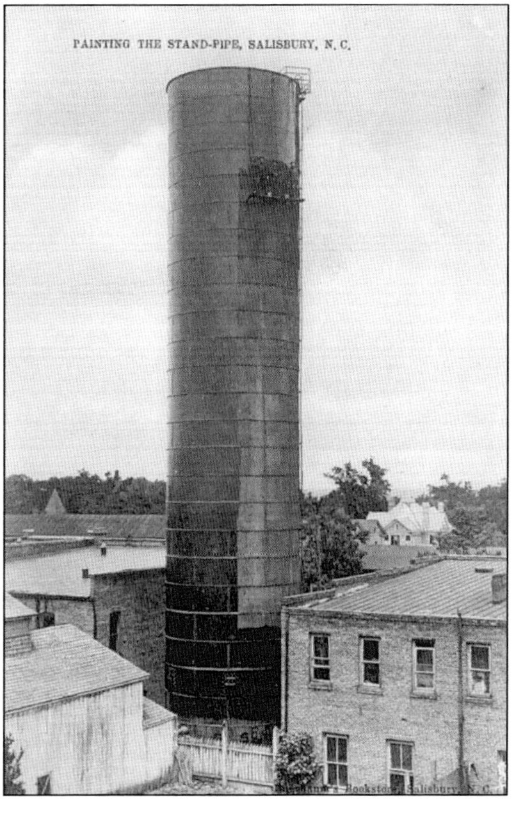

The 150-foot stand-pipe was erected in the first block of Fisher Street after General George Stoneman's Federal raid burned the block in 1865. In 1887, the city contracted to install a public water system throughout the city. The stand-pipe stood until 1949. (Card from Buerbaum.)

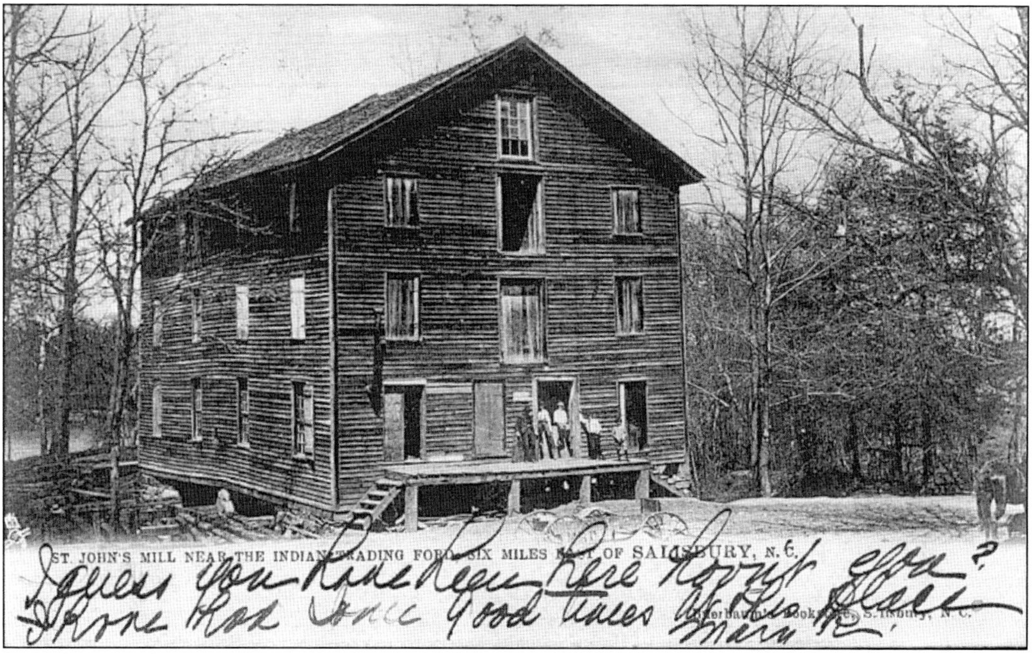

St. John's Mill stood near the site where the Sapona and Saura Indians had built villages at the intersection of two ancient trading paths. Most Native Americans left this area during the colonial era.

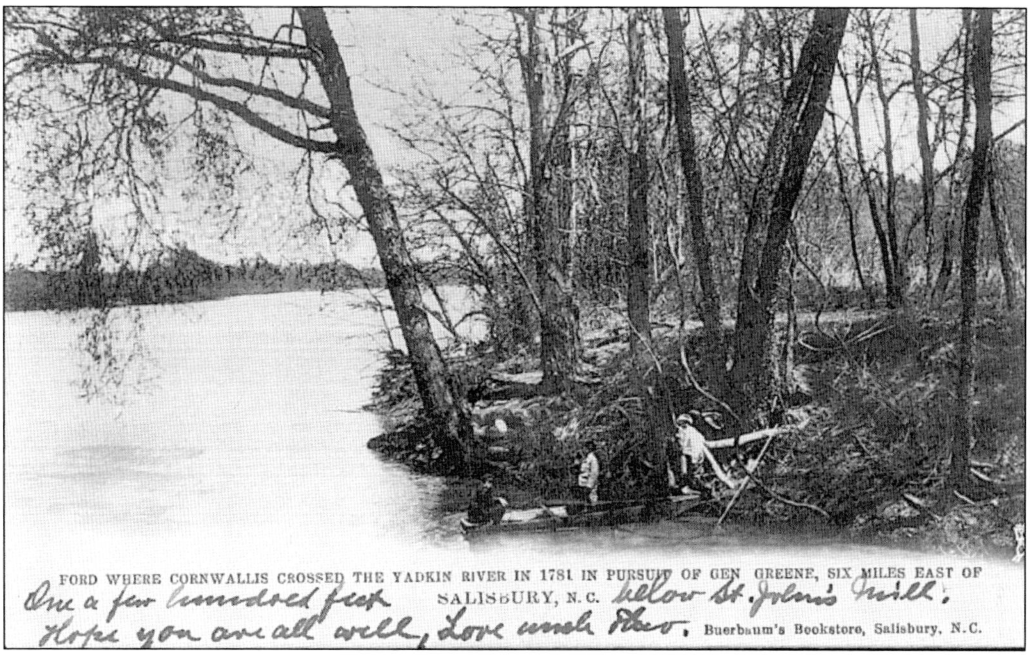

During the Revolution, a retreating Gen. Nathaniel Greene had his spirits boosted when Salisbury tavern keeper Elizabeth Maxwell Steele presented her life savings to the patriots' cause. A sudden rise in the river prevented the British troops from crossing, allowing the American troops to escape and prepare for the Battle of Guilford Courthouse. Buerbaum's note states: "Only a few hundred feet from St. John's Mill. Hope you are all well. Love, Uncle Theo."

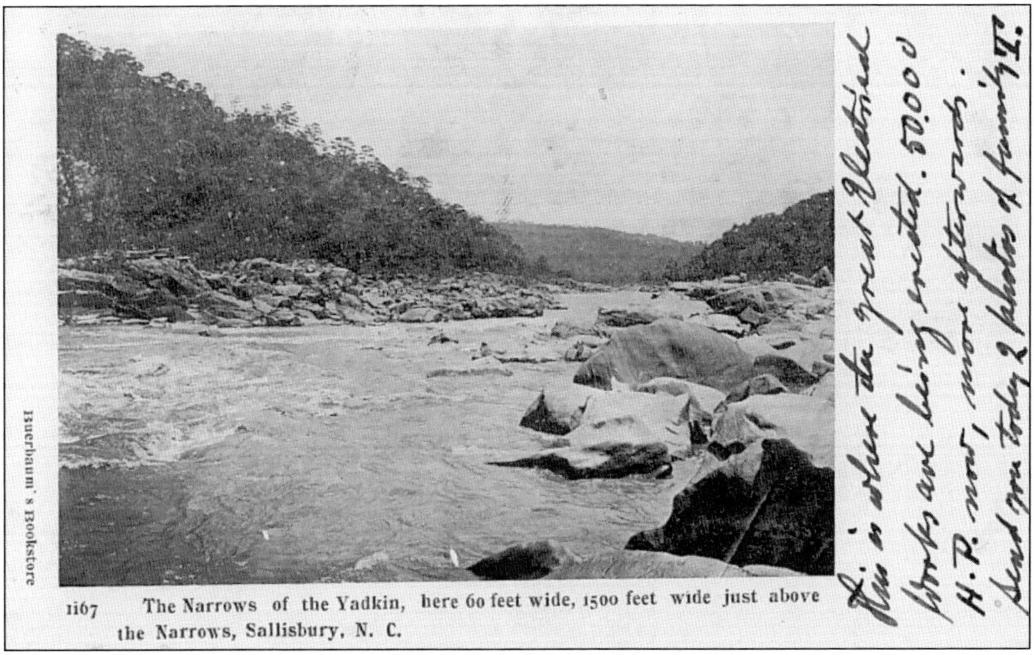

E.B.C. Hambley, whose home was on Fulton Street, was an English mining engineer who had traveled around the world with his work. In 1898, he organized a company to develop the water power at Yadkin Falls, proposing to develop an electric power plant for the distribution of electricity to Salisbury, Albemarle, and Concord. Buerbaum says, "This is where the great electrical works are being erected. 50,000 H.P. now, more afterwards. Send you today 2 photos of family. T."

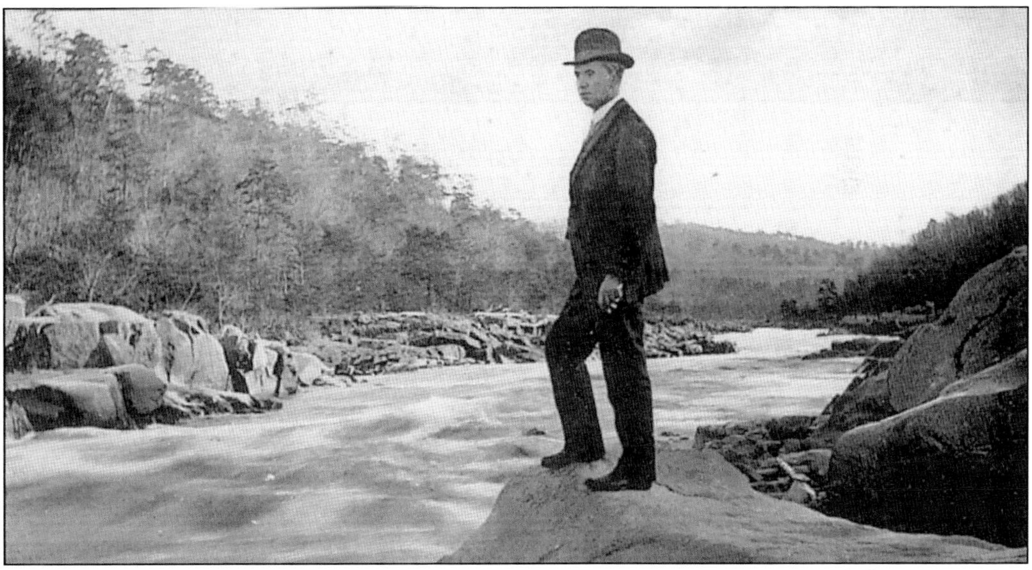

Hambley saw the possibility of long-distance electric power transmission and the potential of the Narrows and Falls of the Yadkin as a power source. He attracted the attention of George I. Whitney, a financier from Pittsburgh, Pennsylvania. Whitney was a financial confidante of Andrew Mellon. The gentleman in this scene is identified by Buerbaum as "Mr. Thornton." (Card from Buerbaum.)

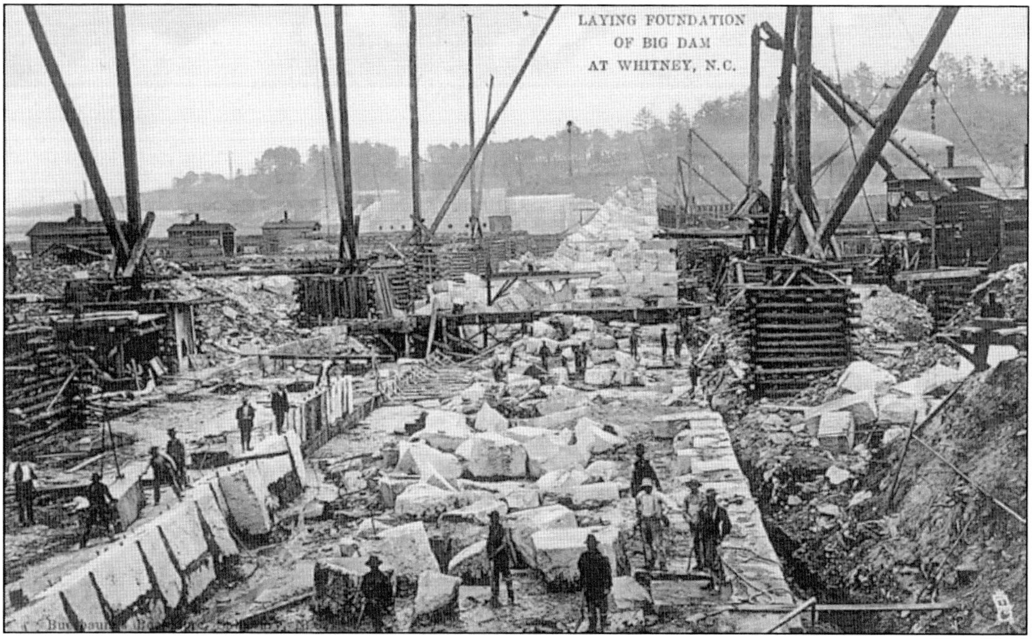

In the late 1890s, George I. Whitney became interested in gold, copper, and granite deposits along the Yadkin River. He began acquiring several thousand acres of potential mineral lands. He then organized eight corporations, each capitalized in excess of $1 million to develop his properties. Salisbury was the headquarters for his various undertakings.

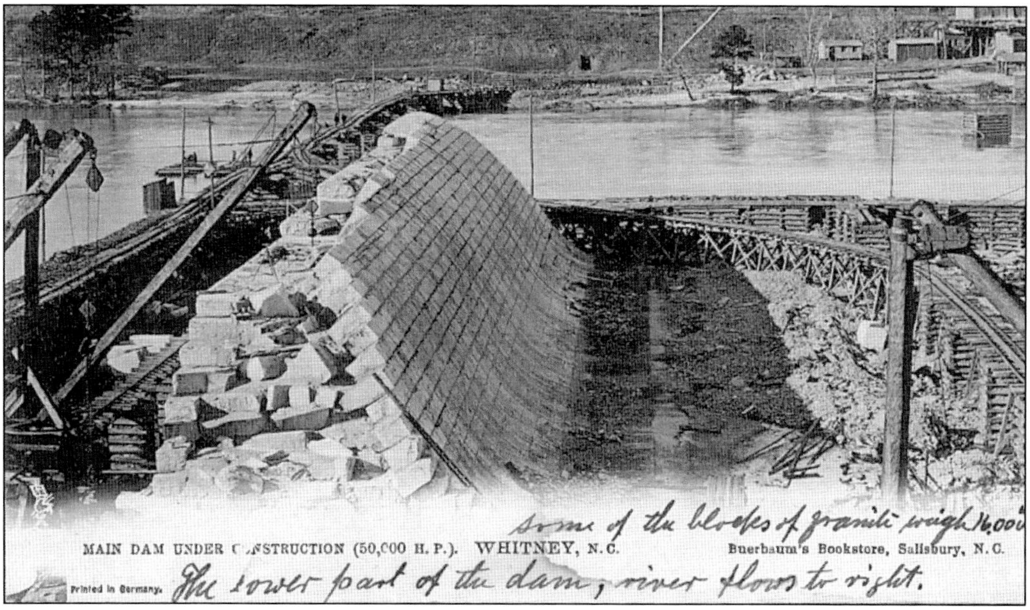

The Whitney Corporations were The Whitney Company, the Whitney Reduction Company, The Yadkin River Electric Power Company, Yadkin Land Company, Yadkin Mines Consolidated Company, The Barringer Gold Mining Company, Rowan Granite Company, and The Yadkin and Virginia Copper and Land Company. In these early years, the companies had limited success, and Whitney conceived the idea of damming the Yadkin River to furnish hydro-electric power for the operation of all these properties. (Card from Buerbaum.)

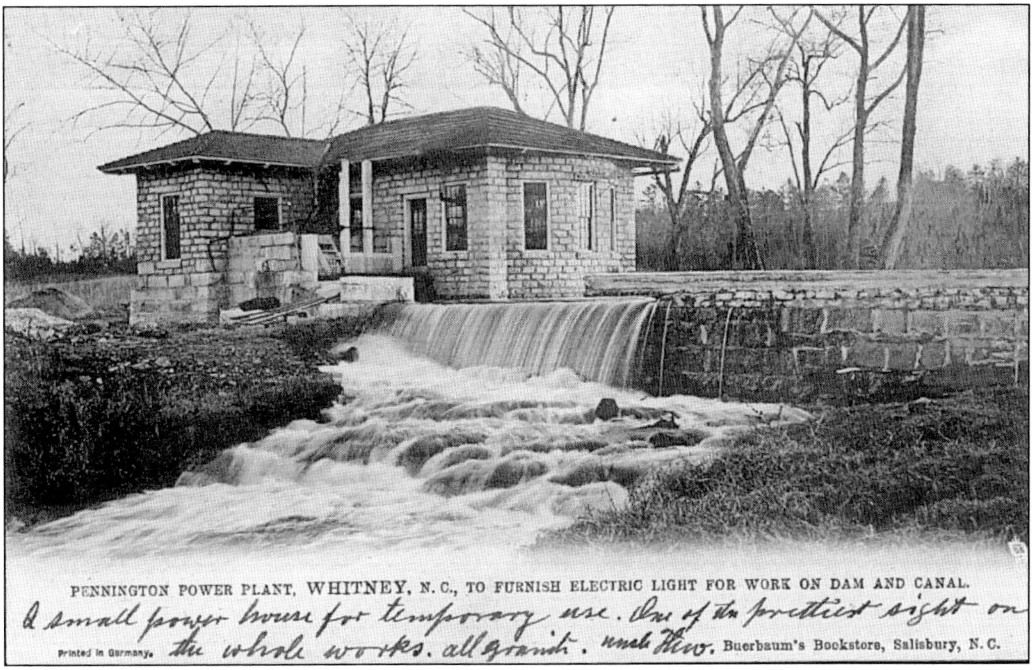

In 1901, Whitney started the erection of the Whitney Dam across the Yadkin River. The completed project was estimated to cost several million dollars. The dam was erected with granite blocks approximately 30 feet high. Plans called for a 5-mile-long canal to divert the water from the dam to the power house at Palmer Mountain, and after passing through the wheels, the water would discharge into the Yadkin River. (Cards from Buerbaum.)

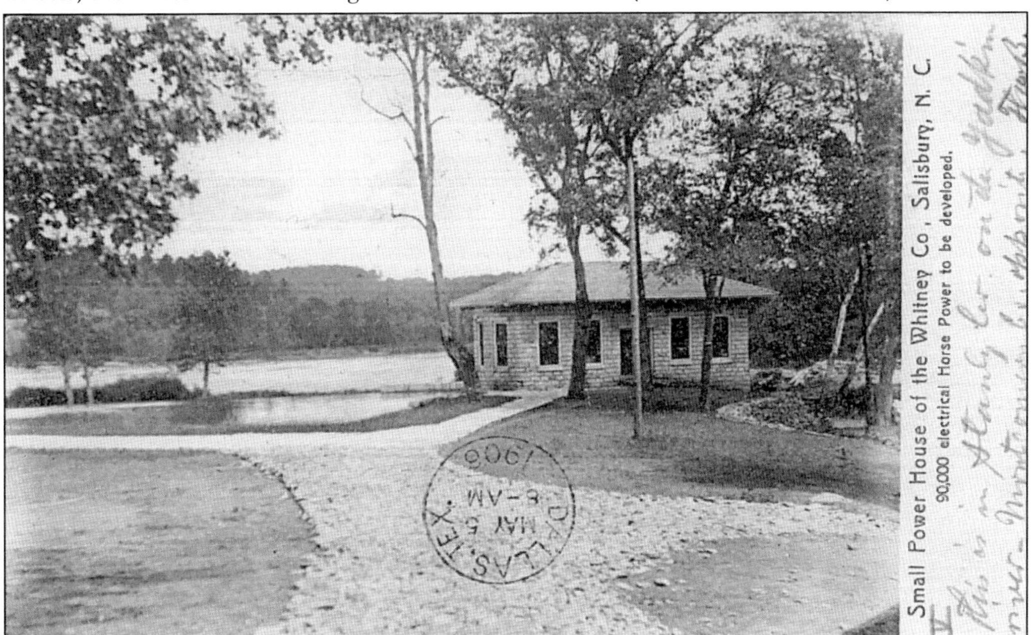

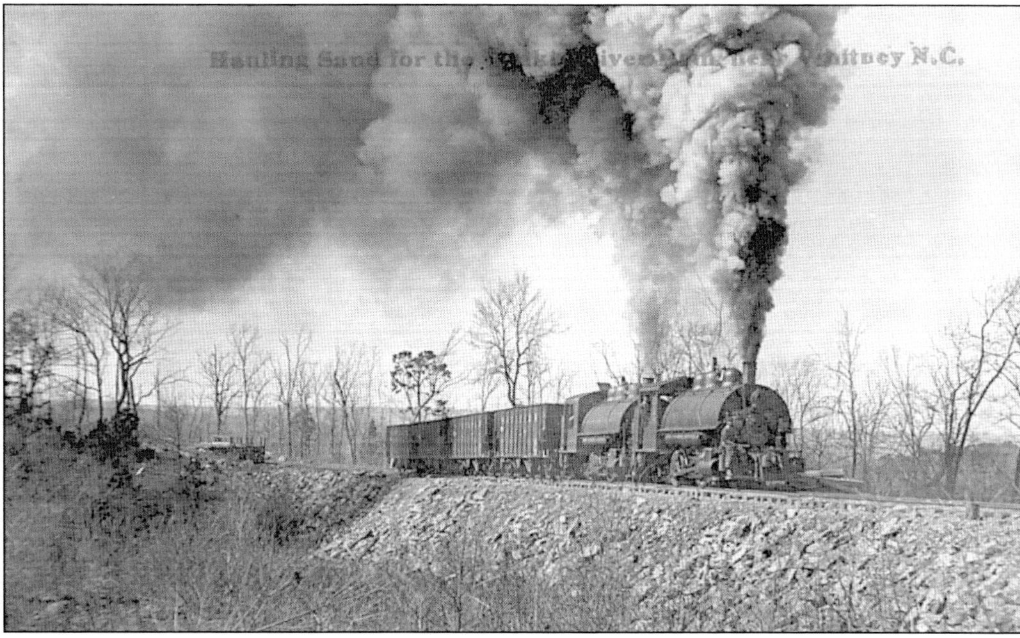

About 1900, the Whitney Company laid out and constructed a standard gage railroad from a point on the Yadkin Railroad known as Hall's Ferry, which was about one mile south of New London. This railroad stretched the 6 miles to the dam, continued to Palmer Mountain, and then continued 4 miles farther to the site of the proposed power house. (Courtesy of the Marian Harter Collection.)

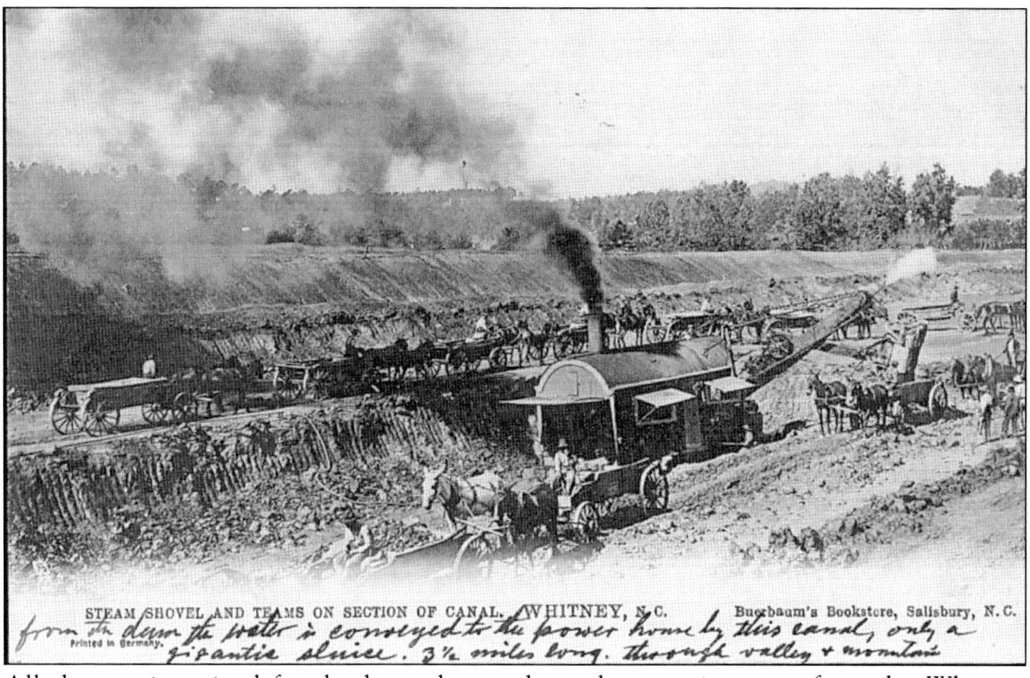

All the granite mined for the huge dam and canal enterprise came from the Whitney Quarry at Granite Quarry. It was transported about 20 miles to the dam site by rail. (Card from Buerbaum.)

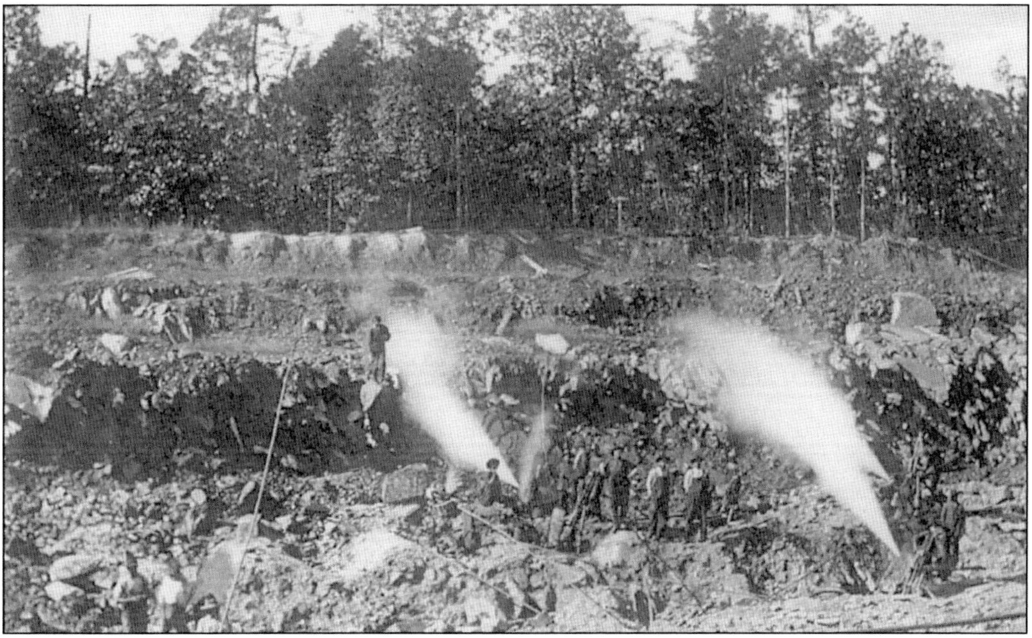

Hoping to revolutionize the cotton manufacturing industry with electric power, the Whitney-Hambley partnership secured the right of way for power lines as far away as Knoxville, Tennessee. (Card from Buerbaum.)

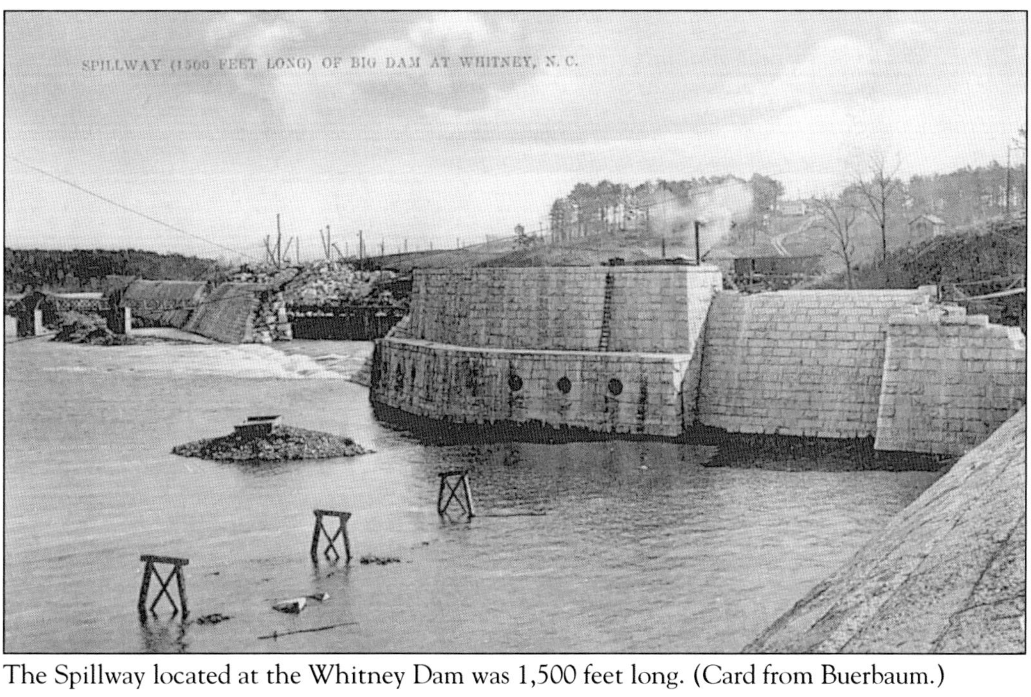

The Spillway located at the Whitney Dam was 1,500 feet long. (Card from Buerbaum.)

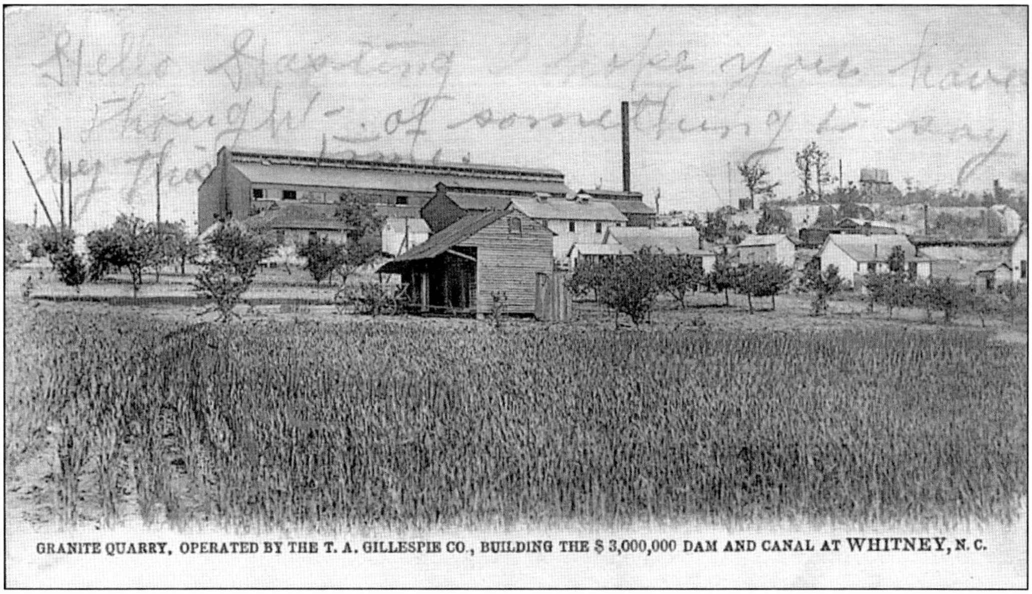

The T.A. Gillespie Company of Granite Quarry was the contractor for the Whitney Dam project. Hundreds of Italian laborers and English stonecutters moved to the community to work in the quarries. The granite was cut at the plant and hauled by rail to the Whitney Station.

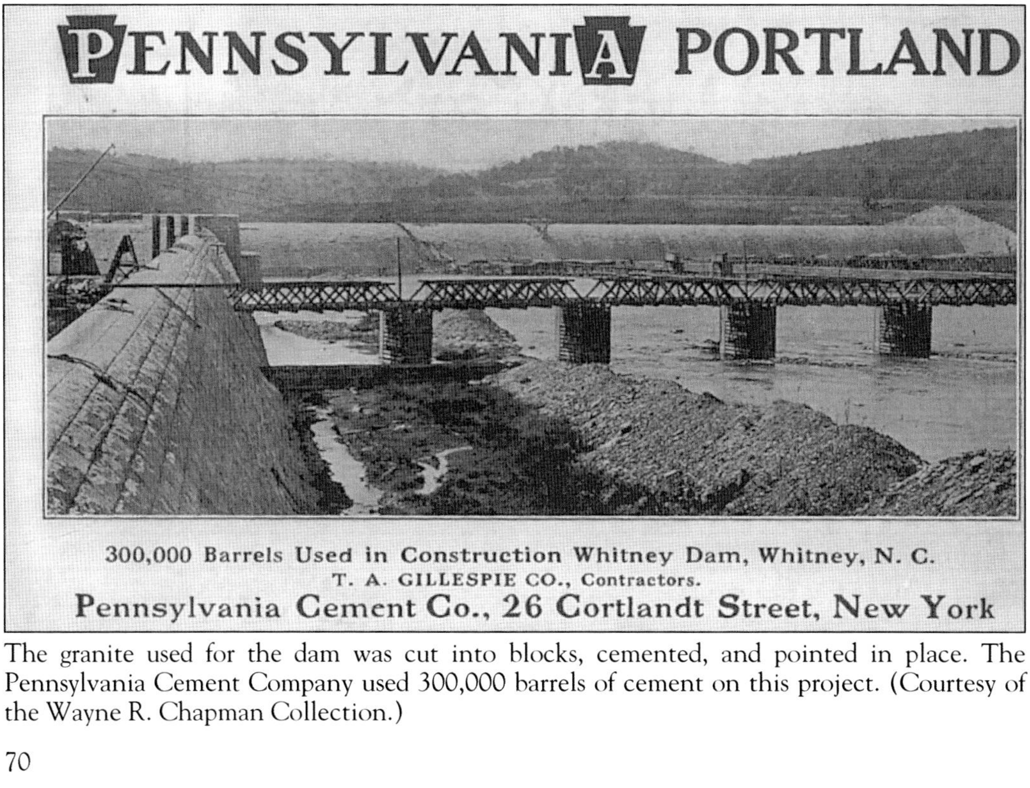

The granite used for the dam was cut into blocks, cemented, and pointed in place. The Pennsylvania Cement Company used 300,000 barrels of cement on this project. (Courtesy of the Wayne R. Chapman Collection.)

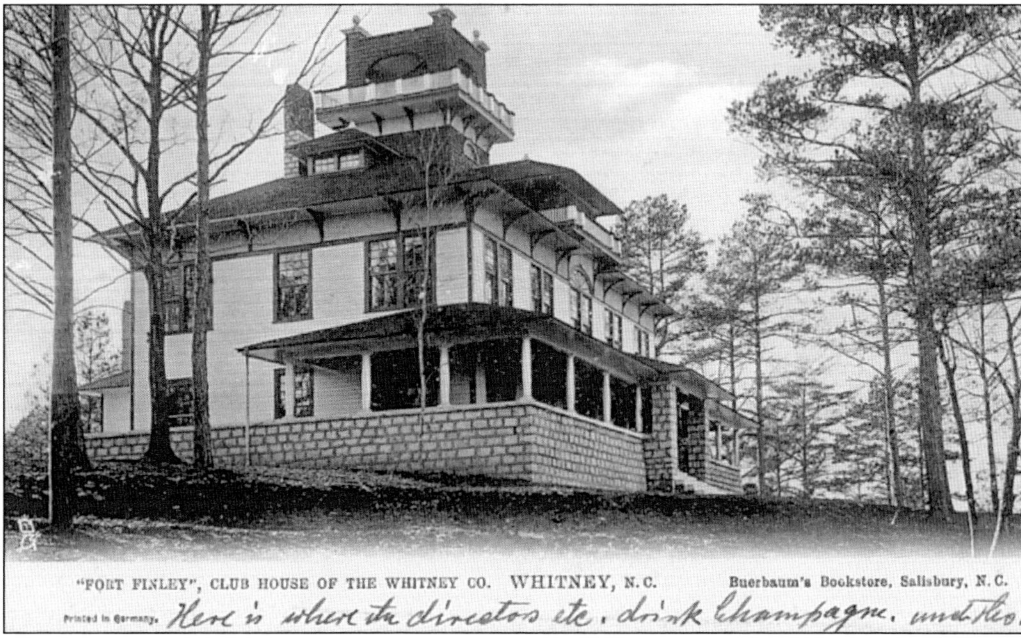

A large clubhouse was erected at the dam site to house the engineers, technical, and office employees. A small town was laid out, roadways graded, a well drilled for a water supply, and several permanent homes were erected for this project. Buerbaum states, "Here the promoters, directors, etc. drink champagne."

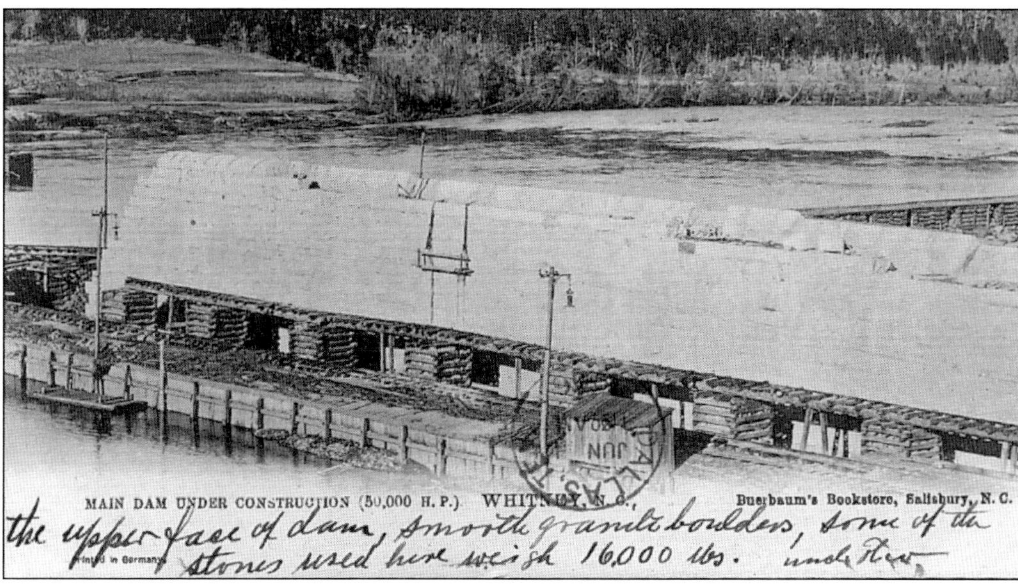

Numerous problems began to plague the project. An accident at the Barringer Gold Mine left eight dead and the company in debt to families and creditors. Barringer never reopened. Two other Whitney mines, the McMackin and the Isenhour, filled with water. Each summer, typhoid dwindled the labor force. Hambley contracted this disease in 1906 and died at age 44. The final blow came in 1908 when Andrew Mellon forced George Whitney into a disastrous sale of Whitney's coal mining stocks, which put Whitney into bankruptcy in 1910. (Card from Buerbaum.)

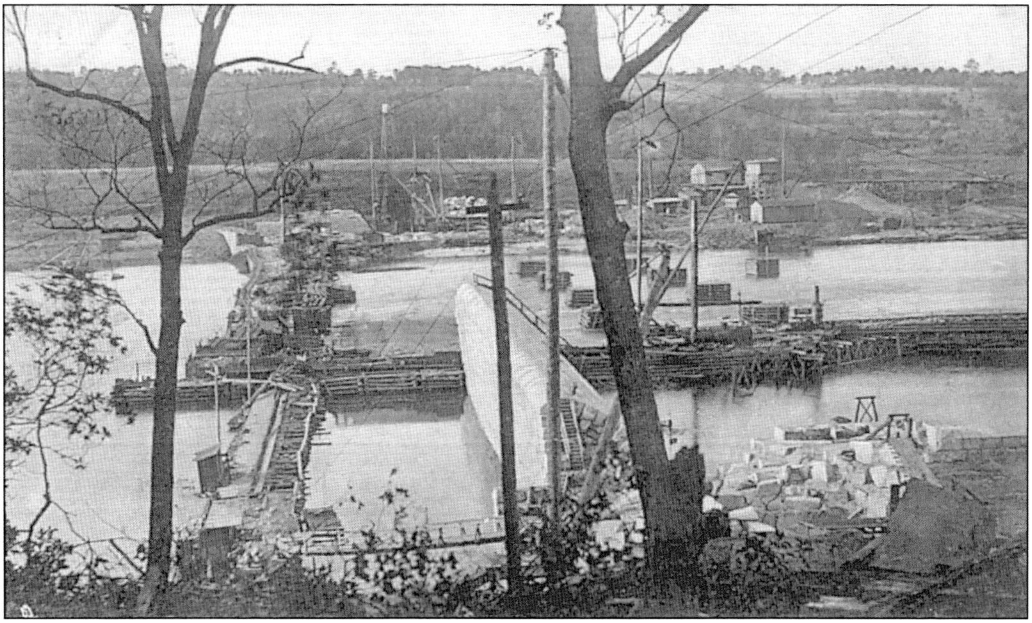

All Whitney workings were sold by receivers to the N.C. Electric and Power Company, which sold Whitney to a French company. In 1915, Alcoa bought the French holdings. The new owners abandoned the Whitney dam site and decided to build their dam downstream. (Courtesy of the Marian Harter Collection.)

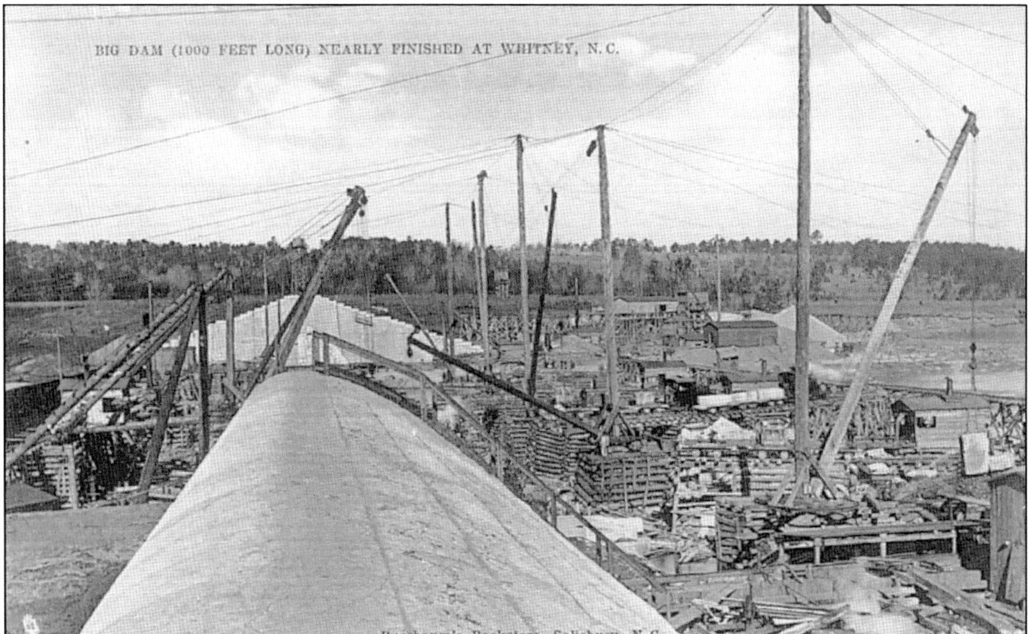

The massive multi-million dollar Whitney dam project was never completed. The incomplete structure can still be seen when the water level is low. (Courtesy of the Sarah Manning Pope Collection.)

Four

RAILWAY

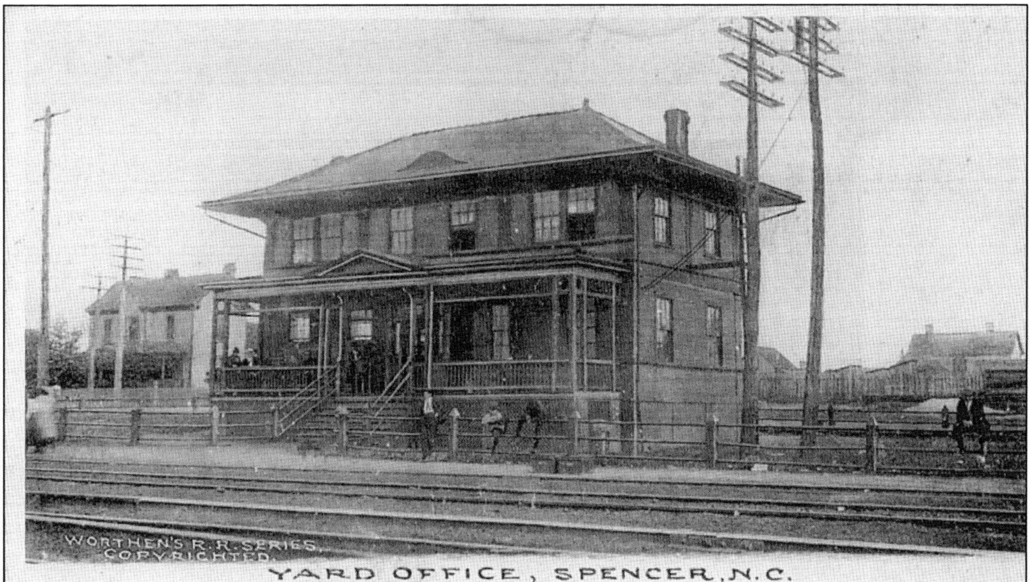

This yard office was built about 1900. The building was located at the back of the Spencer Shops right beside the main line. This building was torn down about 1917–1919. (Courtesy of the Marian Harter Collection.)

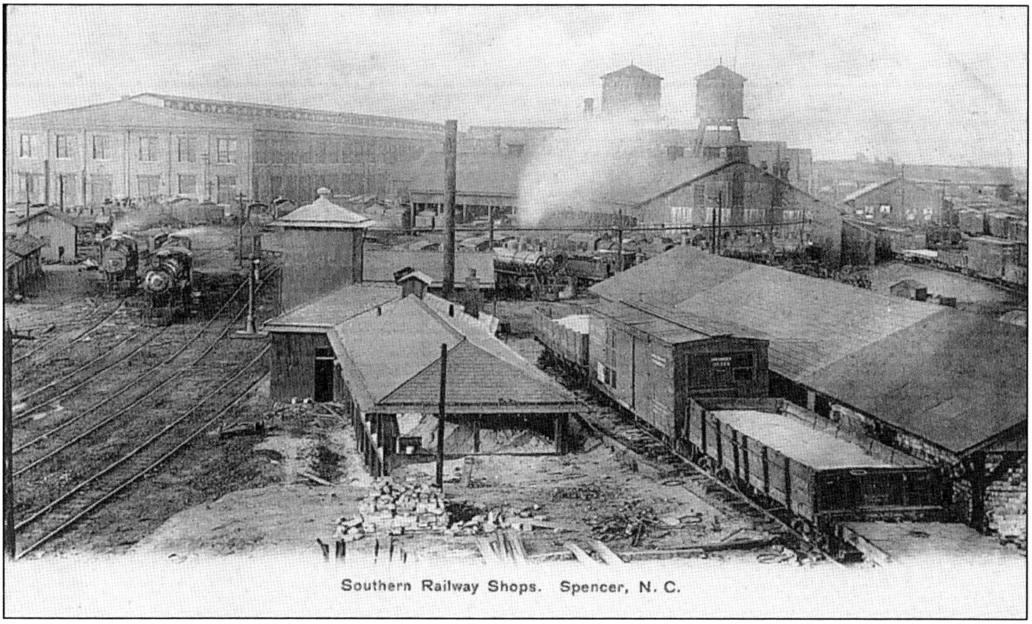

In 1896, 3 miles north of Salisbury, Southern Railroad Company started what became the largest steam locomotive servicing facility between Washington, D.C., and Atlanta, Georgia. Streets were laid out, residences built, and the Town of Spencer—named for Samuel Spencer, president of Southern Railroad—was begun. Today, the facility is known as the N.C. Transportation Museum.

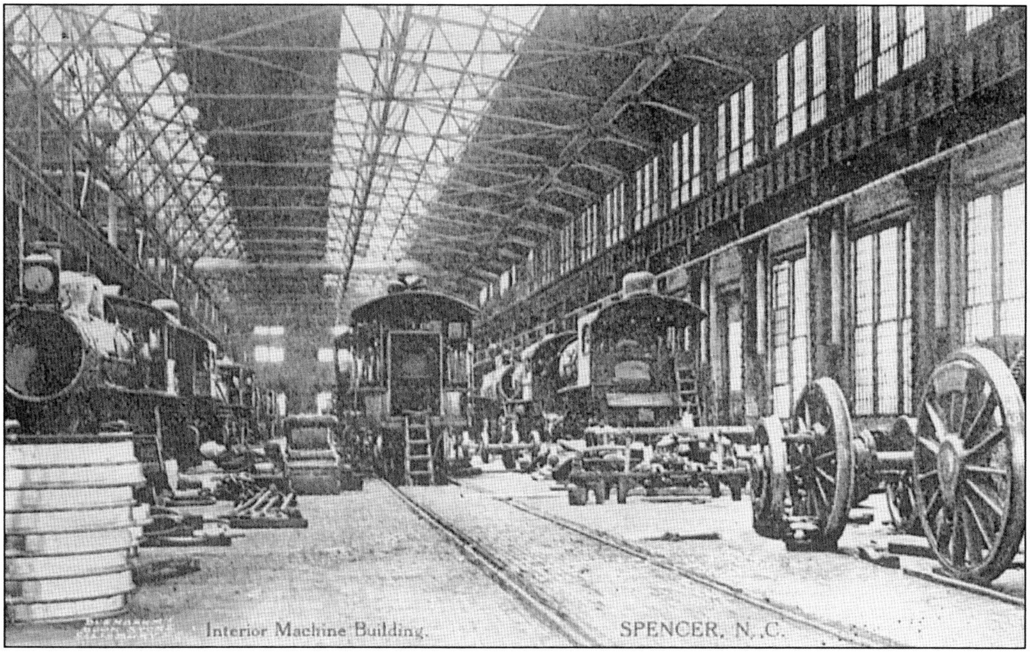

Steam engines would run for about 150 miles before needing to take on coal, water, and sand. In 1905, Spencer Shop's large machine shop was erected. (Card from Buerbaum.)

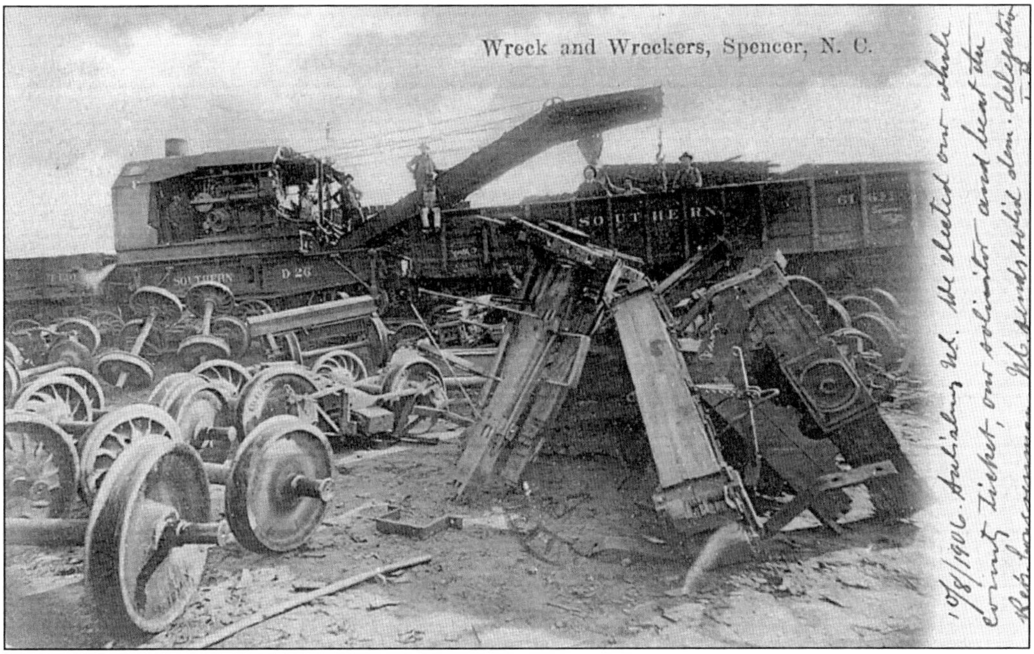

Buerbaum's note on this card states, "We elected the whole county ticket, our solicitor, and beat the Republican Congressman. North Carolina sends solid Democratic delegation." The county had become a Democratic Party stronghold. Buerbaum refrained from commenting on his handiwork at least this once and used his postcards like others—just to send a message.

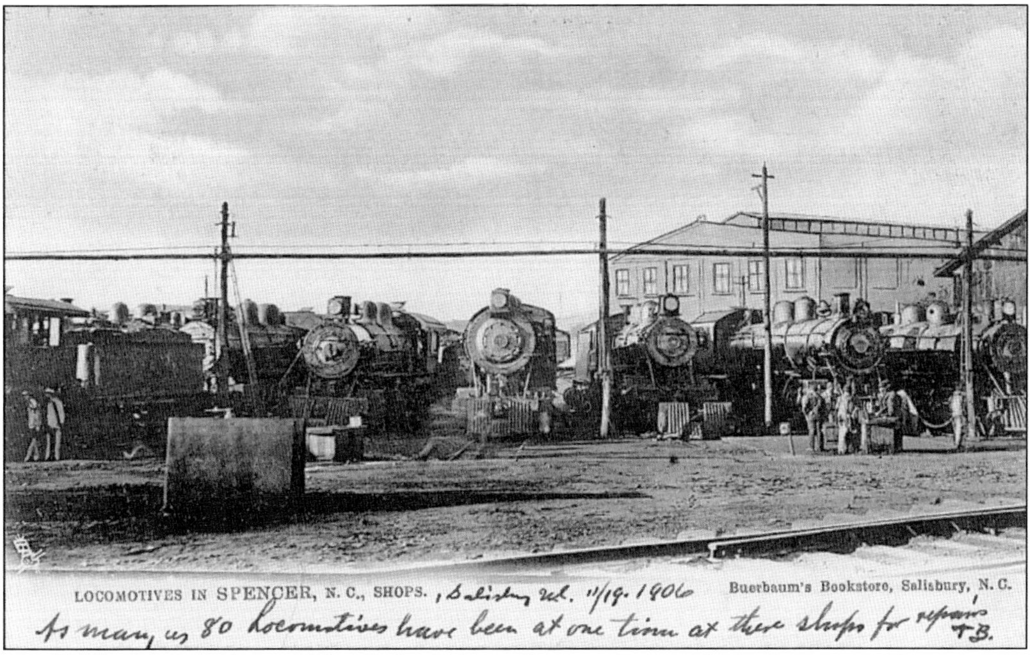

Buerbaum's note on this card showing a lineup of locomotives reads, "As many as 80 locomotives have been at one time at these shops for repairs."

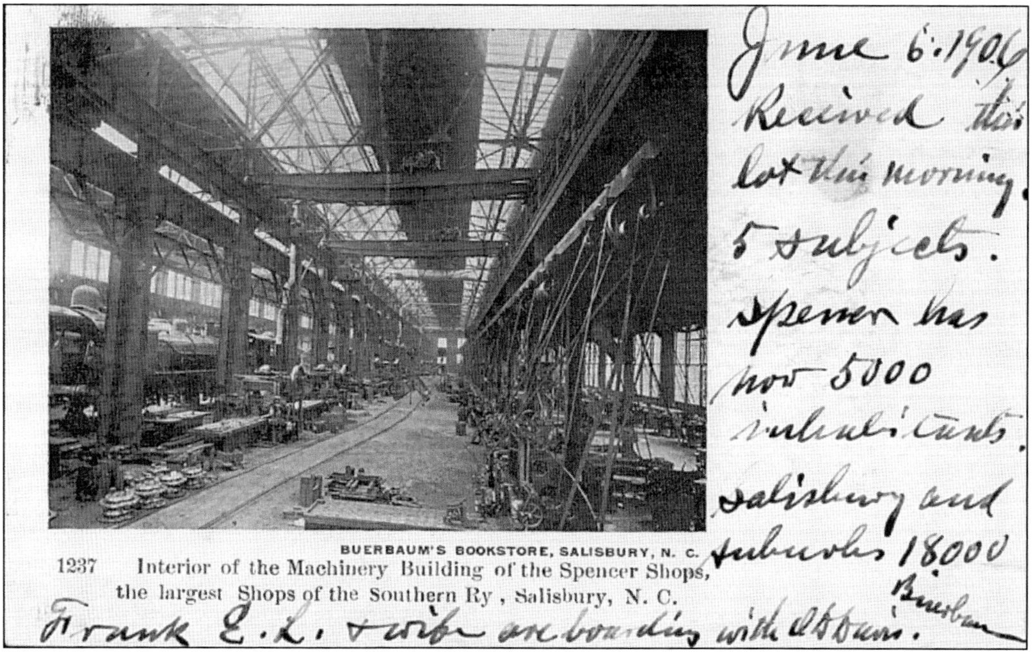

Here, Buerbaum's note states, "Spencer has now 5,000 inhabitants, Salisbury and suburbs 18,000. Frank E.L. and wife are boarding with O.D. Davis." The new railroad town was booming as men crowded in to keep the cinders belching.

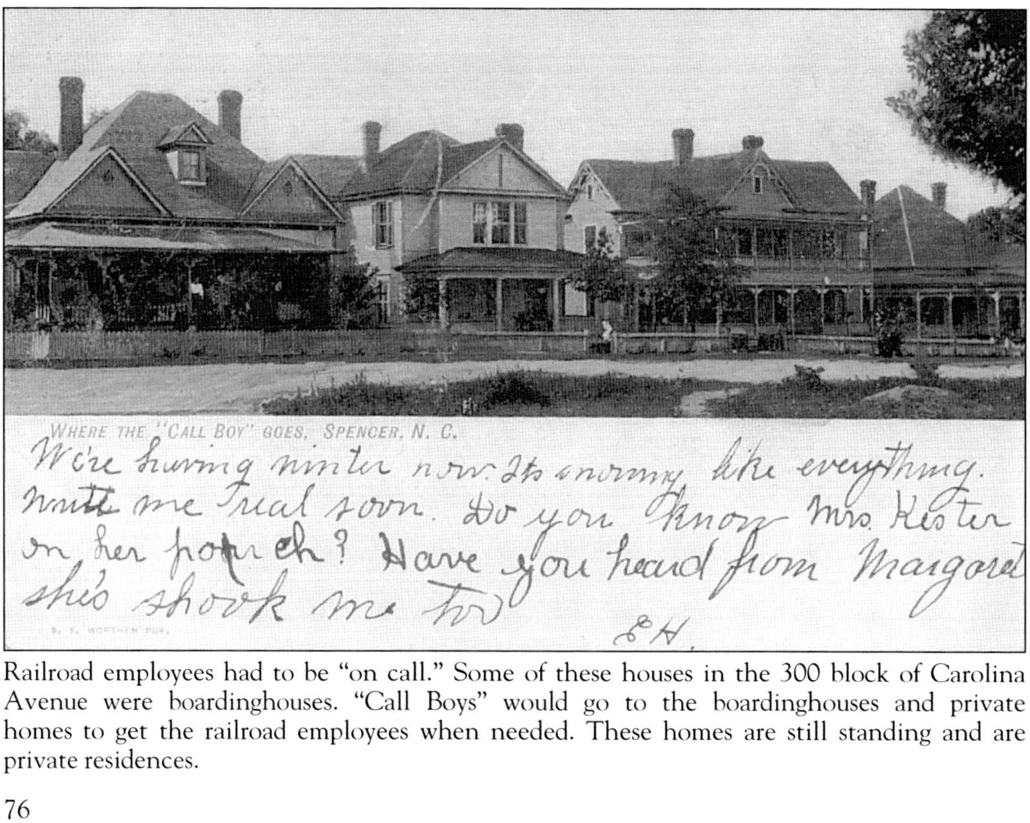

Railroad employees had to be "on call." Some of these houses in the 300 block of Carolina Avenue were boardinghouses. "Call Boys" would go to the boardinghouses and private homes to get the railroad employees when needed. These homes are still standing and are private residences.

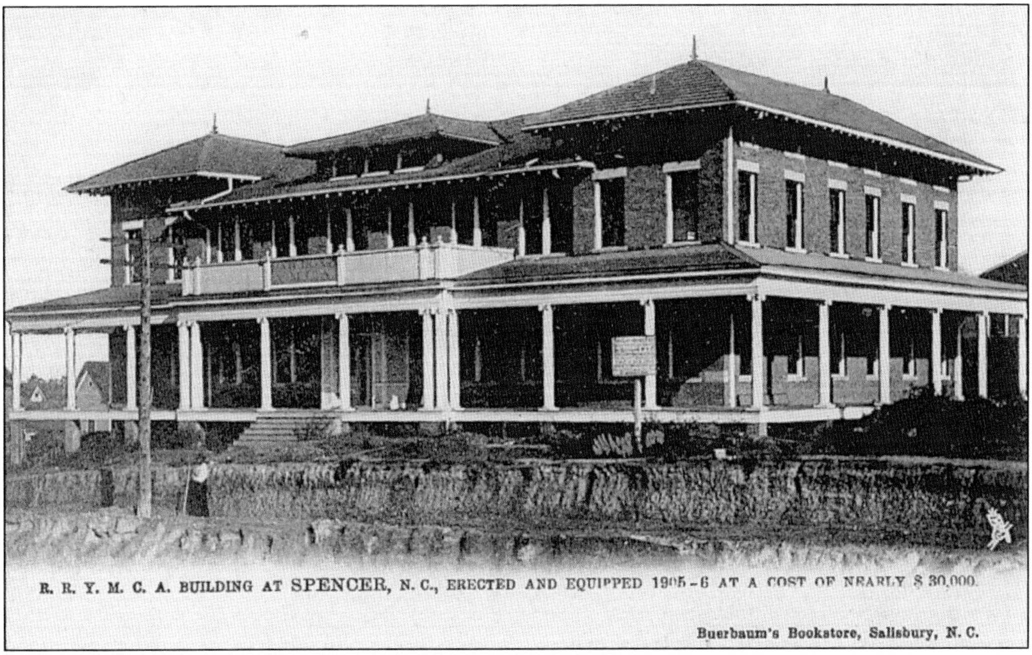

Spencer's Railroad YMCA was subsidized by Southern Railroad. It offered 24-hour-a-day, 365-days-a-year service to the railroad employees. Men could come at any time and order a meal. This facility closed in 1968 and was demolished in 1970. The Spencer City offices are now in this location.

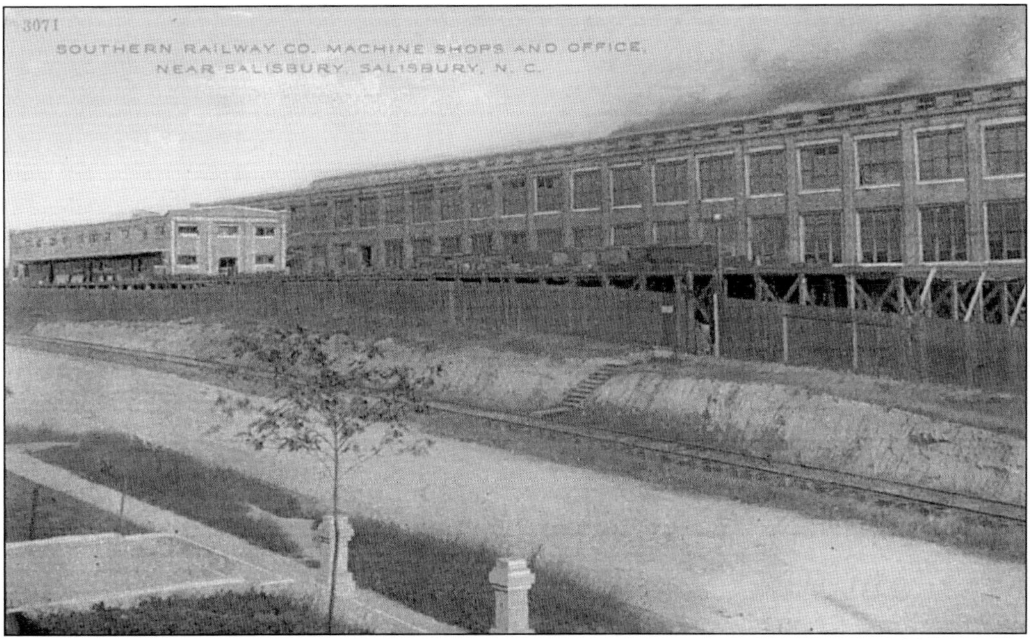

The original Spencer Shops included a 15-stall roundhouse, a small machine shop, a blacksmith, a boiler shop, two car repair sheds, a storehouse, a paint house, and an oil house. This view was taken from the yard of the Railroad YMCA.

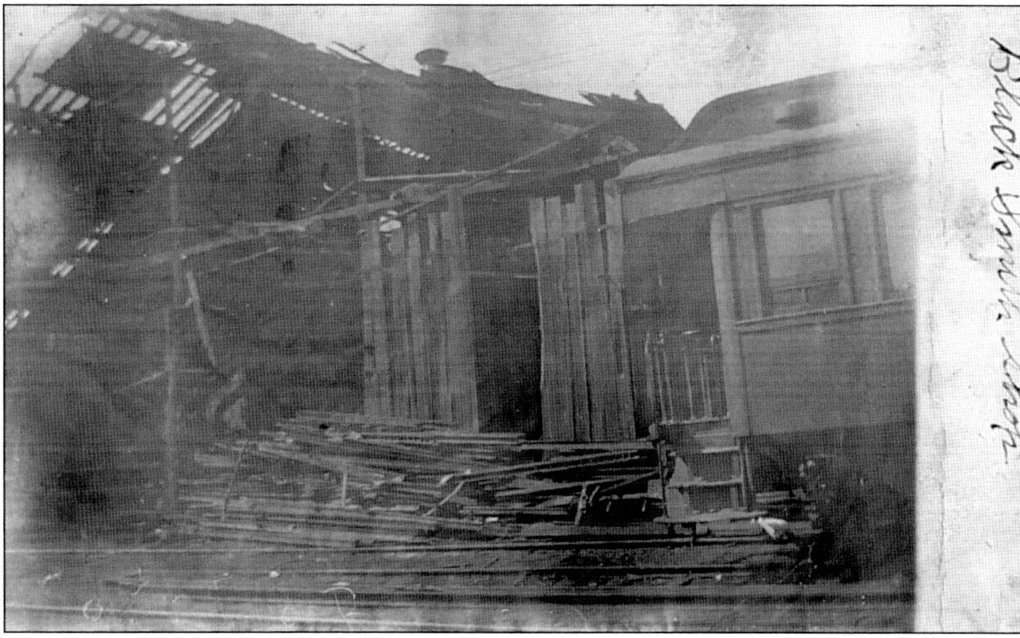

On October 1, 1908, a caboose near the Spencer Shop's powder house caught fire. The powder house, which was located near the blacksmith shop was filled with gunpowder, dynamite, railroad torpedoes, and other explosives. The resulting explosion killed two men and injured numerous others. The explosion was felt all over the town. The blacksmith shop is pictured.

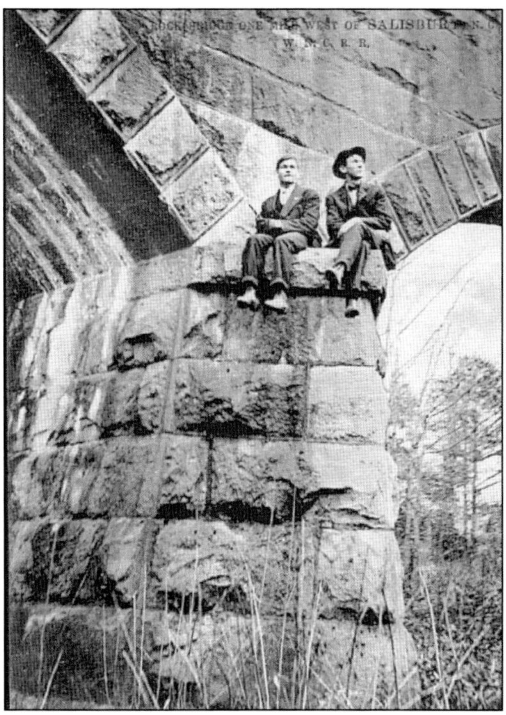

The double-arch bridge was erected to carry the Western N.C. Railroad across Grant's Creek. It was constructed in 1856–1857 by William Murdoch, a Scottish stonemason who had helped build North Carolina's State Capitol and Charleston, South Carolina's Fort Sumter. Because the bridge was so expensive, the railroad's directors asked a New York engineer to appraise it. His opinion was that nothing short of an earthquake would ever remove the bridge. The bridge is still standing. (Card from Buerbaum.)

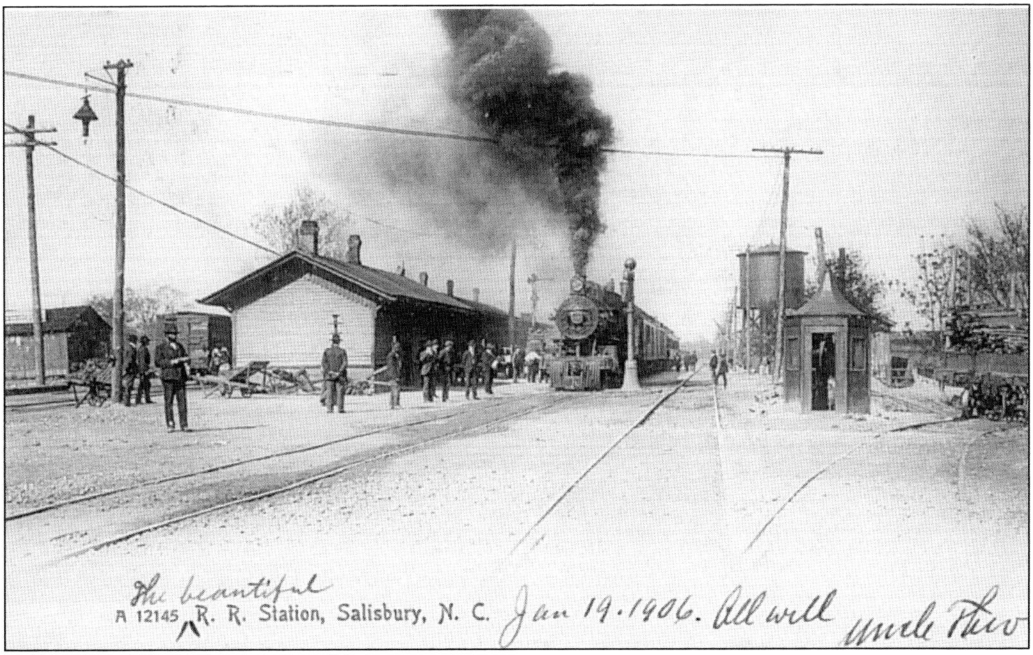

This card shows Salisbury's original railroad station. The small building on the right with the door was the watchman's shanty. When a train started out, the watchman came out with a hand sign to stop any traffic on Council Street. The water tank supplied water to the water spout beside the engine. In March 1907, this depot was torn down. (Card from Buerbaum.)

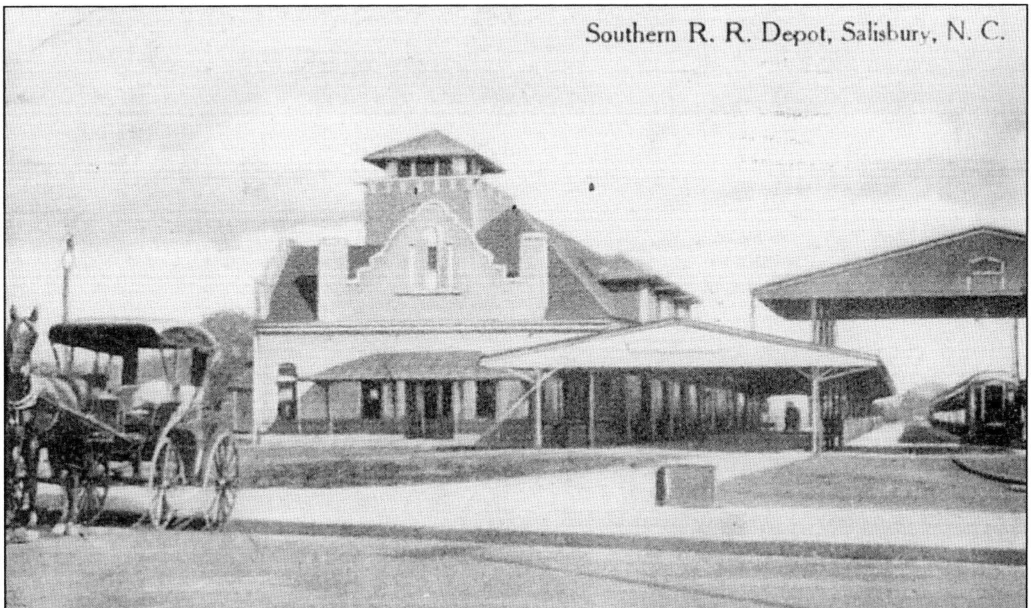

Salisbury's Spanish mission–style depot was called the most beautiful depot between Washington, D.C., and Atlanta, Georgia. The shed on the right was designed to protect passengers from weather. The vent in the shed was to allow smoke from the engines to escape.

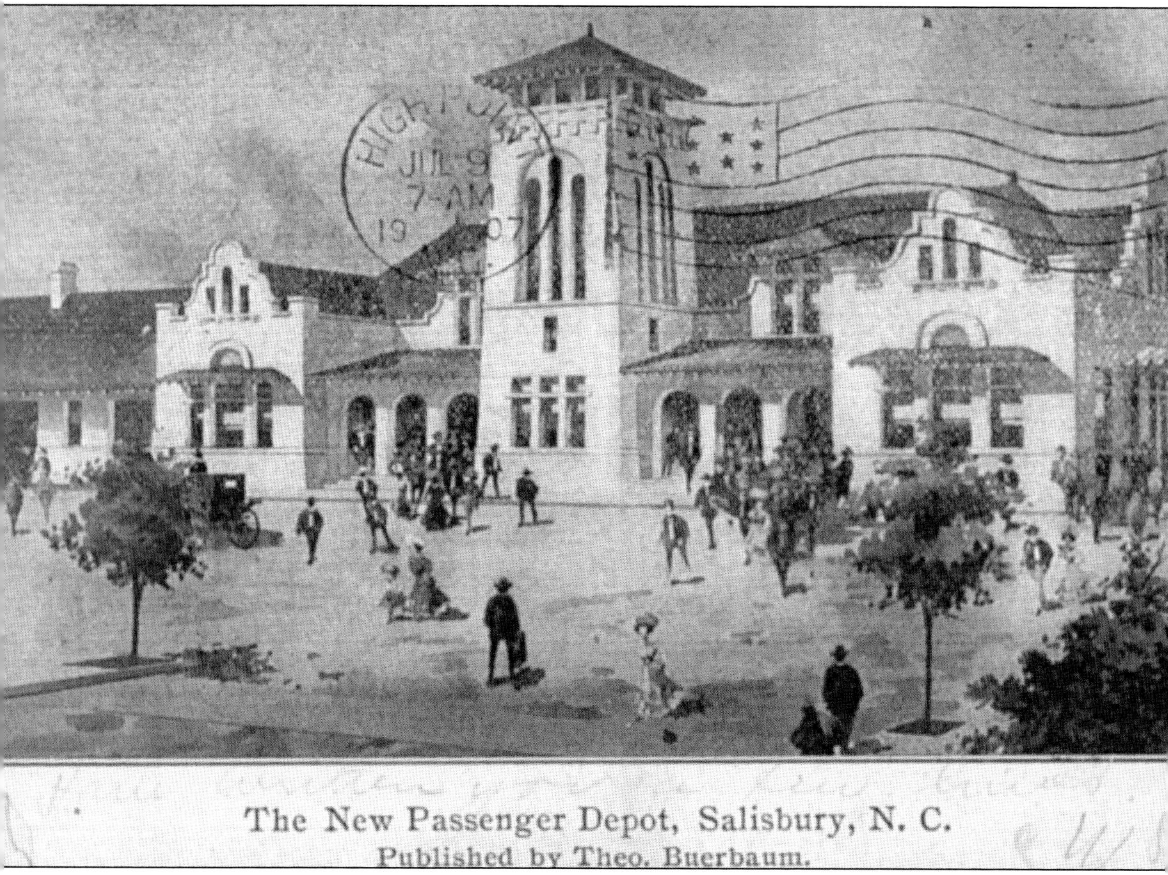

Built in 1908, the depot has been at the center of town activities. It now houses Historic Salisbury Foundation and is known as the Tom E. Smith place.

Five

MILITARY

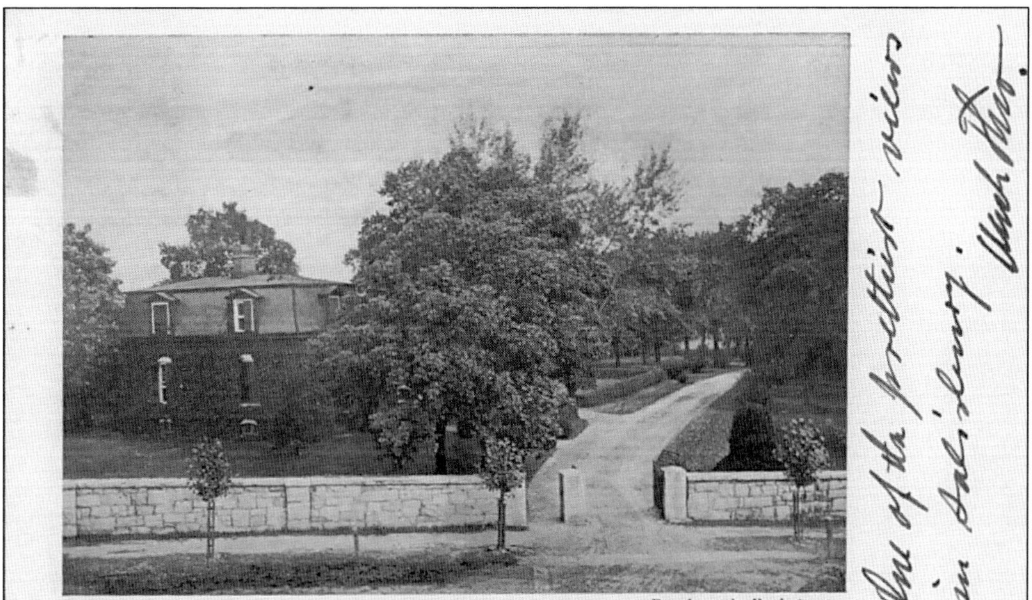

The National Cemetery in Salisbury was established in 1865 on land the federal government purchased from Joseph Horah. The cemetery holds an unknown number of Union soldiers who died at the Confederate prison and were buried in trenches outside the prison gates. Buerbaum says, "One of the prettiest views in Salisbury. Uncle Theo."

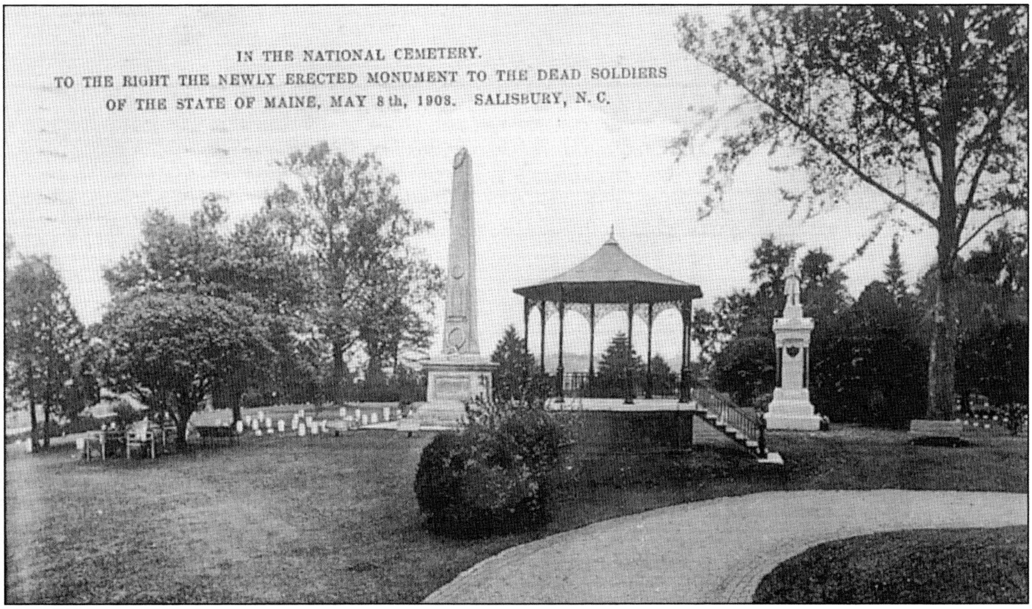

This 19th-century, cast-iron gazebo stood for decades in the National Cemetery. When it was scrapped, Edgar Temple rescued it and had it moved to his family home in the Milford Hills section of Salisbury. It was later moved to complement Salisbury's Bell Tower, which stands along Innes Street.

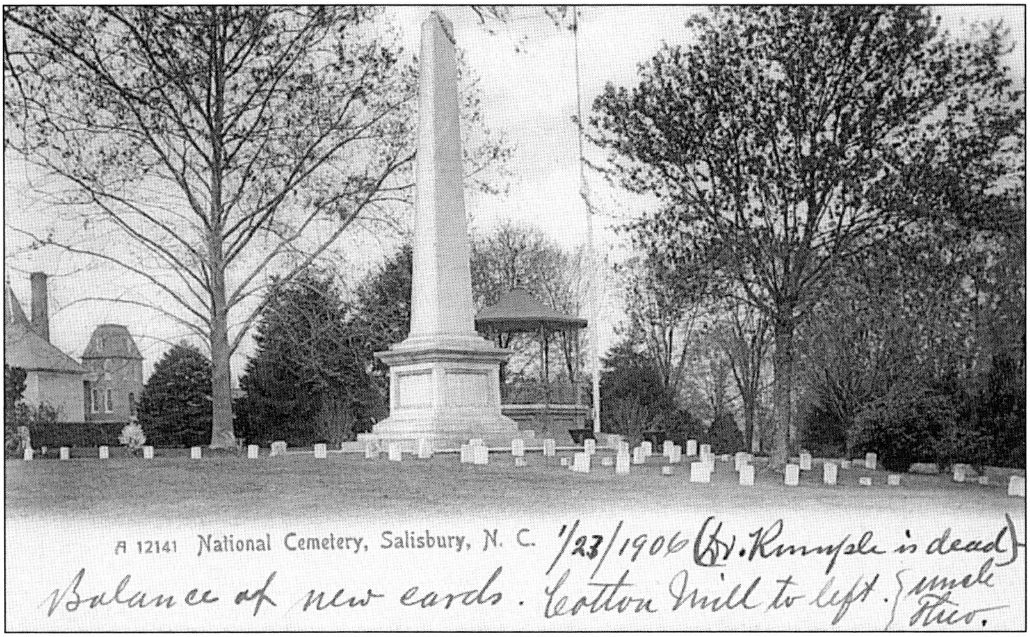

The U.S. government erected this monument in 1876 in memory of the soldiers who died while held in the Salisbury Prison from 1864 to 1865. Buerbaum's note reading "Dr. Rumple is dead" refers to Rev. Jethro Rumple, D.D., who was the pastor of Salisbury's First Presbyterian Church for 46 years. Rumple performed home missionary work in the North Carolina mountains and also authored *History of Rowan County* in 1881. He died January 20, 1906. (Card from Buerbaum.)

The National Cemetery's Pennsylvania monument was dedicated on November 16, 1910. It is topped by a bronze statue of a Prisoner of War, which stands 8 feet high. The memorial is made of white granite from Mount Airy quarries, Georgia marble, and Italian marble. (Card from Buerbaum.)

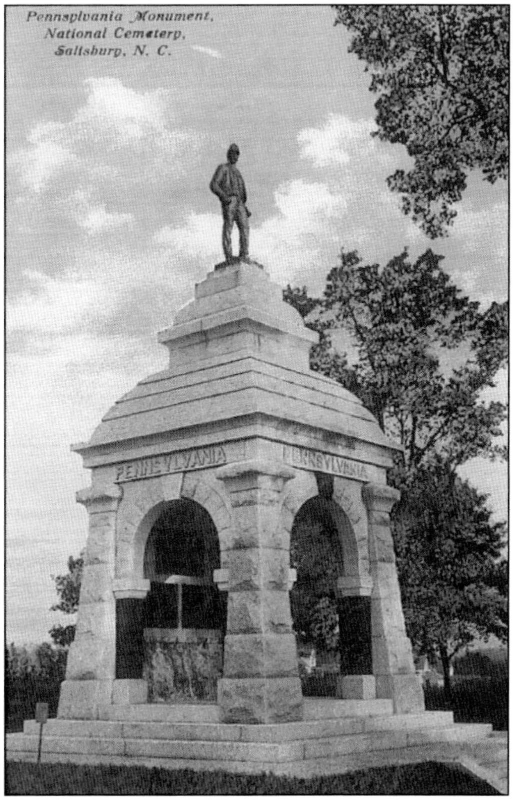

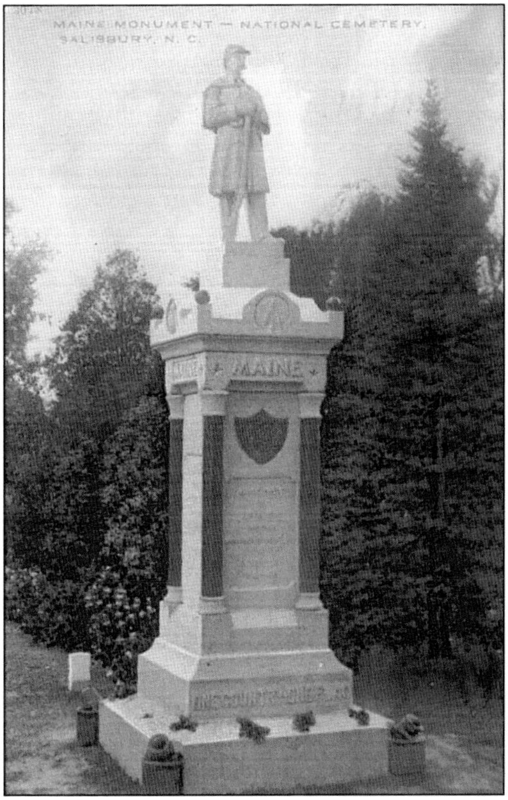

The state of Maine erected a monument from Maine granite on June 8, 1908. Maine and Pennsylvania were the only two monuments erected in the cemetery by northern states in memory of their soldiers who died at the Salisbury Prison.

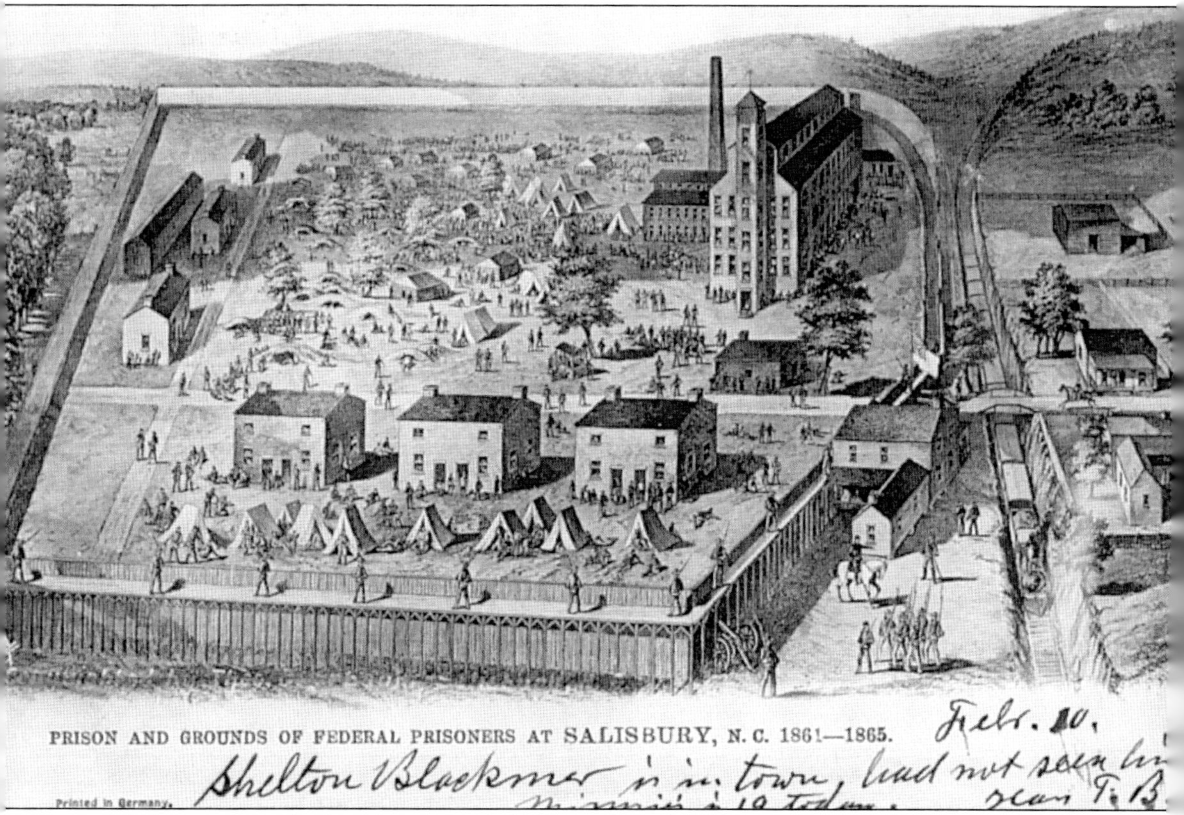

Salisbury artist Charles Kraus painted the image of the Confederate prison from memory 21 years after the prison burned. Salisbury's prison burned during General Stoneman's raid on April 17, 1865. On close inspection, the upper, right-hand corner of the card reveals a tunnel, the preferred method of escape by most Union soldiers. (Card from Buerbaum.)

In 1903, Salisbury's Robert F. Hoke Chapter, United Daughters of the Confederacy commissioned Frederick Ruckstuhl to create a memorial with an artistic, as well as patriotic significance. The sum of $10,000 had to be raised. The statue was completed and put on exhibition in Paris. It was then placed in a warehouse for four years until all the money was raised. The monument has two bronze figures above a Rowan County pink granite pedestal. The Angel, "Fame," holds a dying Confederate soldier. (Card from Buerbaum.)

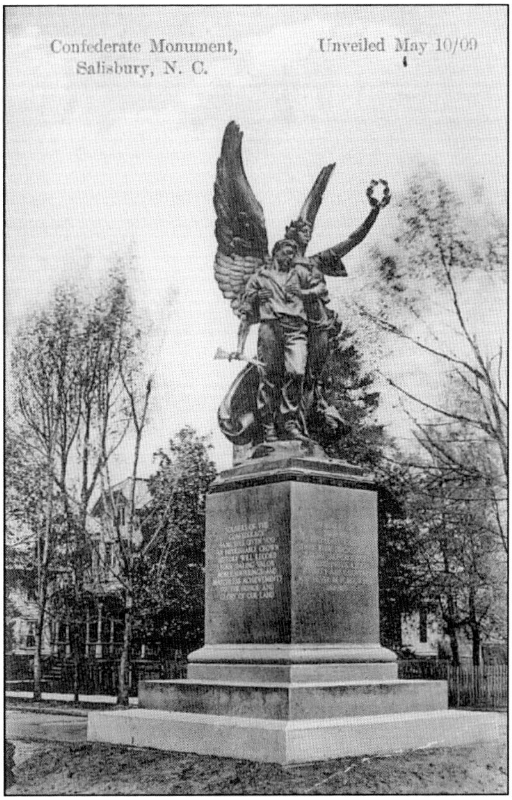

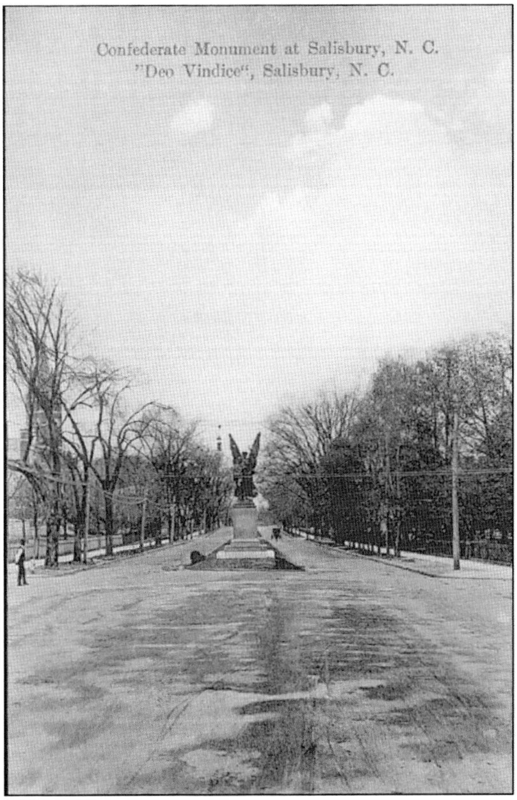

On May 10, 1909, the Confederate monument was dedicated before a crowd of 4,000. A procession met at the Empire Hotel and was led by Mrs. T.J. "Stonewall" Jackson. This was Mrs. Jackson's last public appearance. Six hundred school children placed floral tributes at the base. The monument was unveiled by Frances Fisher (Christian Reid) Tiernan, who recited "Gloria Victus," which she had written. "Deo Vindice" is translated as "With God as Protector." (Card from Buerbaum.)

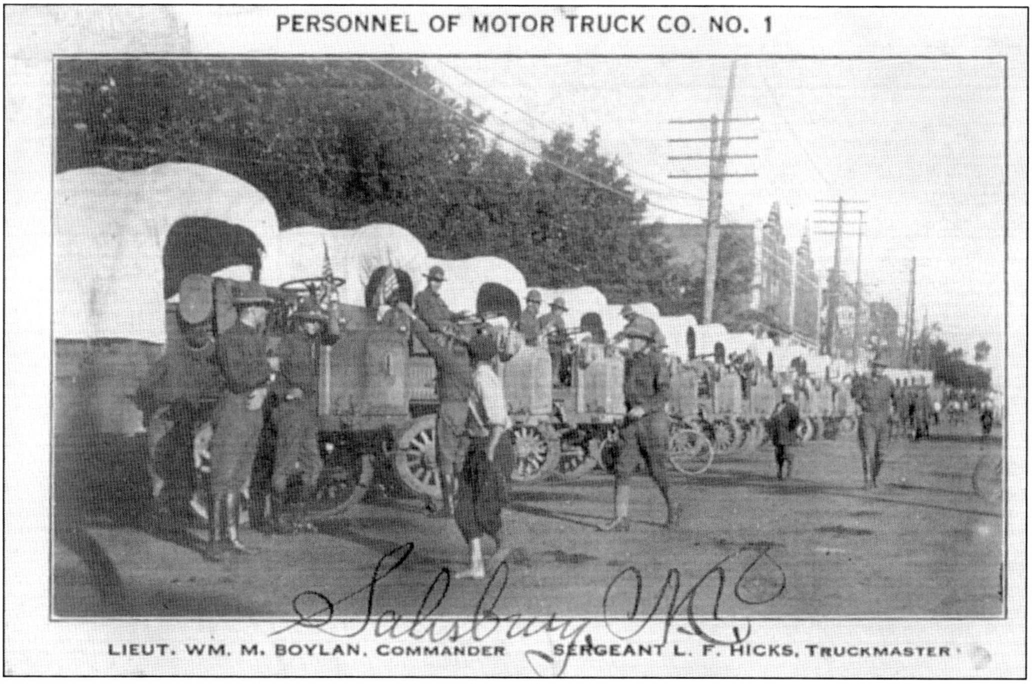

The United States went to war with Germany in 1917. In July of that year, the National Guard was called to active duty, and Rowan County men prepared to leave. Drills and maneuvers were given on East Innes Street. In September, Rowan's second quota of men left for Fort Jackson with Lt. Samuel C. Hart. A local American Legion Post here would later carry his name. This card is postmarked September 24, 1917. (Courtesy of the Marian Harter Collection.)

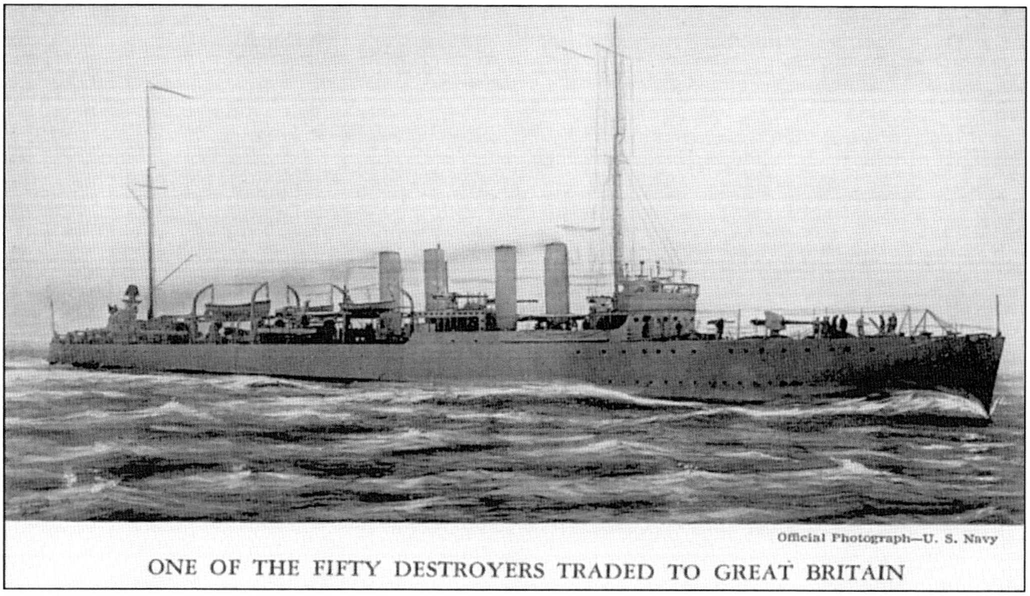

Salisbury's English Speaking Union sponsored this destroyer from 1940 to 1945. It was one of 50 destroyers the United States lent England in exchange for the use of air space and naval bases. In 1950, Lt. Commander M. Beechinge of the Royal Navy and British Consul T. McDonald presented the ship's log book to the Salisbury City Council.

Six

Social Services

Schools, Government Buildings, Nazareth Orphan's Home, and Medical Buildings

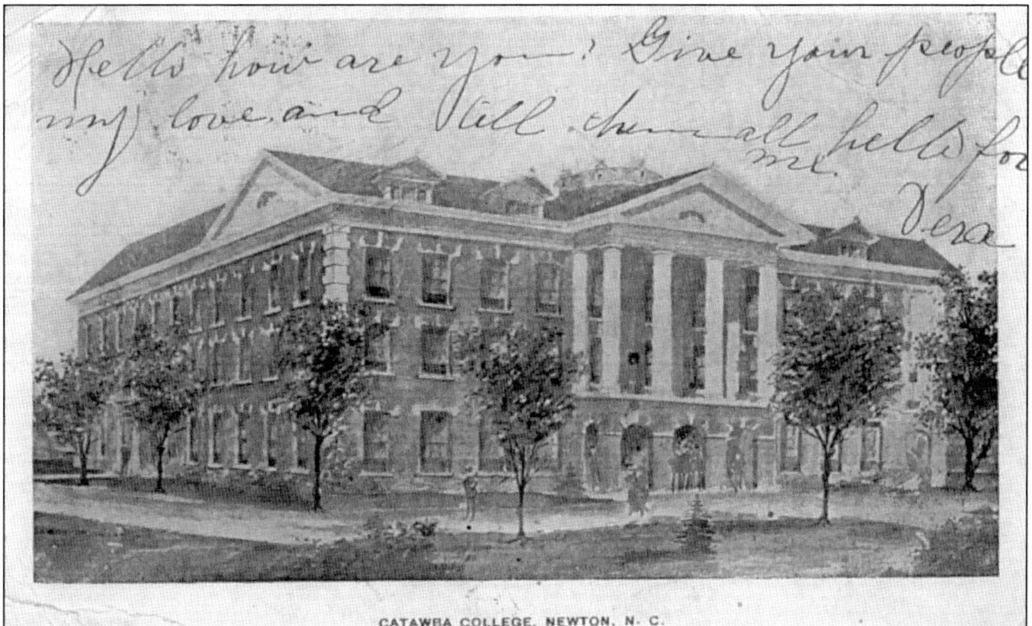

This view is the Old Main Building in Newton, North Carolina. Salisbury's Catawba College was founded there in 1851 and operated in Newton until closing in 1923. It reopened in Salisbury in the fall of 1925.

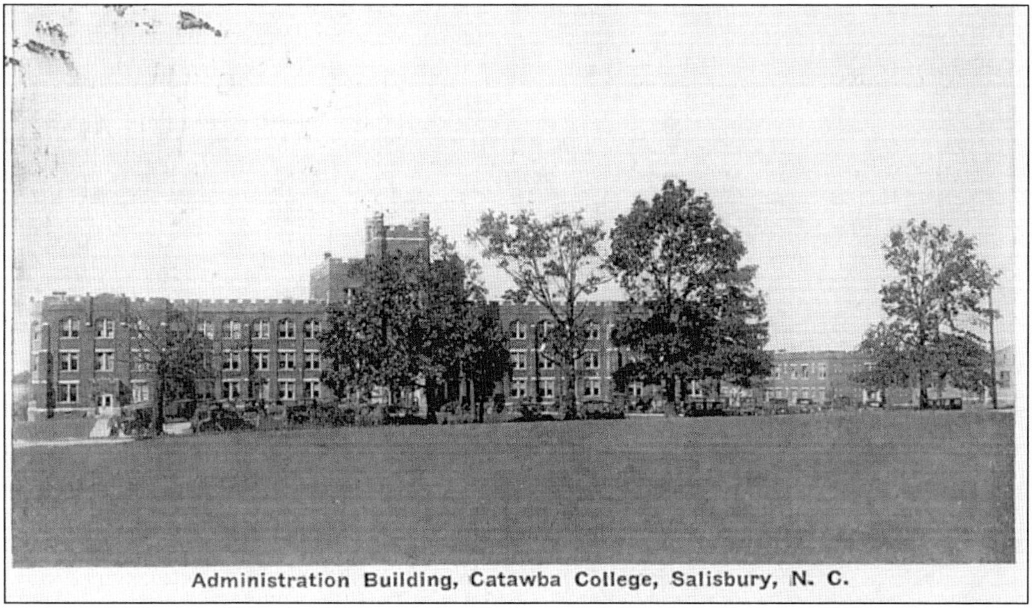

The Hedrick Administration Building was named in honor of Mr. J.T. Hedrick of Lexington, a church leader and trustee of the college. The building was built as Faith Hall in 1917 to house the Salisbury Normal and Industrial Institute, but the institute never moved into the facility. When local church leaders prevailed on the North Carolina Classis of the Reformed Church to move Catawba College to Salisbury, the property was purchased to house the college. It housed a dormitory for men, staff apartments, the library, dining facilities, an auditorium, classrooms, faculty offices, and all administrative offices.

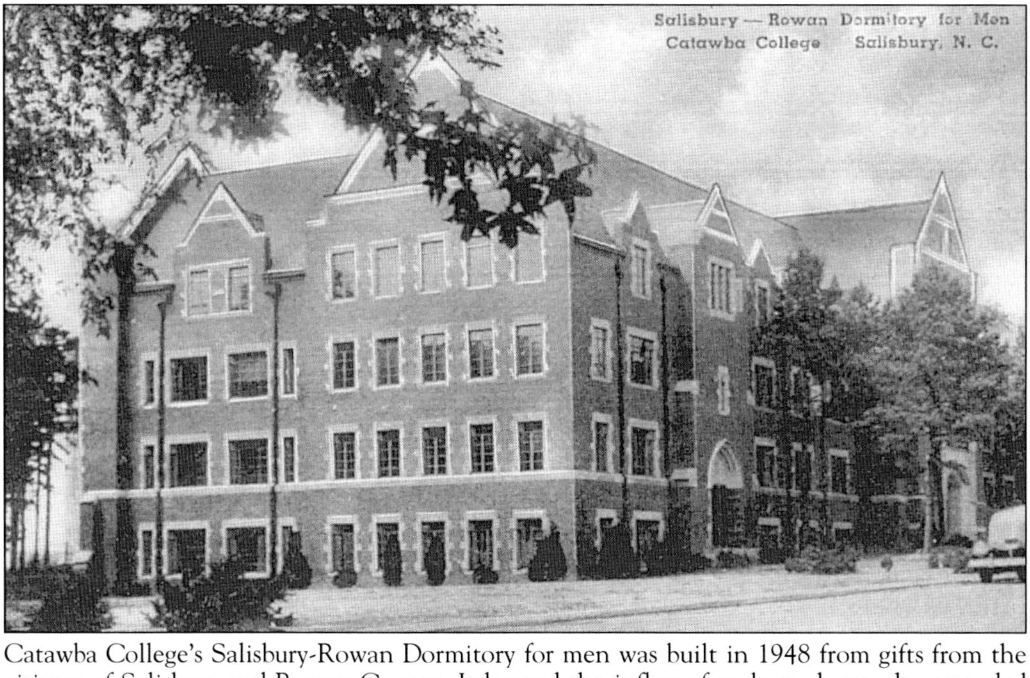

Catawba College's Salisbury-Rowan Dormitory for men was built in 1948 from gifts from the citizens of Salisbury and Rowan County. It housed the influx of male students who attended college on the G.I. Bill following World War II.

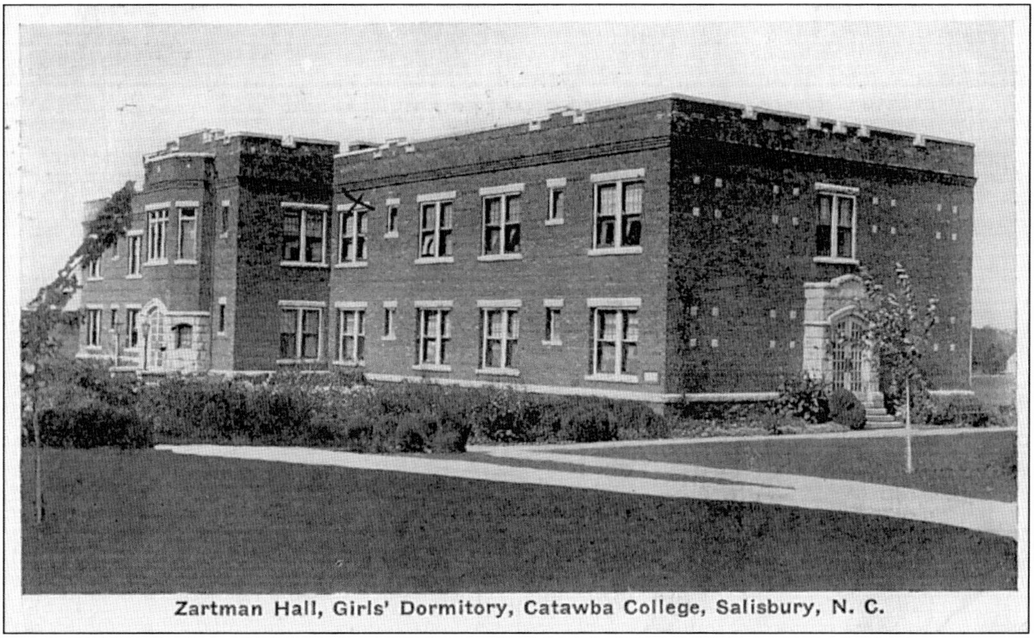

Zartman Hall at Catawba College was built in 1926 as the first women's residence hall on Catawba's campus and was named for Elizabeth Conrad Zartman. It was built with funds provided by the Women's Missionary Society of the Reformed Church. In 1988, the hall was modernized and renamed Barger-Zartman Hall in honor of Zeda Barger of Rockwell.

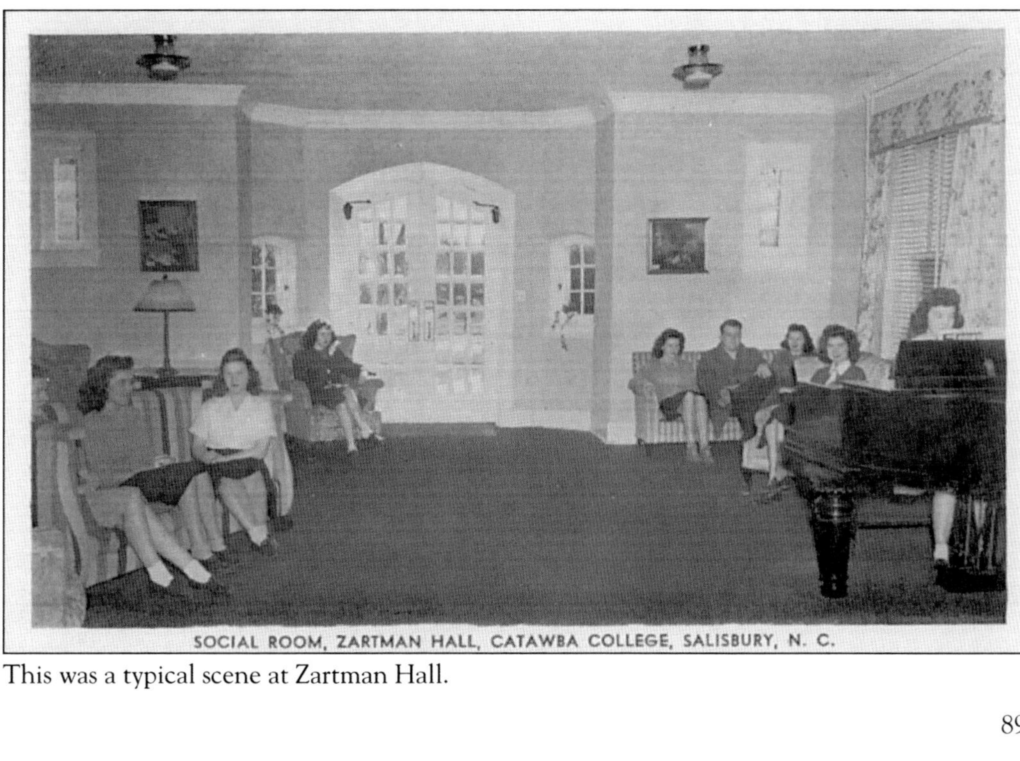

This was a typical scene at Zartman Hall.

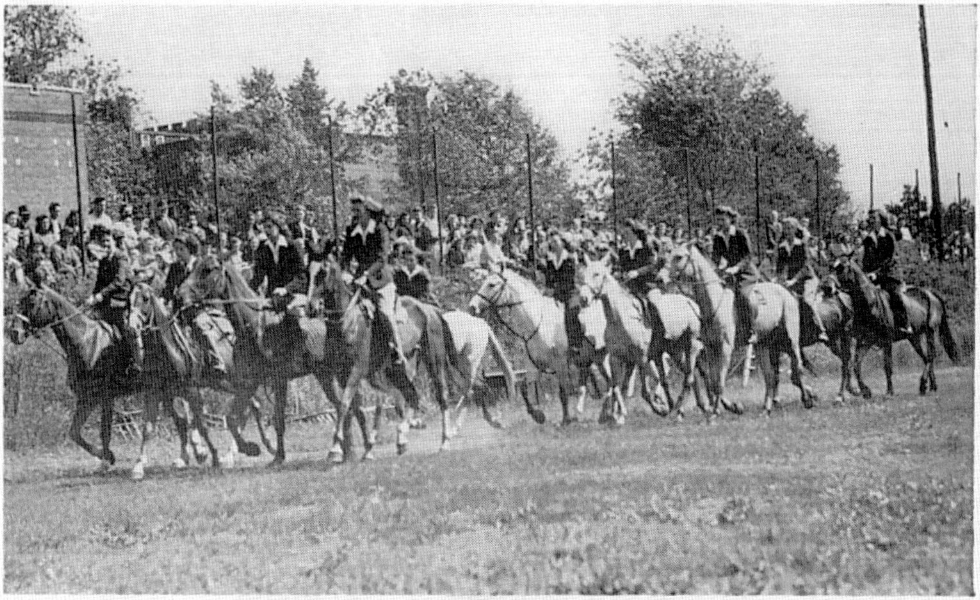

HORSE SHOW — CATAWBA COLLEGE, SALISBURY, N. C.

Catawba College's Horse Show was an annual event of the Women's Athletic Association. Noted trainer and instructor Mr. June Fisher, who operated Meadowbrook Stables, was in charge of the program. This photo appeared in the 1946 college yearbook, the *Sayakini*.

RAHAUSER DINING HALL, CATAWBA COLLEGE, SALISBURY, N. C.

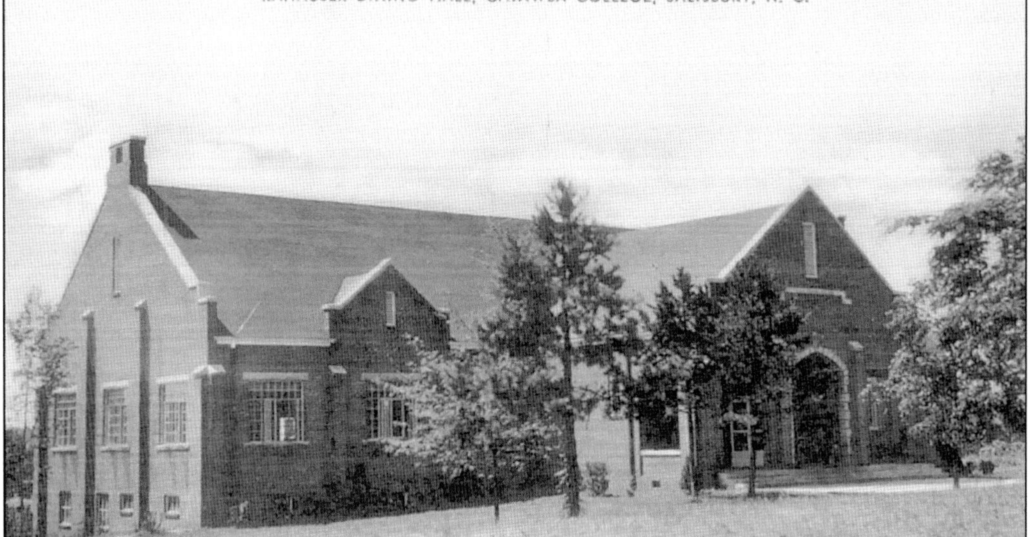

The college dining hall was officially titled the Rahauser Refectory in honor of Rev. Frederick Rahauser, a minister of the German Reformed Church, and it was built in the summer of 1938. In May of that year, Trustee Lotan Corriher of Landis, chairman of the building committee, approached Wagoner Construction Company and asked them to design and build a new dining hall that would be completed for the opening of the school in the fall of 1938. Corriher's gift of $10,000 and Rev. Rahauser's daughter Amelia's gift of $5,000 substantially funded the construction.

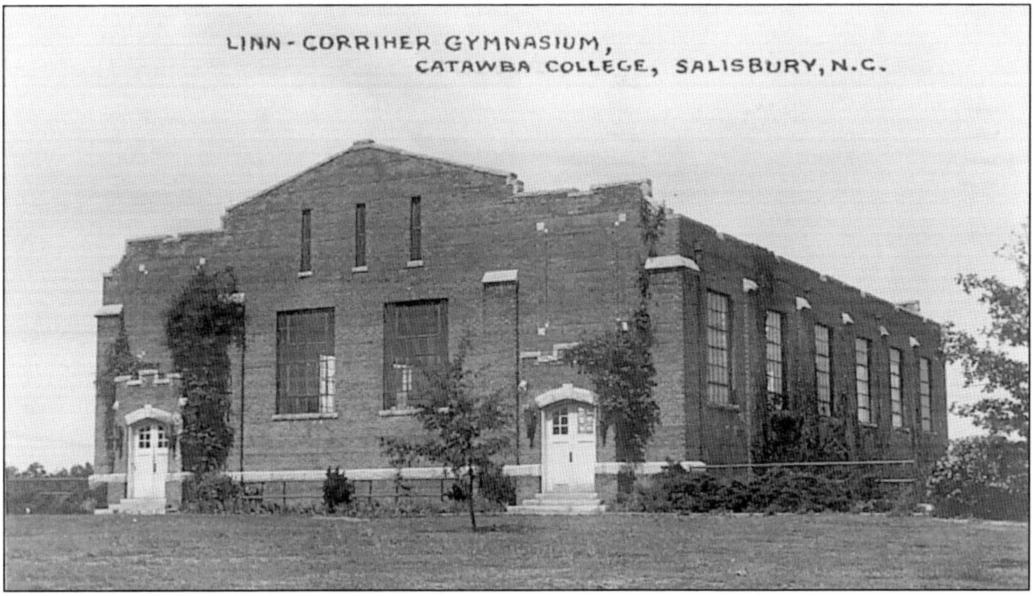

Catawba's Linn-Corriher Gymnasium was named in honor of two Landis trustees, J.P. Linn and L.A. Corriher. The gym was used for home basketball games from 1926 until the late 1950s when the college's games were moved to Boyden High School's new gym. Even then, the Linn-Corriher Gym was the location for physical education classes, intramural competition, formal dances, and graduation services until the completion of the Abernathy Physical Education Building in 1970.

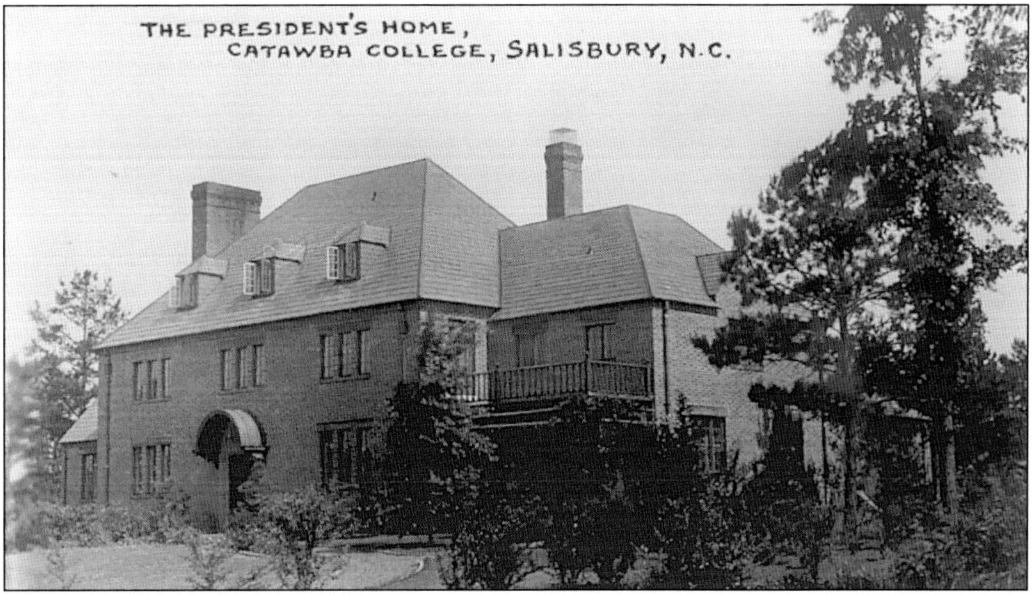

The President's House on the campus of Catawba College was built in 1930–1931. It was designed by the brother-in-law of Dr. Elmer Hoke, Catawba's first president in Salisbury. Dr. Hoke and his family only lived in the new house for a few months prior to his sudden death in the spring of 1931 at the age of 38. The building was originally named the Jacob Crawford Clapp House in honor of Dr. J.C. Clapp, who had been president of Catawba College from 1860 until 1900.

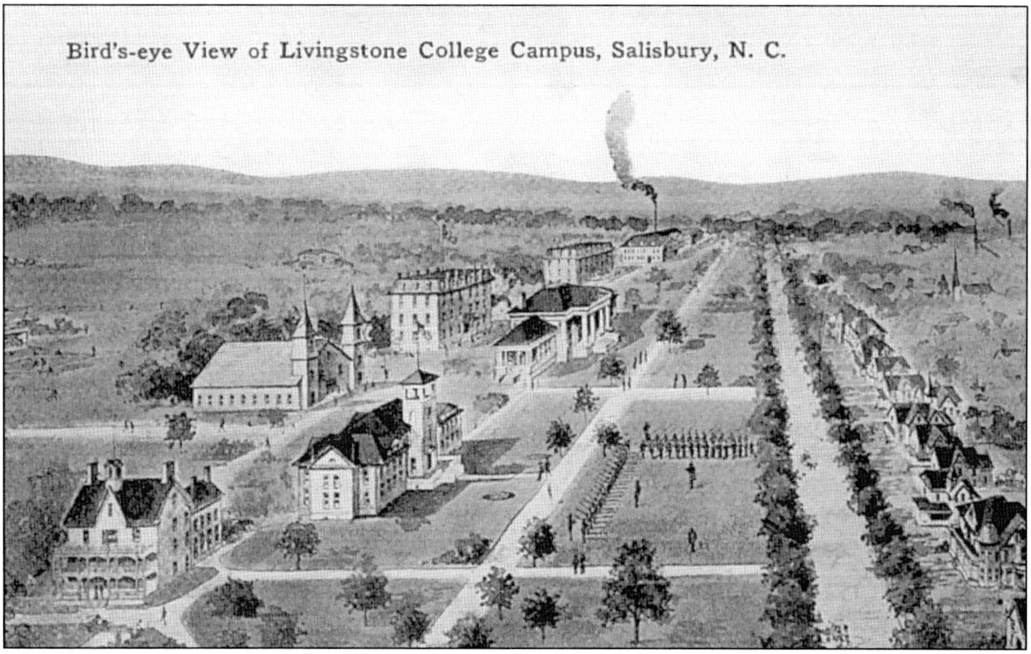

Joseph Charles Price suggested trustees change the name of Zion Wesley College to Livingstone College to honor African missionary, explorer, and abolitionist David Livingstone. The college was founded in 1879.

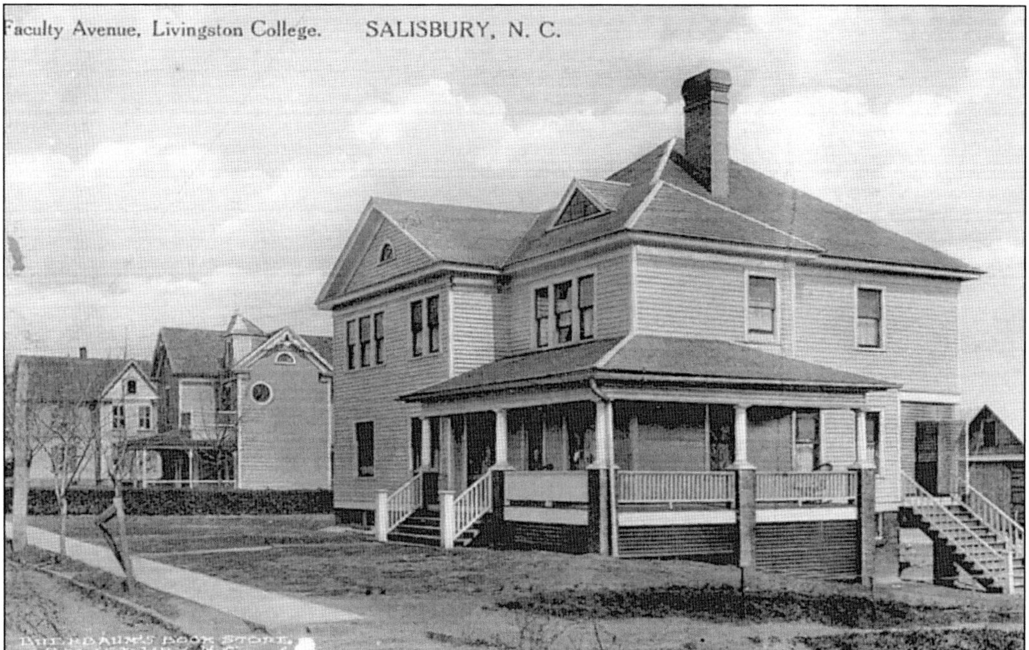

Monroe Street was where most of the faculty of Livingstone resided. The name "Faculty Avenue" was not the true name of this street but was a commonly accepted term.

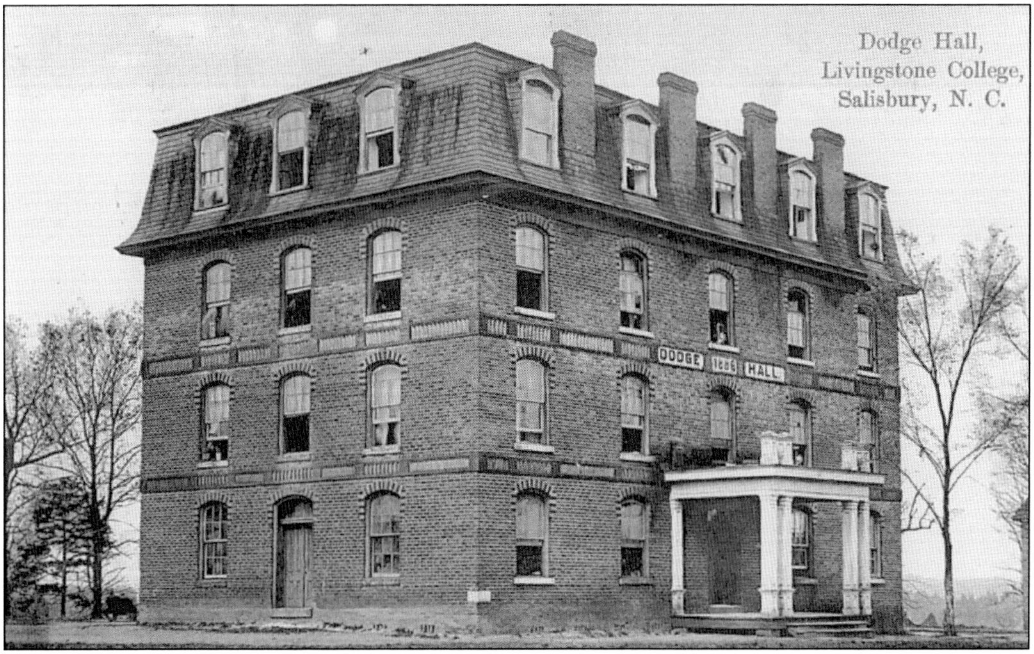

Dodge Hall was built in 1886 and was the first brick building constructed on the Livingstone College campus. The bricks were fashioned from clay pits located on the campus. Students helped with the brick making.

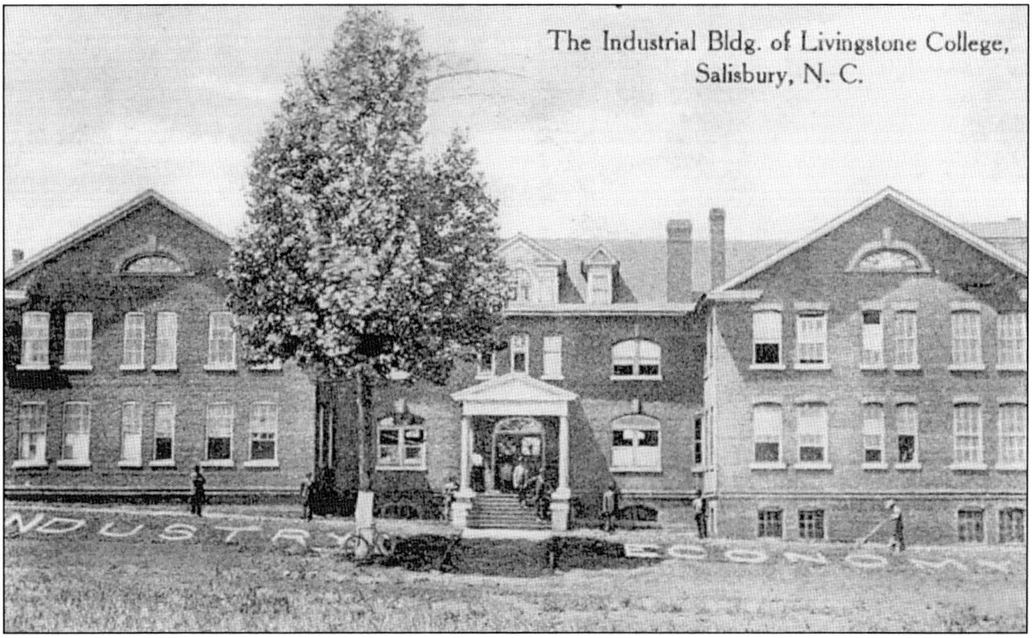

Livingstone's Industrial Building, later called Ballard Hall, was constructed in 1887. This building housed the industrial department in the early years. Part of the top of this building has been destroyed. Major renovations have been done to the building, which now houses the Student Services Center and campus bookstore.

Carnegie Library, built in 1907, was named in honor of Andrew Carnegie, the philanthropist. His gifts to schools and universities totaled in the millions of dollars, and many communities across the United States have libraries because of his generosity. (Card from Buerbaum.)

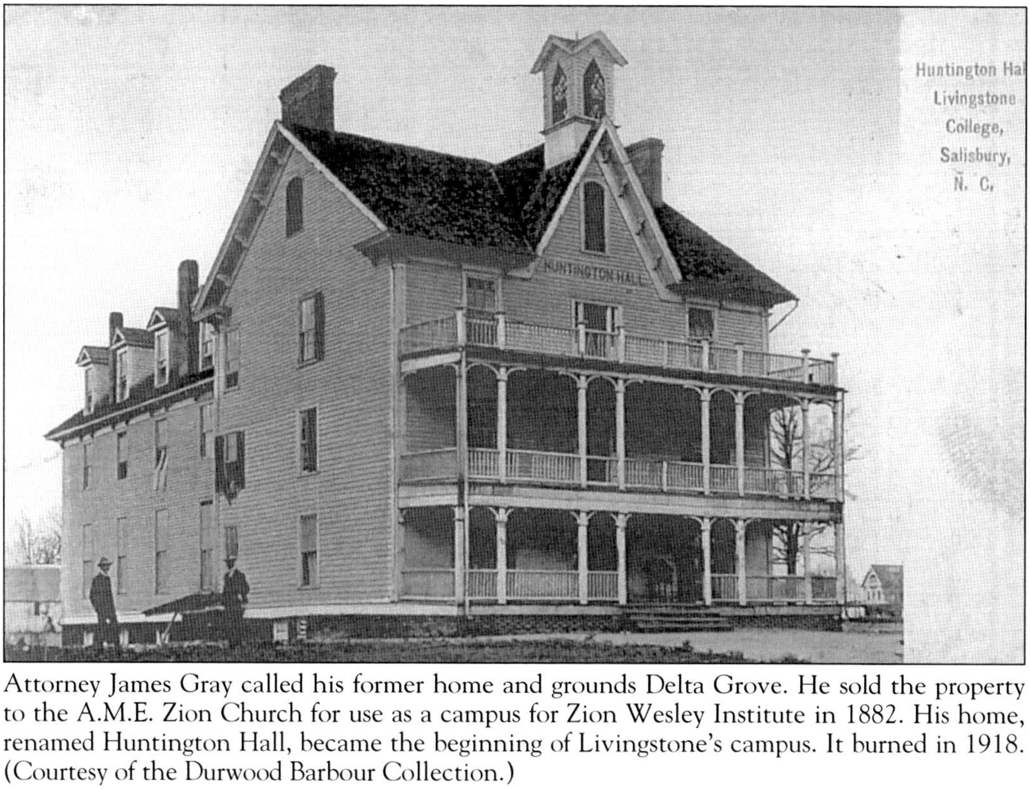

Attorney James Gray called his former home and grounds Delta Grove. He sold the property to the A.M.E. Zion Church for use as a campus for Zion Wesley Institute in 1882. His home, renamed Huntington Hall, became the beginning of Livingstone's campus. It burned in 1918. (Courtesy of the Durwood Barbour Collection.)

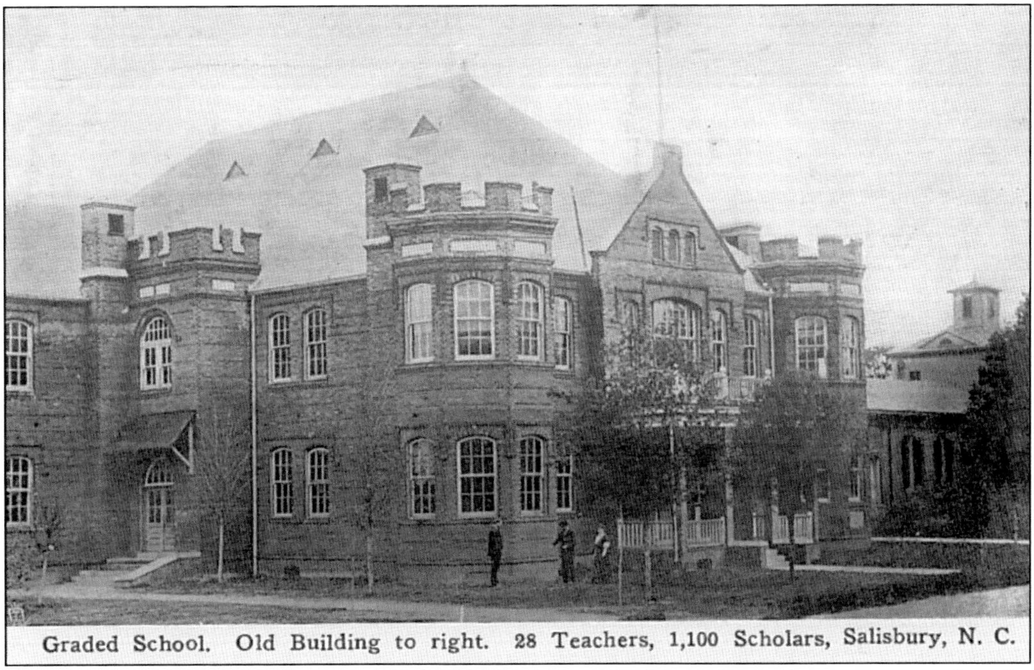

Salisbury's Graded School at 314 North Ellis Street was built in 1904 and was connected to the Old Ellis Street School. These buildings and a third on the North Ellis-West Liberty corner became Frank B. John Elementary School when Boyden High School opened in 1926. (Card from Buerbaum.)

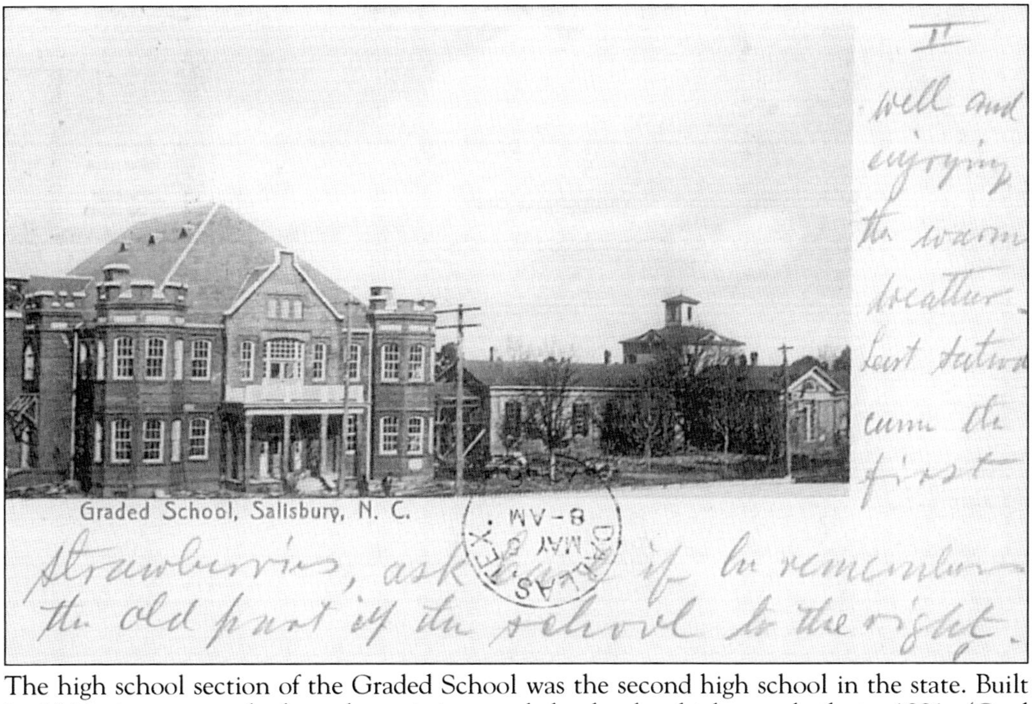

The high school section of the Graded School was the second high school in the state. Built in 1904, it was attached to the existing graded school, which was built in 1881. (Card from Buerbaum.)

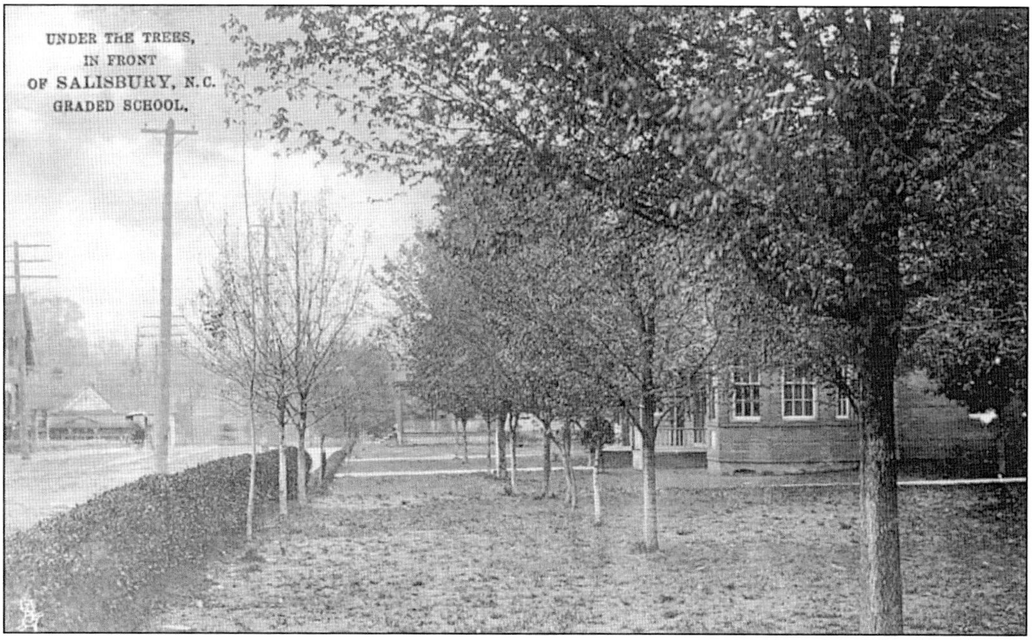

This is a view of the yard in front of the Graded School, showing the dirt street and the beautiful tree-lined walkway.

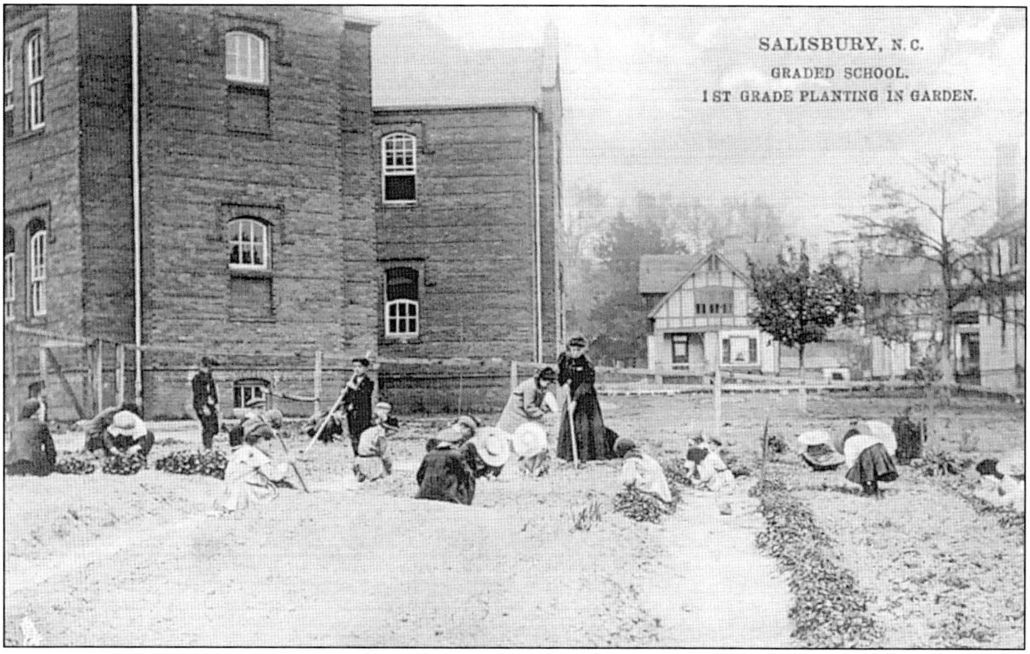

The first graders are shown here planting a garden in the rear of the addition to the school. The addition was built to provide room for a library, auditorium, offices, and classrooms.

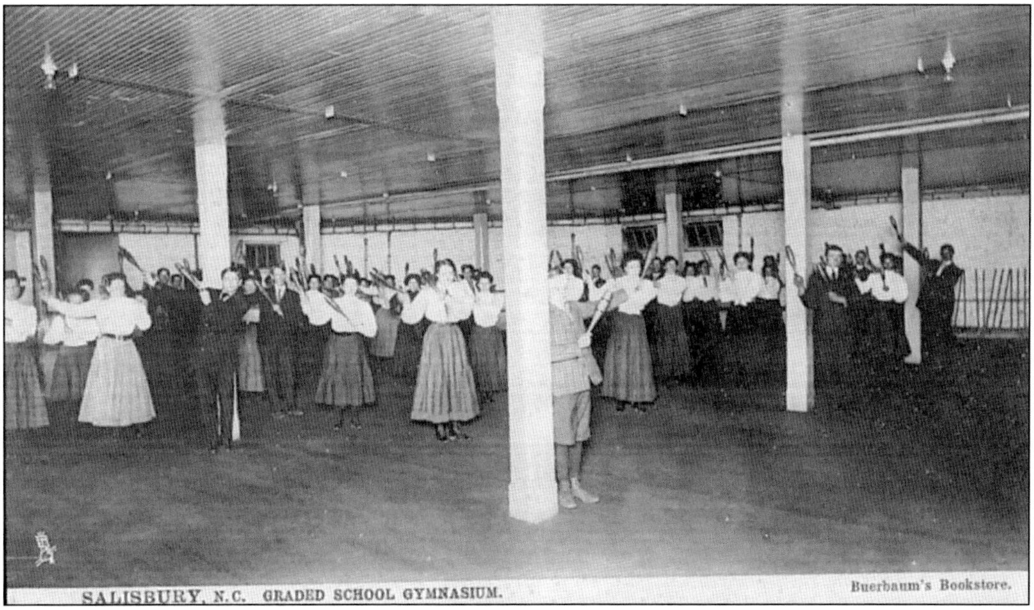

These views show the latest in educational practices of the time—organized physical education and laboratory teaching in the sciences. Above, this large group of students in the Graded School Gymnasium are using "Indian clubs." The clubs were made of metal or wood and were swung singly or in pairs for exercising the arms. Below, the array of chemicals available for this class is fascinating. Fortunately, the students at the tables are wearing protective aprons in case of an accident.

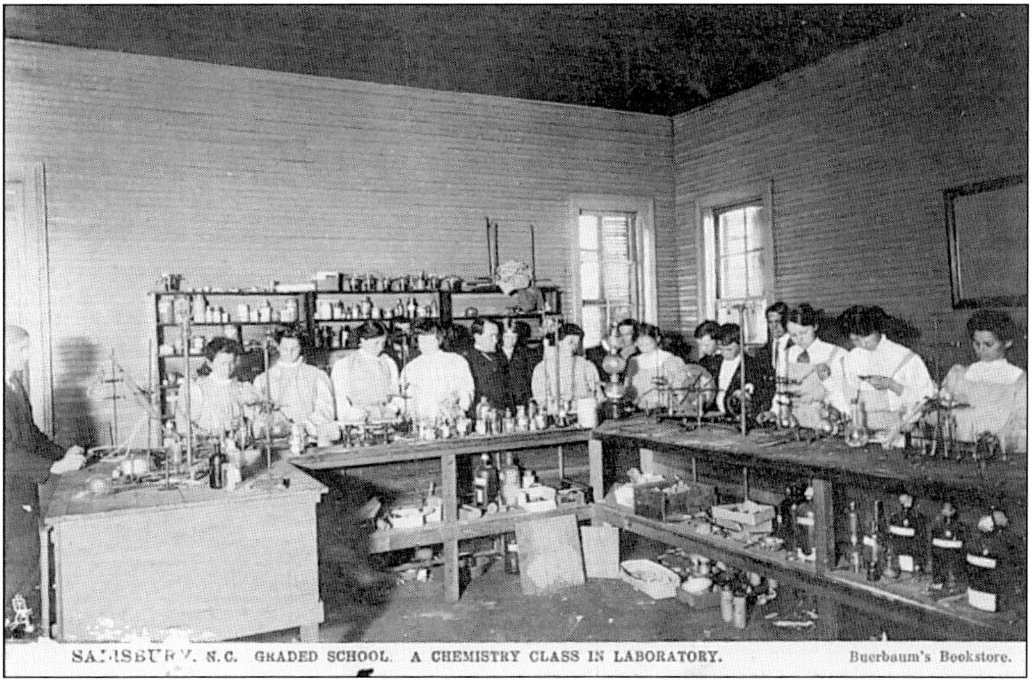

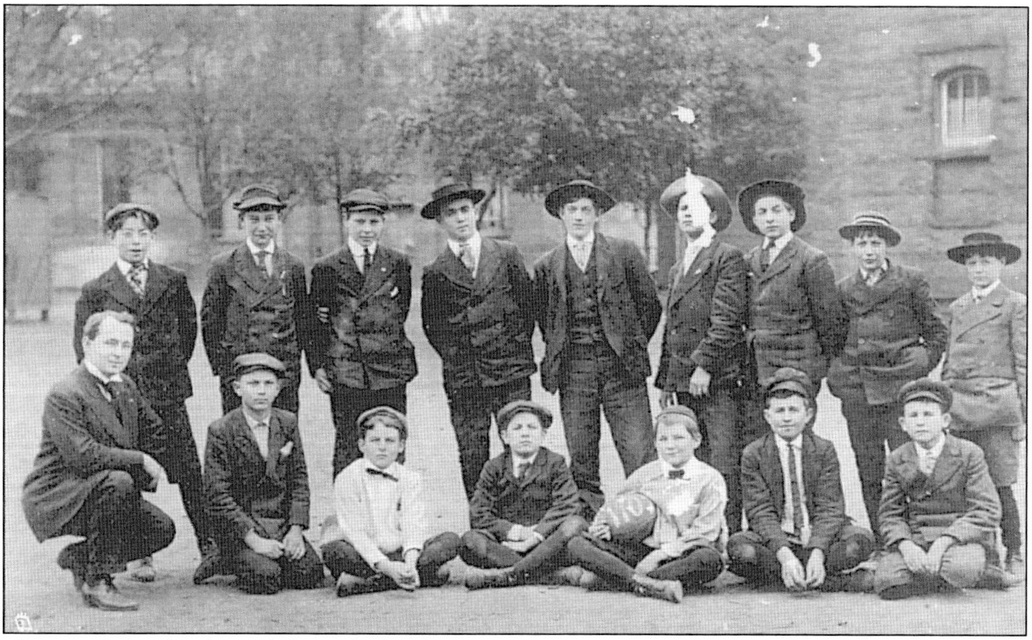

The Graded School's eighth grade football team dressed up for its team photo. The young man seated third from right is holding a football dated 1907.

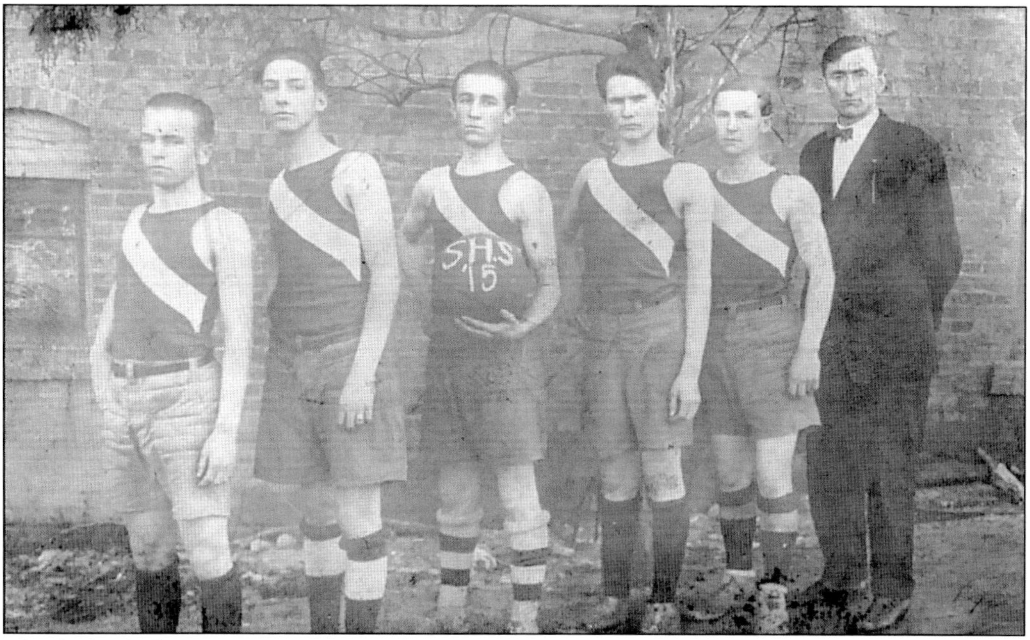

The basketball team at Spencer High School is pictured here in 1915. Sterling Stoudemire, who would later become a professor at the University of North Carolina, is second from left. The gentleman in the suit is probably the coach. (Courtesy of the Marian Harter Collection.)

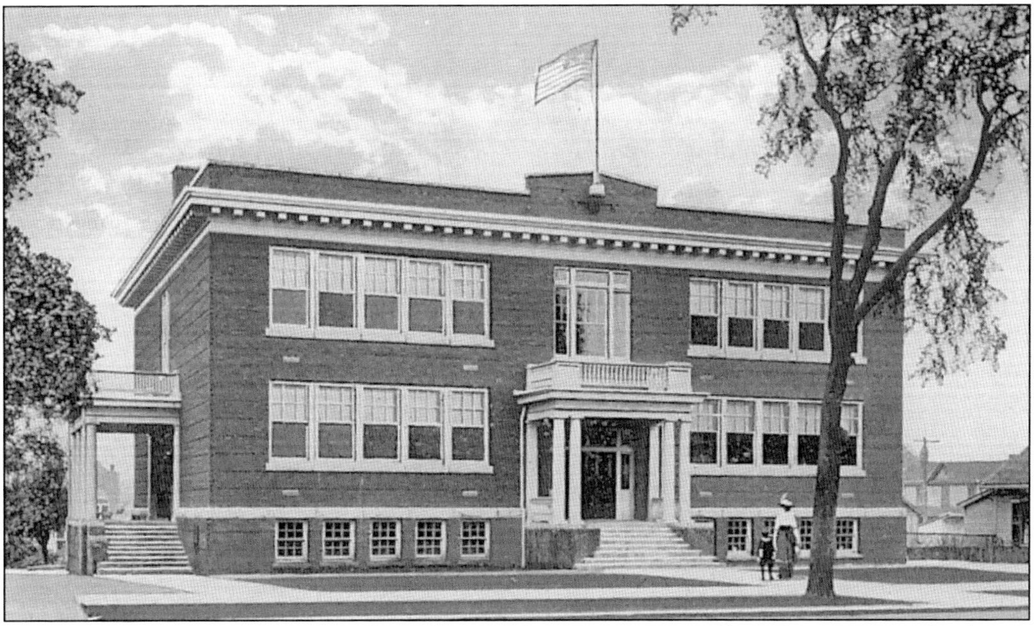

The Innes Street School, which later became known as A.T. Allen Elementary School, was named for Arch Turner Allen. Allen was the superintendent of the Salisbury Public Schools from 1910 to 1917 and later served in the North Carolina State Department of Education. This school was located in the 300 block of East Innes Street.

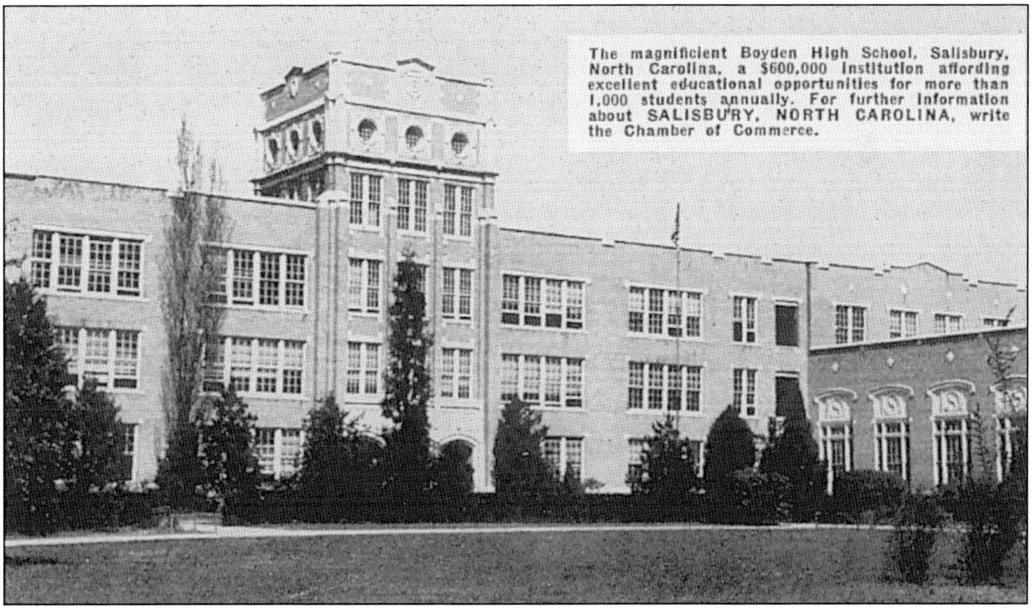

Boyden High School was named for Col. Archibald Henderson "Baldy" Boyden in 1926. A great supporter of education, Henderson helped create the first public school for African Americans in Rowan County. The school's name was later changed to Salisbury High School.

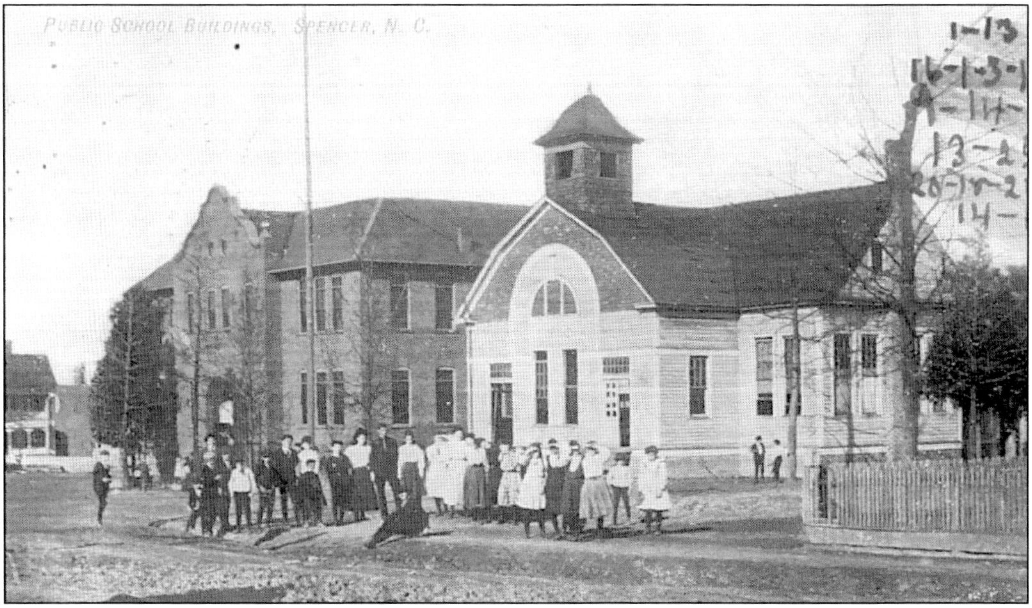

The first classes here were held in January 1901. In 1906, a two-story, brick building with a truncated hip roof was erected to replace the wooden structure. The Spencer Public School was for Spencer residents only. A disastrous fire consumed the brick portion of the building in 1925. Students who thought they would get to miss classes were disappointed when the town's churches provided classroom space. In 1937, Spencer became part of the Rowan County School System.

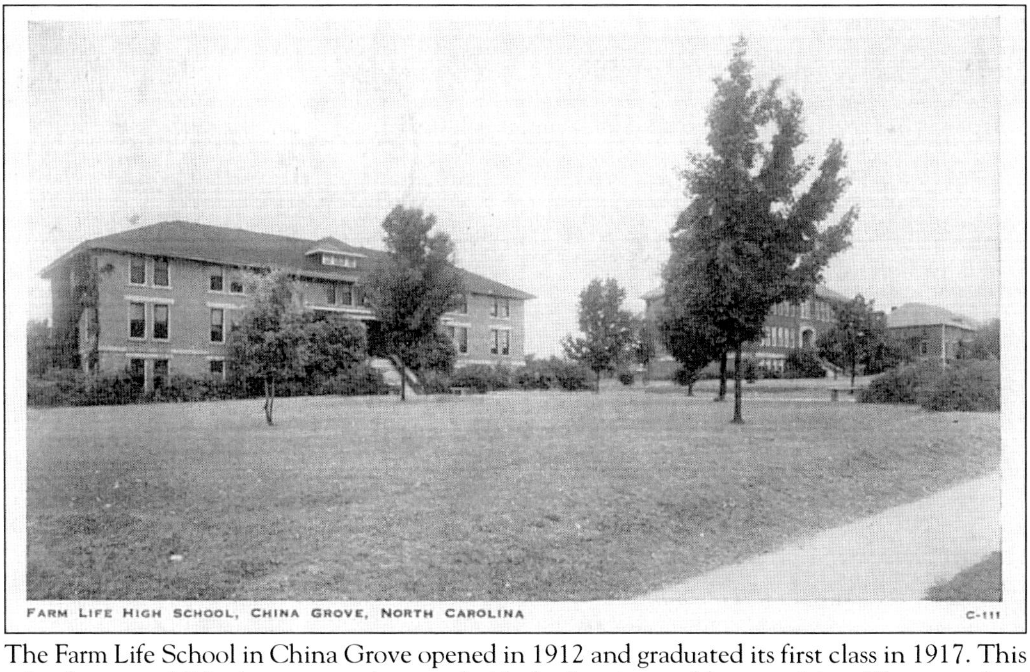

The Farm Life School in China Grove opened in 1912 and graduated its first class in 1917. This school was established to prepare boys and girls for farming and homemaking. Classes such as farm crops, animal husbandry, farm management, and dairying were included in the schedule. The school became China Grove High School in 1934.

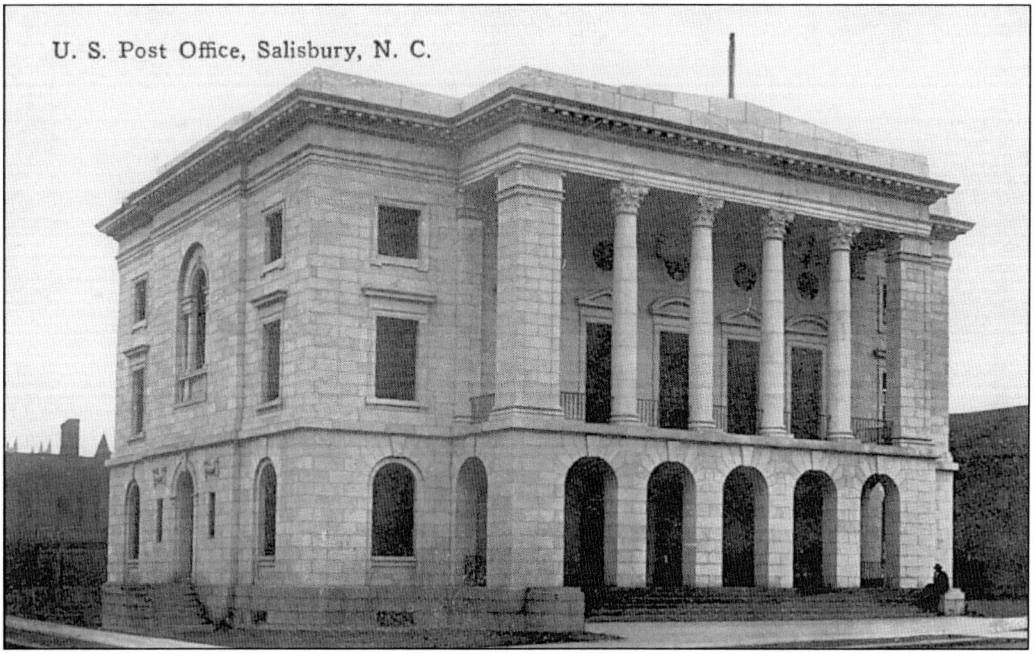

The post office at 130 West Innes Street was built in 1911 of white Italian marble. The renovated building in 1932 was declared a memorial to the late Sen. Lee Overman, whose last efforts were on behalf of the erection of this massive building for Salisbury. (Card from Buerbaum.)

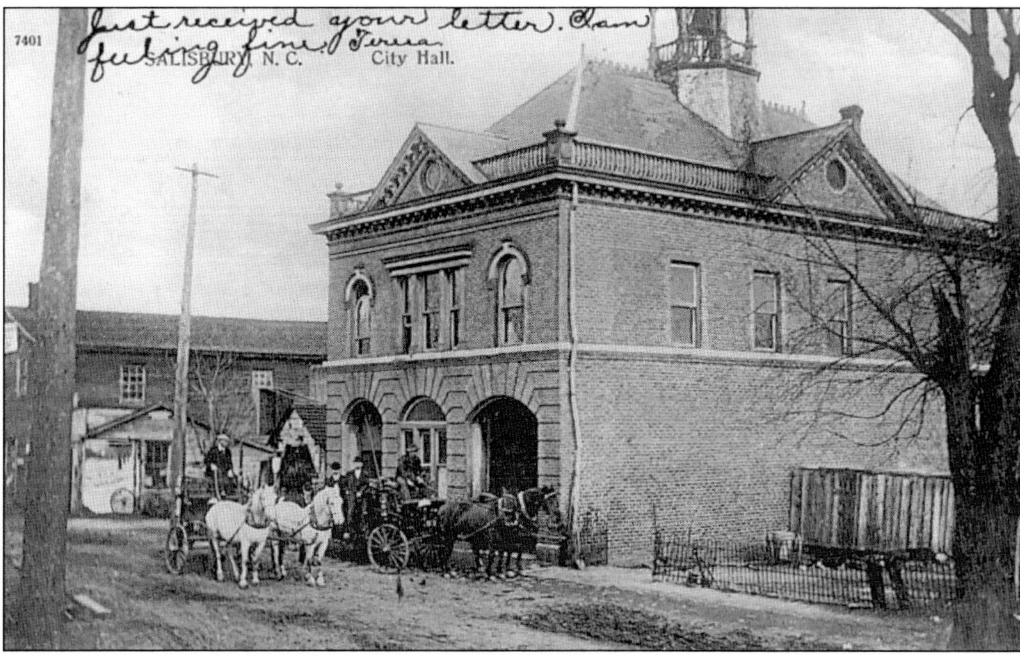

Salisbury's old city hall was located at 117 South Lee Street. The structure was built in 1896 and housed police, fire, sheriff, and the jail. A steam pump was kept ready with horses in case of fire. The structure has also housed the Firehouse Restaurant and Mill's Florist. (Courtesy of the Marian Harter Collection.)

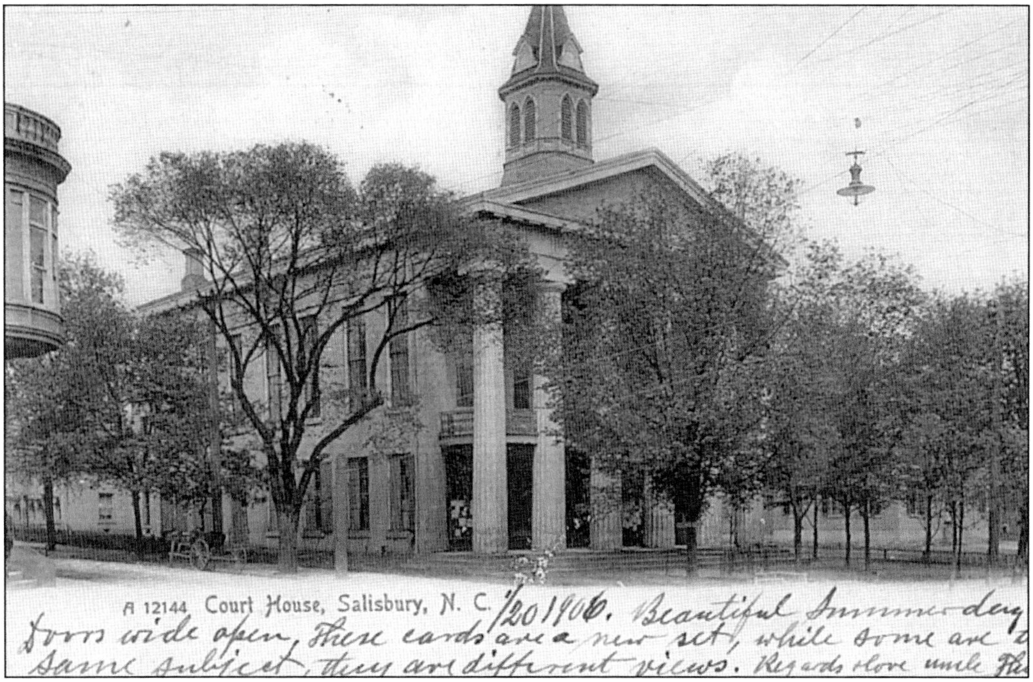

Salisbury's courthouse was built in 1856. In 1865, the building was spared by Union general George Stoneman during his raid on Rowan County. In 1860, the cupola was added to house the town clock and bell. In 1914, the building was turned into a community center. (Card from Buerbaum.)

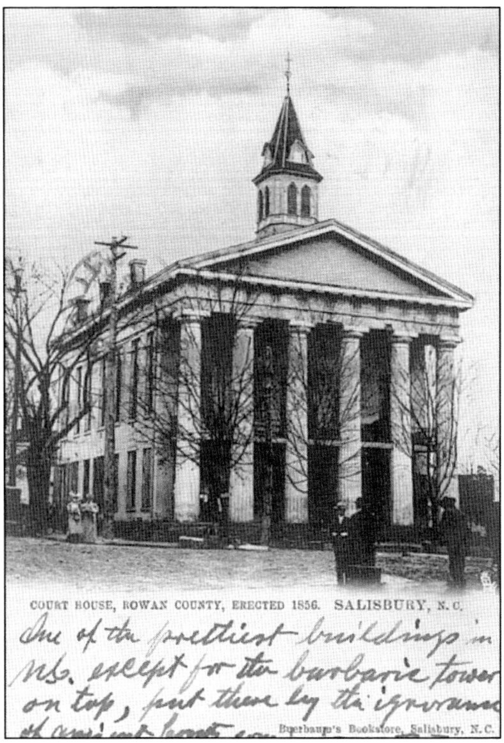

Extensive repairs had to be made to this building 20 years after it was erected. Unfortunately, water leaked around the cupola. Buerbaum's note offers his strong opinion of the tower—"One of the prettiest buildings in N.C. except for the barbaric tower on top, put there by the ignorance of ancient County Commissioners. T.B."

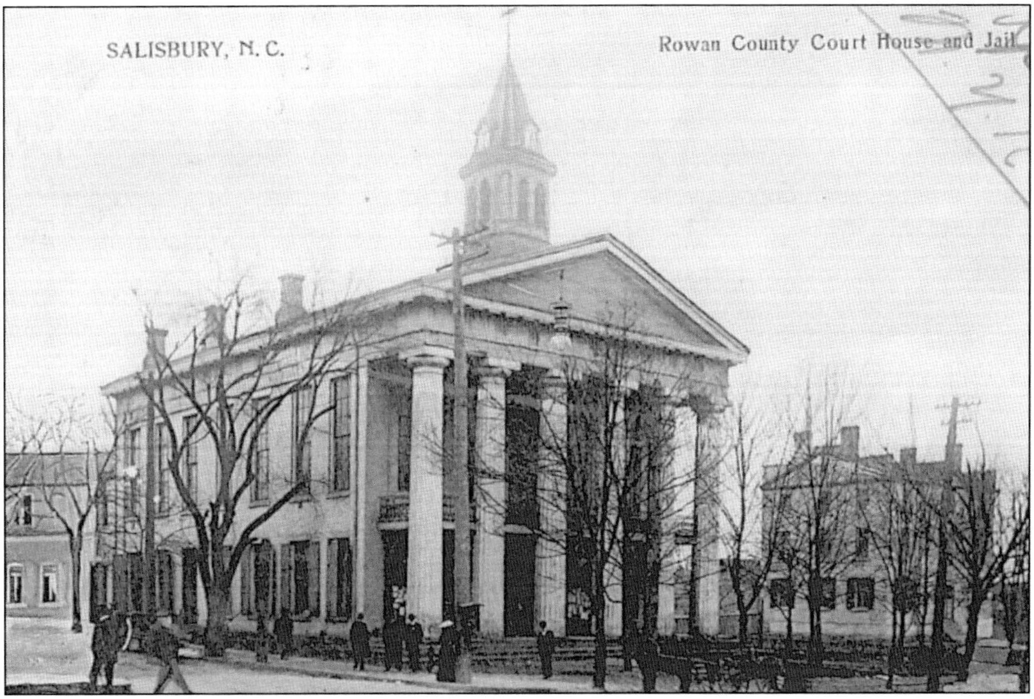

The three-story building to the right was the county jail, which was built in 1833. Until the 1890s, some executions took place behind the jail in a fenced area. The jail was demolished in 1912.

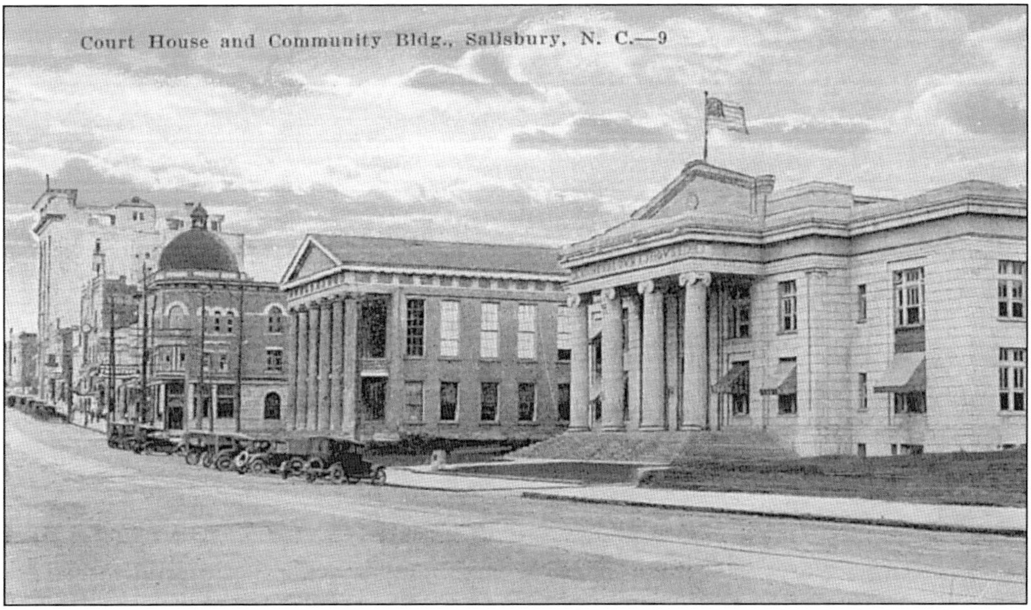

The massive new courthouse was built in 1914 beside the former courthouse, known for most of the 20th century as the Community Building. It housed spaces for civic groups, as well as the Rowan Public Library. The cupola on the Community Building had been removed in this view.

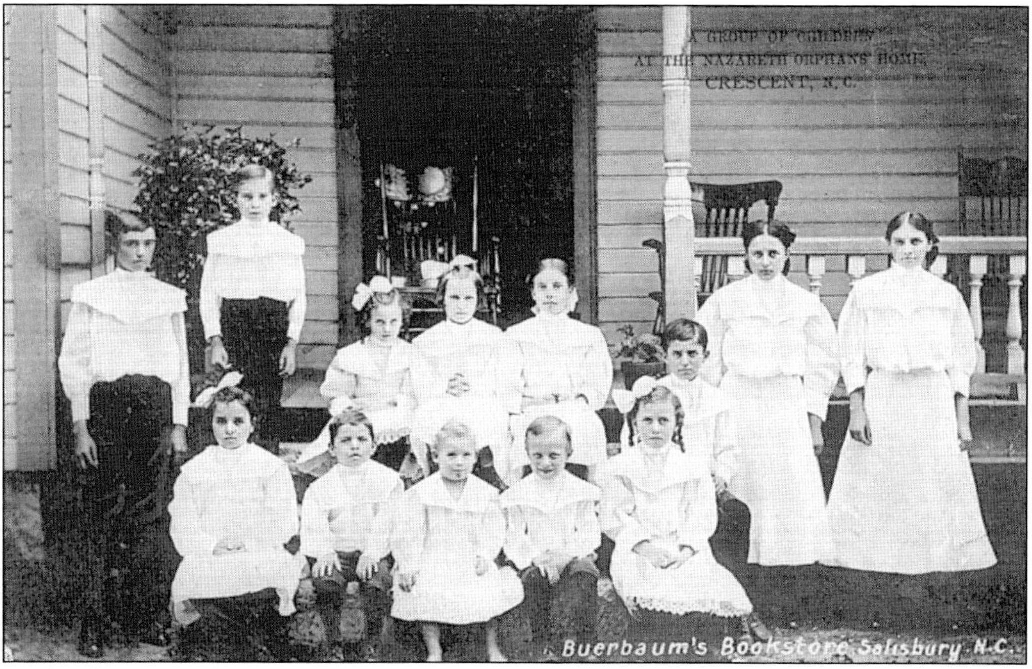

Rockwell's Nazareth Orphan's Home opened in 1906 when Miss Mary Abbot and children moved into the McNairy farmhouse. The home had been open for two years when these children posed.

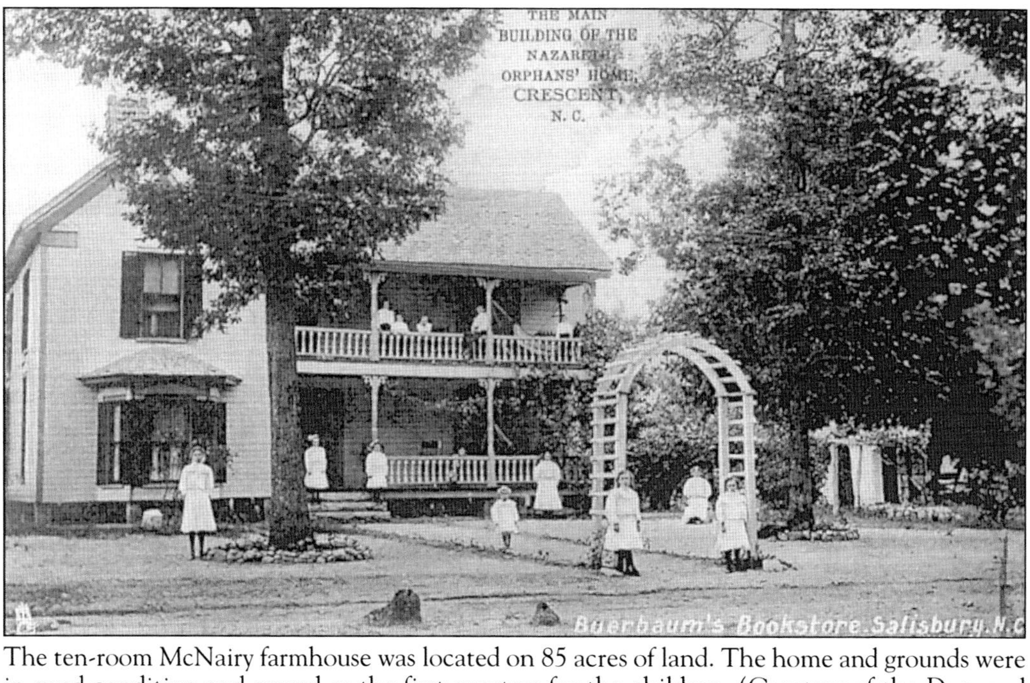

The ten-room McNairy farmhouse was located on 85 acres of land. The home and grounds were in good condition and served as the first quarters for the children. (Courtesy of the Durwood Barbour Collection.)

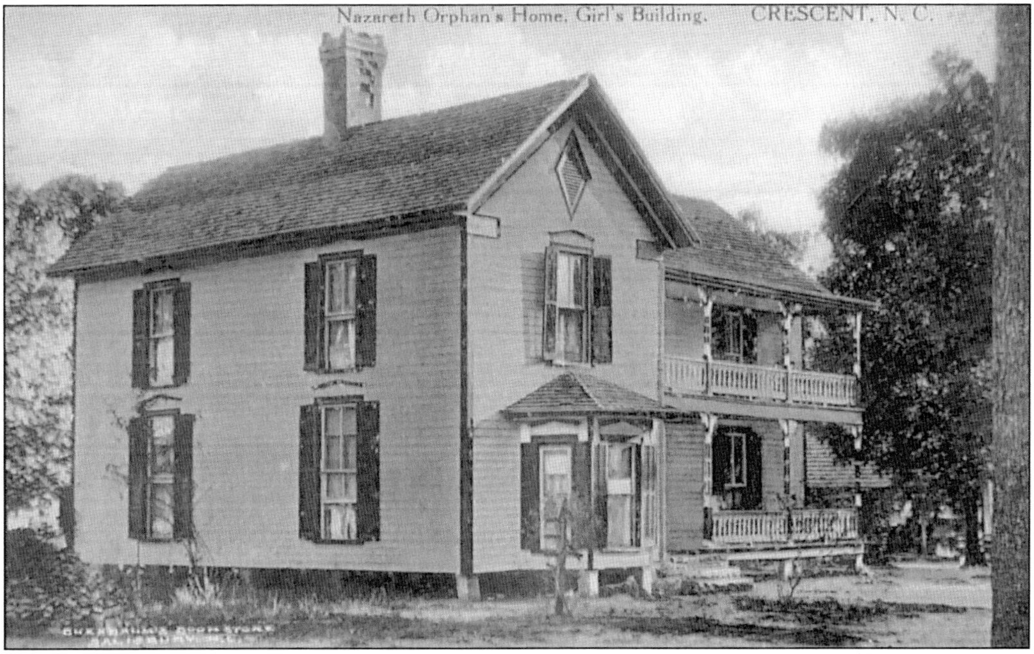

This image was taken before the Payne Building dormitory for girls was erected in 1925. In later years, when the Payne Building was demolished, a sealed copper box was discovered in the cornerstone. The box included a tribute to Rev. J.M.L. Lyerly, the Nazareth Orphan's Home founder, and writings by John T. Wyatt, known as "Venus of Faith," who was instrumental in the beginning of the town of Faith.

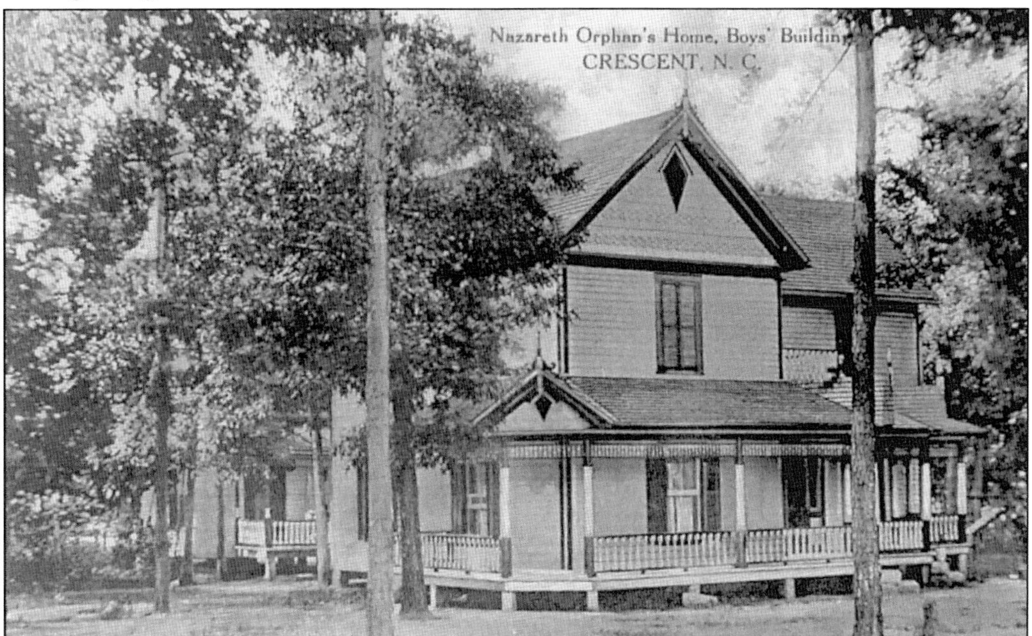

The Lyerly Building for boys was built in 1913–1916. The building was named for Ray P. Lyerly, the superintendent of the home from 1932 to 1943. (Courtesy of the Durwood Barbour Collection.)

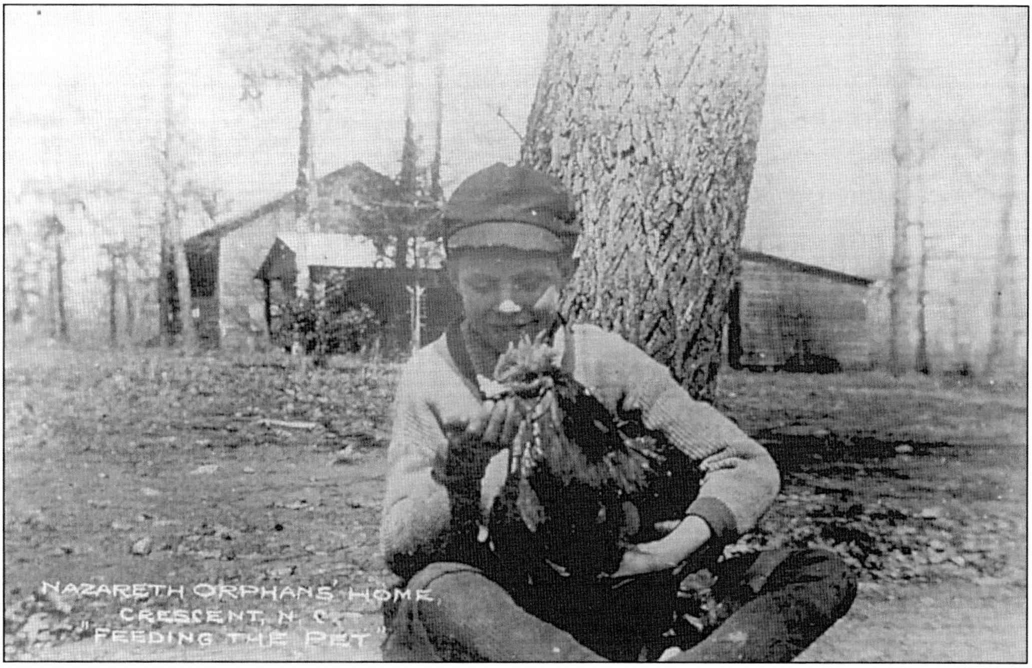

Farm animals and children inevitably become friends. This young man is feeding his pet hen. (Courtesy of the Durwood Barbour Collection.)

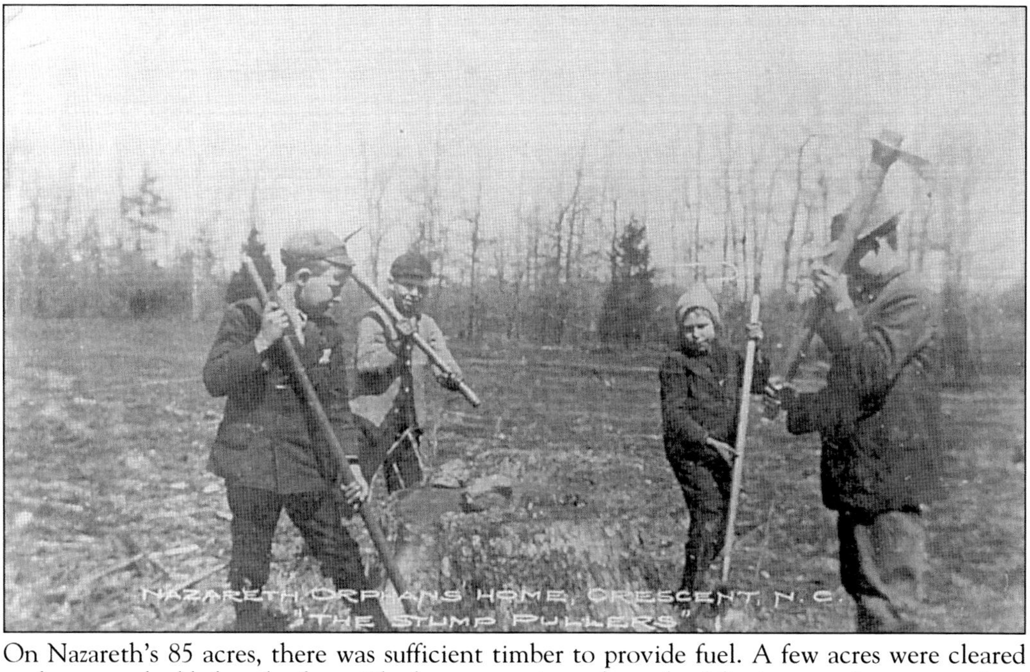

On Nazareth's 85 acres, there was sufficient timber to provide fuel. A few acres were cleared each year and added to the farm. The boys were given the task of digging out the stumps, thus, the name the "Stump Pullers." (Courtesy of the Durwood Barbour Collection.)

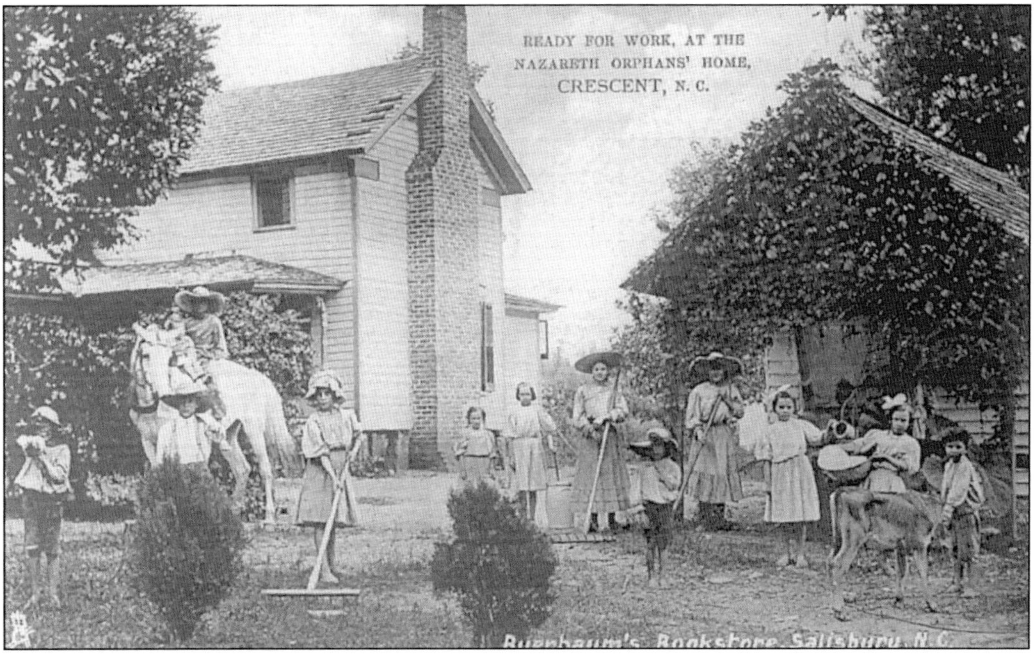

The home produced much of its own meat and dairy products, as well as corn, fruit, sweet potatoes, and Irish potatoes. The superintendent, matron, and children did all the farming. (Courtesy of the Durwood Barbour Collection.)

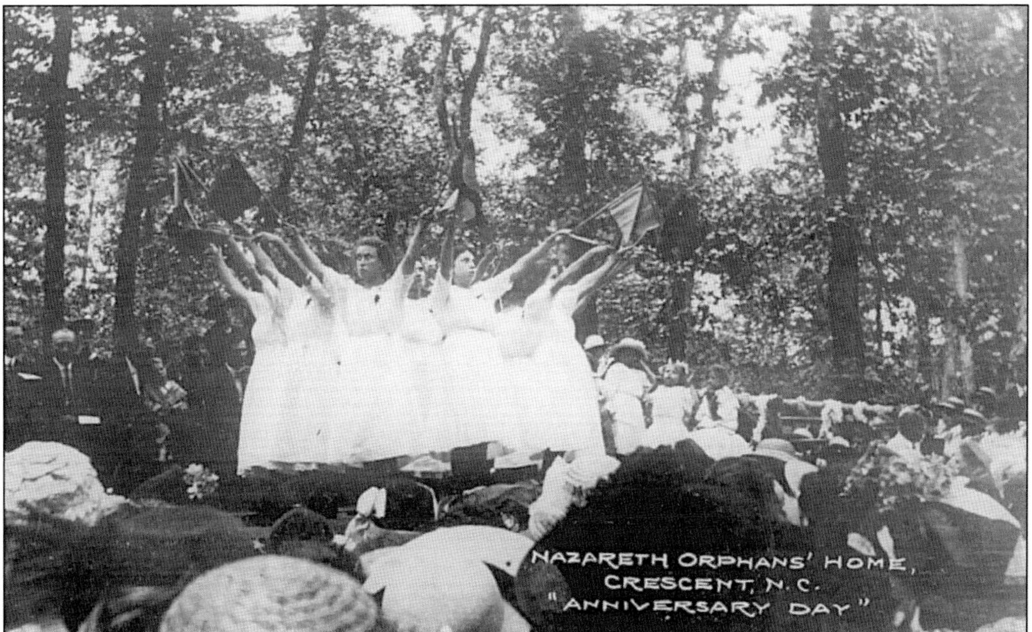

Nazareth's first Anniversary Day celebration was held September 12, 1907. The children gave recitations and sang. Many donations were received to support the home, and Anniversary Day became an annual affair. (Courtesy of the Marian Harter Collection.)

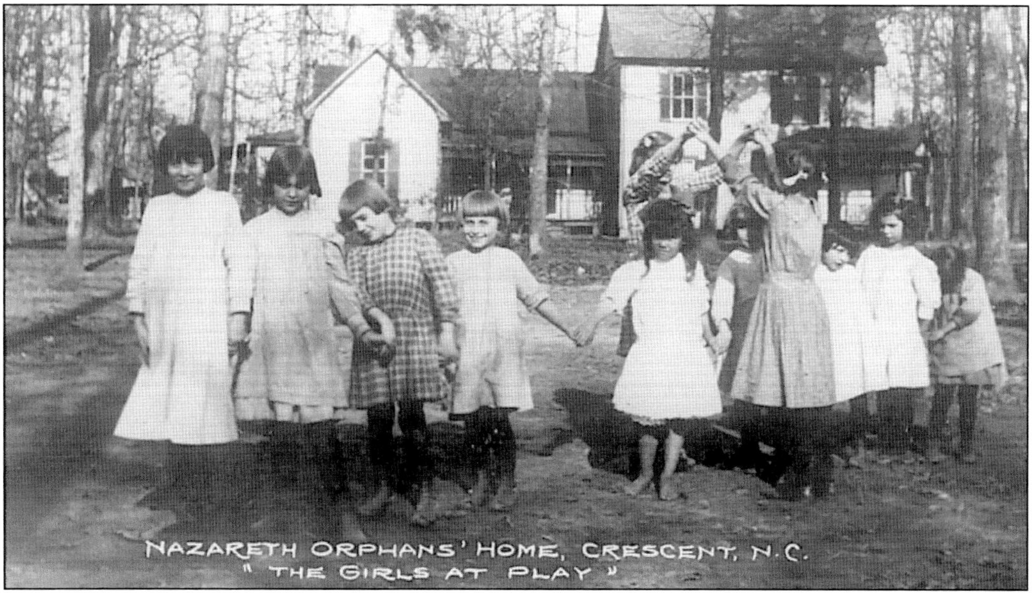

Beautiful, happy girls play "London Bridge is Falling Down." (Courtesy of the Wayne R. Chapman Collection.)

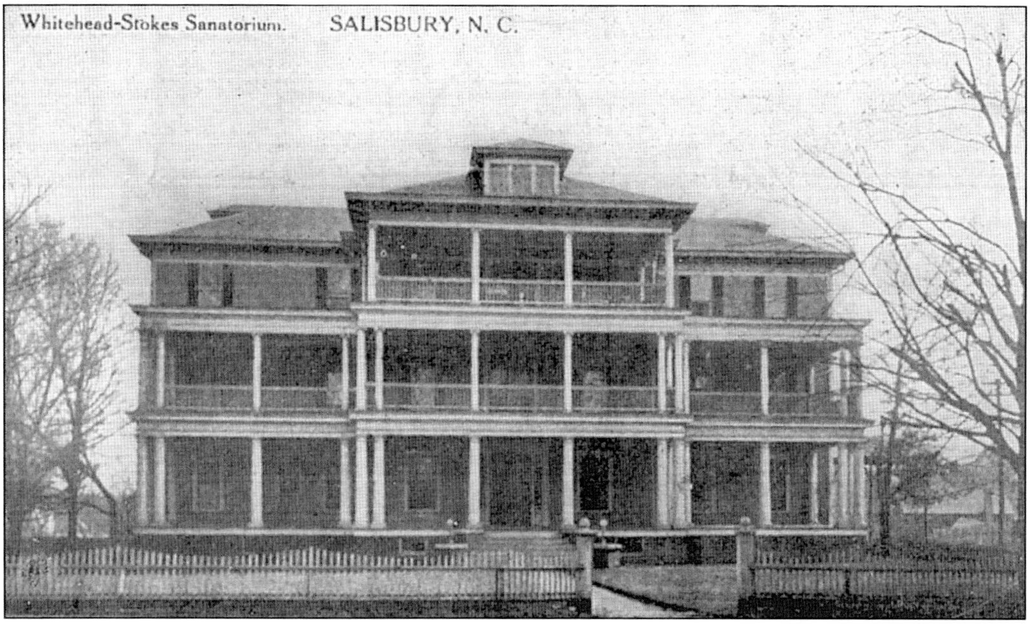

Back when doctors made house calls in horse and buggies, a Salisbury native, Dr. John Whitehead, dreamed of establishing a hospital for Salisbury. Dr. Whitehead picked Dr. J. Ernest Stokes of Johns Hopkins as his associate in the enterprise and then erected a frame building on the northeast corner of Fulton and Liberty Streets. The highly skilled physicians made the Sanatorium the leading hospital in the state. People came from throughout the South to Salisbury for medical care.

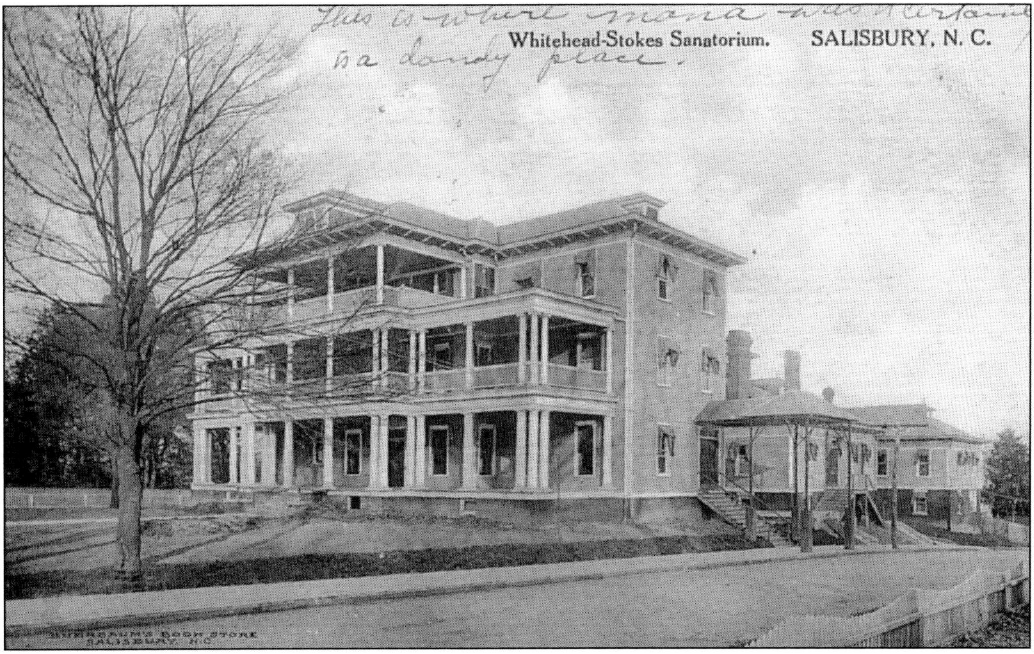

The 40-bed Whitehead-Stokes facility was enlarged to 60 beds. Features included two large screen porches, an elevator, an ambulance entrance, and a kitchen on each floor. A nurse's training school began in 1903. By 1921, demands on the facility were such that the need for a larger hospital was recognized.

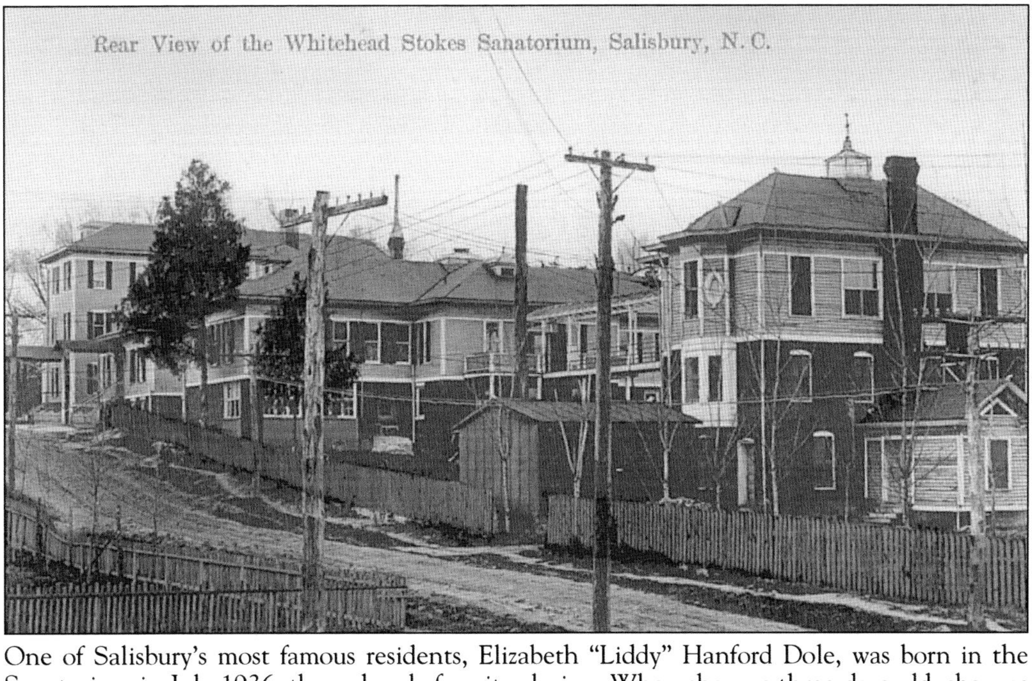

One of Salisbury's most famous residents, Elizabeth "Liddy" Hanford Dole, was born in the Sanatorium in July 1936, three days before its closing. When she was three days old, she was transferred by ambulance in her bassinet and was the ninth patient to enter the new hospital, Rowan General, on Mocksville Avenue.

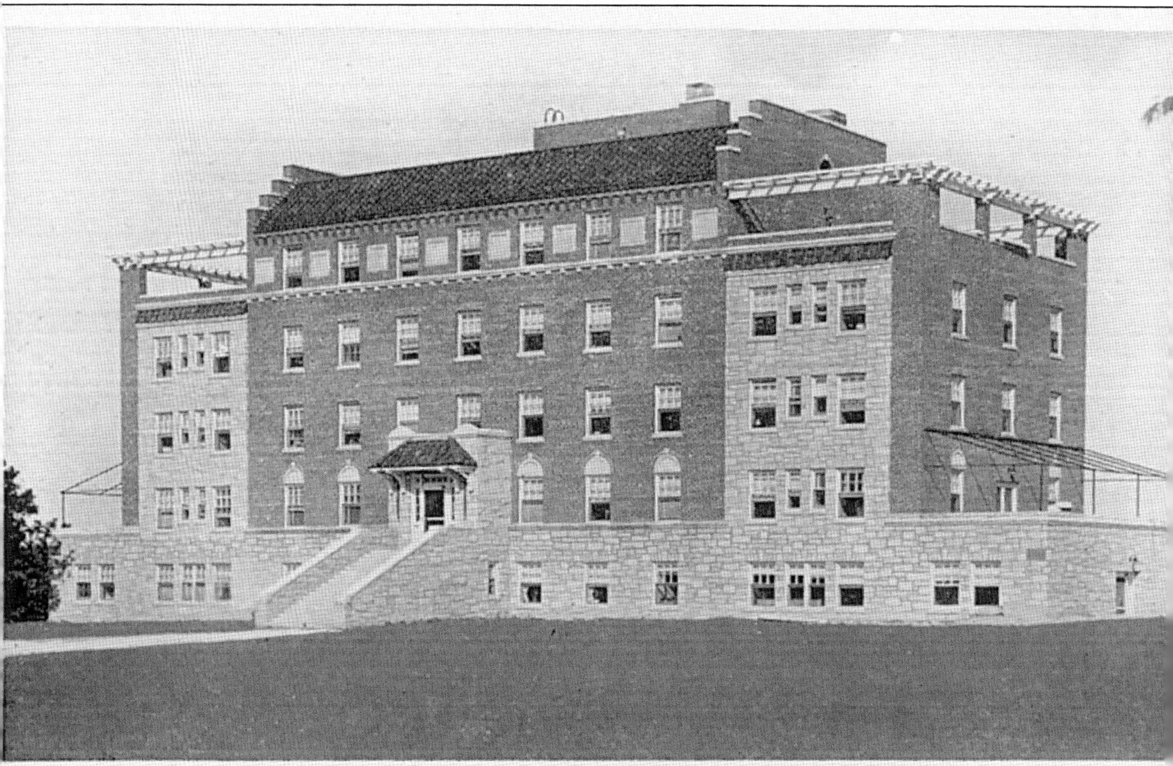

Rowan General Hospital, Salisbury, North Carolina

The Henderson family donated land on Mocksville Avenue for Rowan General, which was occupied on August 1, 1936. Numerous citizens and the Duke Foundation made donations to make the new hospital possible. The hospital's name soon changed to Rowan Memorial Hospital, and the complex is now known as the Rowan Regional Medical Center.

Seven

CHURCHES

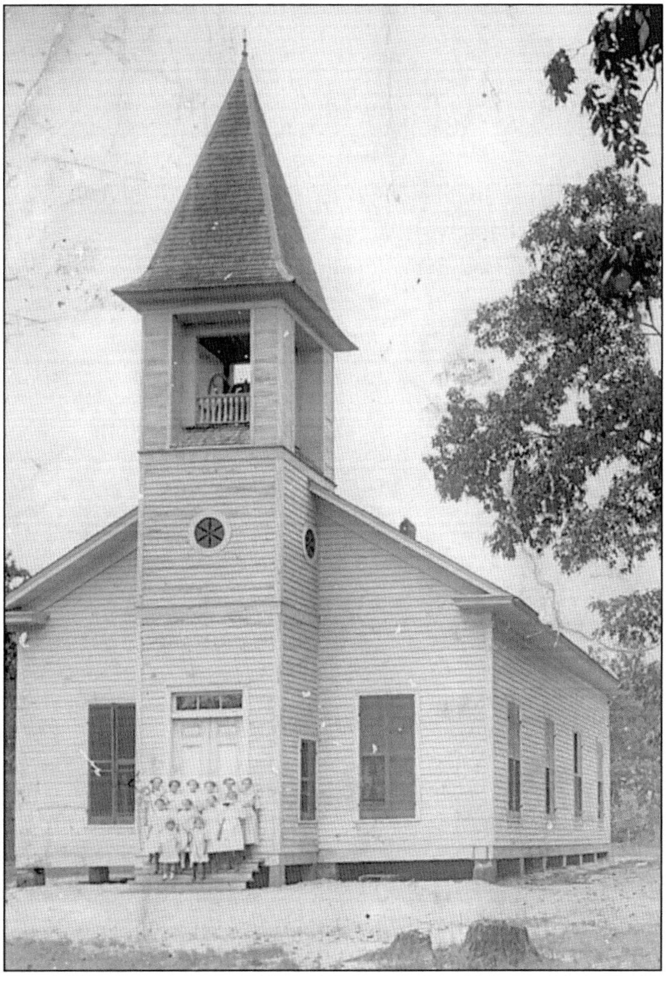

Salem Lutheran Church began with a log structure in 1850. The white frame building pictured, built in 1882, was completely destroyed by fire just before Easter sunrise services on April 9, 1950. The 100th anniversary of Salem was celebrated in 1950 with the dedication of a new brick church, which was also destroyed by fire on January 31, 1979. The current church was completed in 1980 and is located on Sherrill's Ford Road. (Courtesy of Jean Waller.)

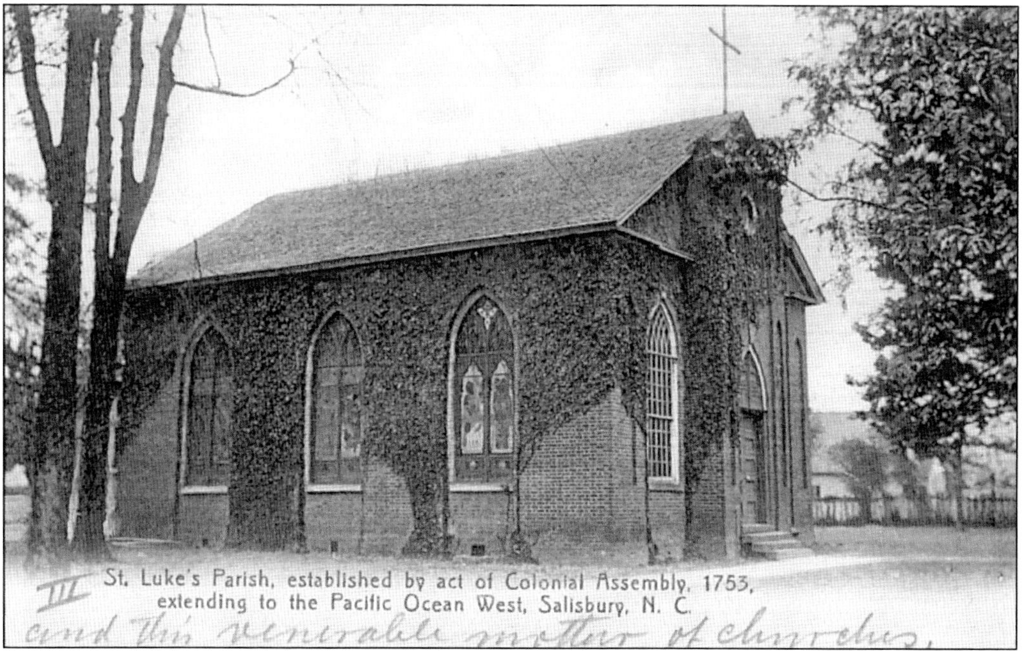

St. Luke's Episcopal Church was built in 1828 and is the oldest existing church building in the city of Salisbury. Funds for the erection of this church were raised by subscription and the rental of pews. The practice of pew rental was discontinued when the War Between the States began. In 1906, Buerbaum called this church the "Venerable mother of churches."

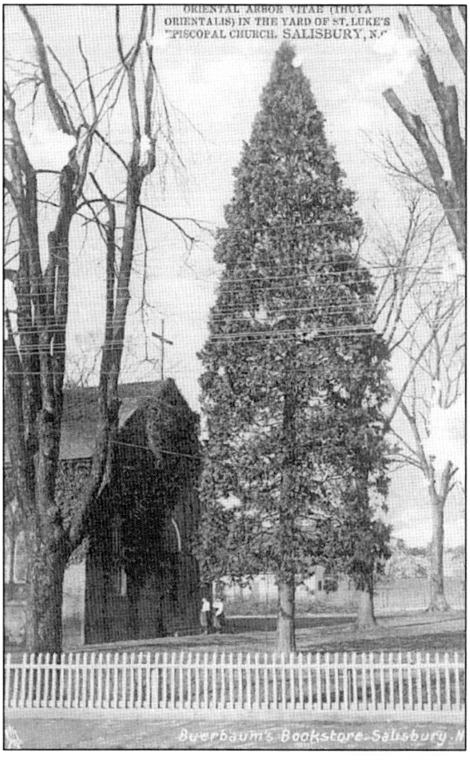

This beautiful conifer, called an incense cedar, was brought from Asia by Wade Hampton of South Carolina and presented to Julia Smyth of Salisbury, who planted it in the church yard in 1855. (Card from Buerbaum.)

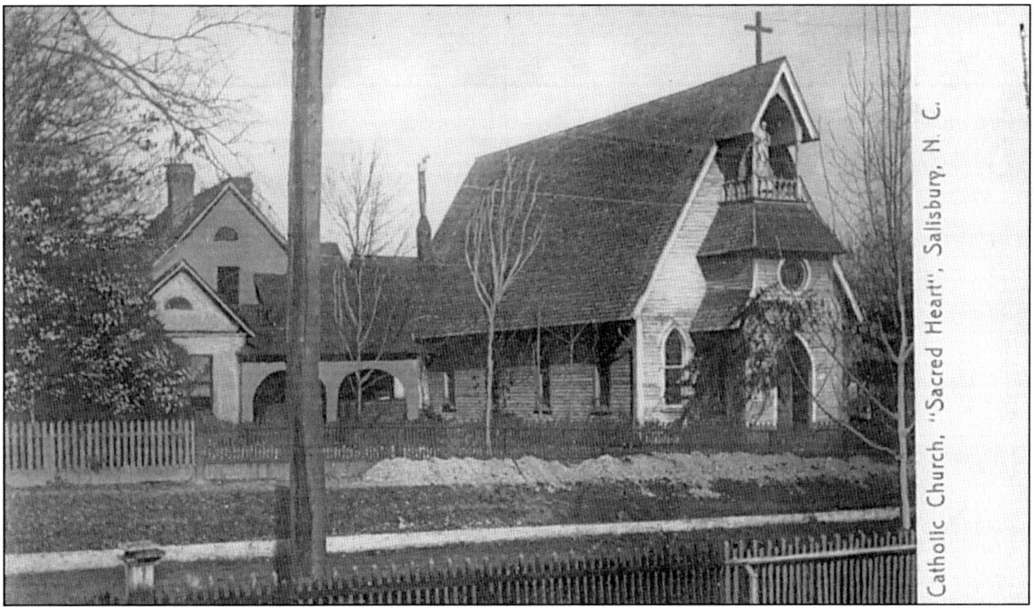

Frances Tiernan (Christian Reid) donated a lot on the corner of Council and Fulton Streets for Sacred Heart Catholic Church. The plans called for an Alpine-Swiss design, consisting of a high-pitched roof and narrow windows. The church was completed in 1882 and was replaced in 1940. In 1910, the Sisters of Mercy from Belmont purchased adjacent property and built a school, which can be seen in this view.

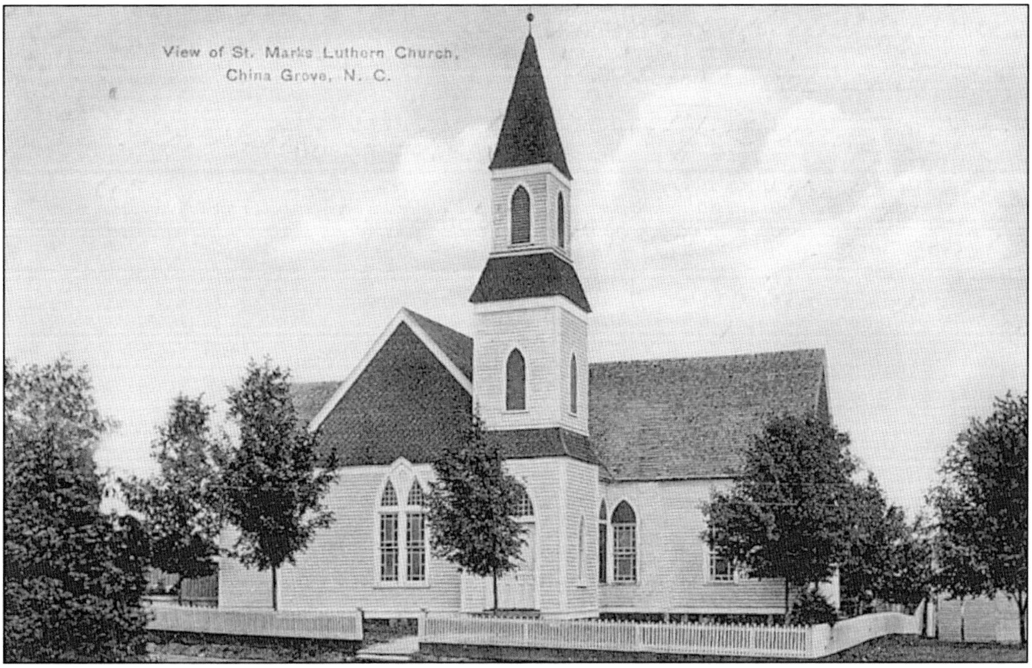

St. Mark's Lutheran Church in China Grove was organized in 1894 and was part of a three-church parish, which included Lutheran Chapel and Center Grove in Kannapolis. I. Frank Patterson donated the land for the construction. In 1902, the church became independent. This old frame structure was torn down, and the current building was erected in 1917.

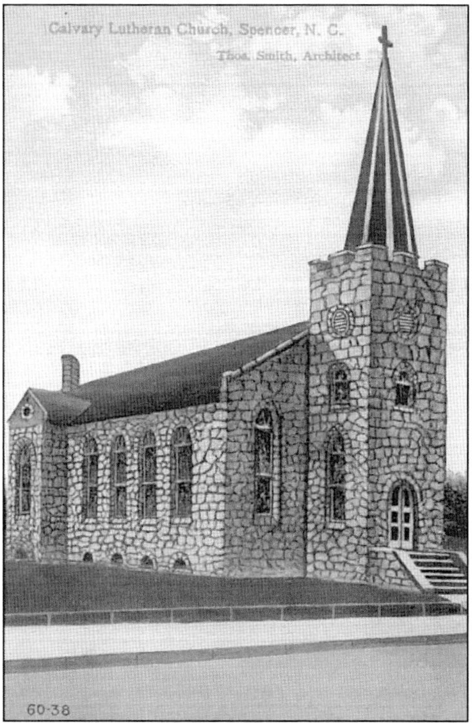

Prior to the establishment of Calvary Lutheran Church, Lutherans in Spencer walked to Christ Lutheran Church in East Spencer. A plank walkway was constructed that ran from the corner of Fourth Street and Carolina Avenue going north to Depot Street, then turned 90 degrees and continued to the Southern Railroad tracks. The dedicated Lutherans had to dodge falling cinders and sooty moisture from the steam. Work on this stone church began in 1913 on South Carolina Avenue in Spencer. The current church building was completed in 1962 and is located at Fifth Street and Carolina Avenue.

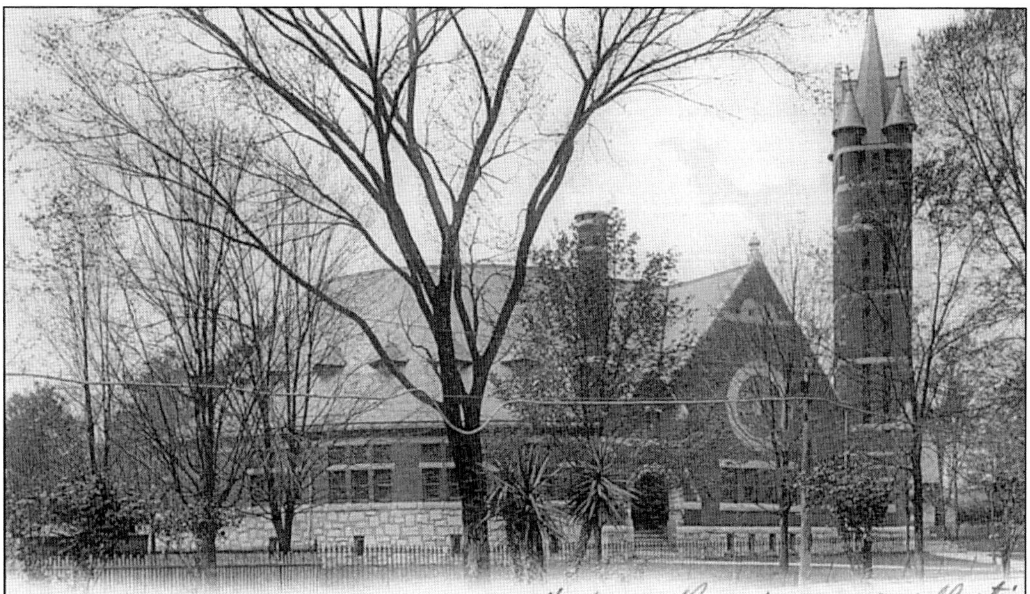

Salisbury's First Presbyterian Church, built in the ornate Richardsonian Romanesque style, was located at the corner of Jackson and West Innes Streets. The church building was torn down when the current church at Fulton and West Innes Streets was built in 1969. Fortunately, the bell tower was preserved and is the site of an annual New Year Eve's celebration. (Card from Buerbaum.)

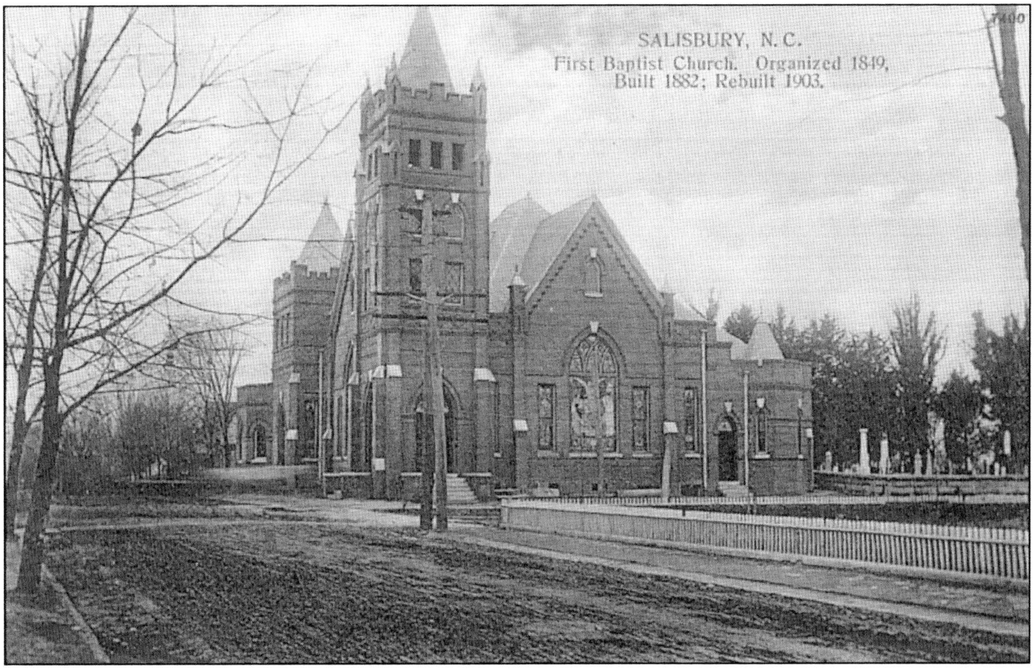

Salisbury's First Baptist Church was organized in 1849. In 1882, a one-room brick structure was built at North Church and West Council Streets. In 1903, this larger church was built on the same site. The present church at 200 South Fulton Street was completed in 1952. The 150th anniversary was celebrated in 1999 and members walked from the original church site to the present Fulton Street site.

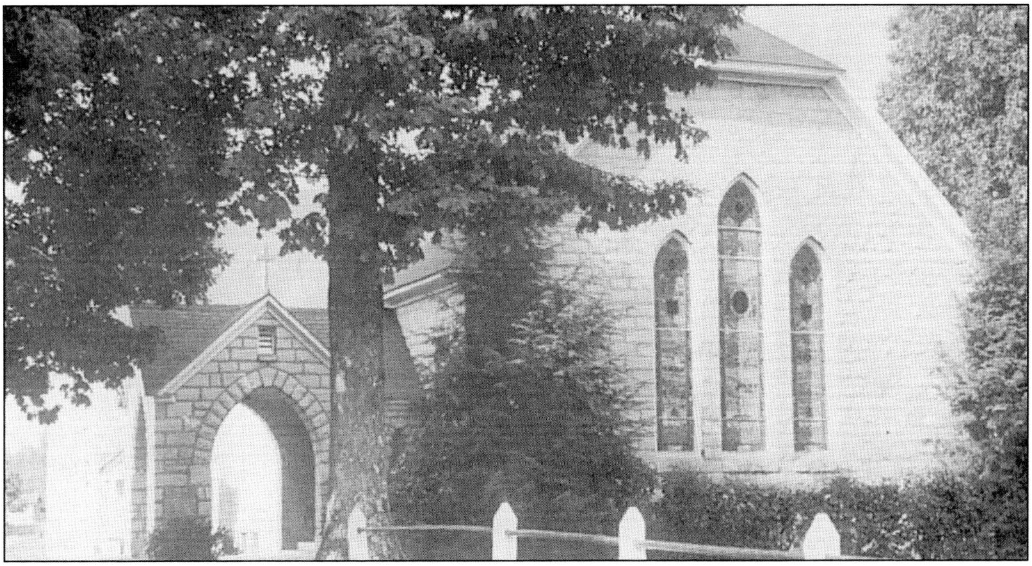

Shiloh Methodist Church began in 1881 in Granite Quarry. The congregation met in a school building until 1889 when a church was finally built. That frame church burned in 1912, and a new church was built, which served the congregation until 1937. When the new church structure was completed, the old structure was moved and attached to the new building and now functions as the educational building.

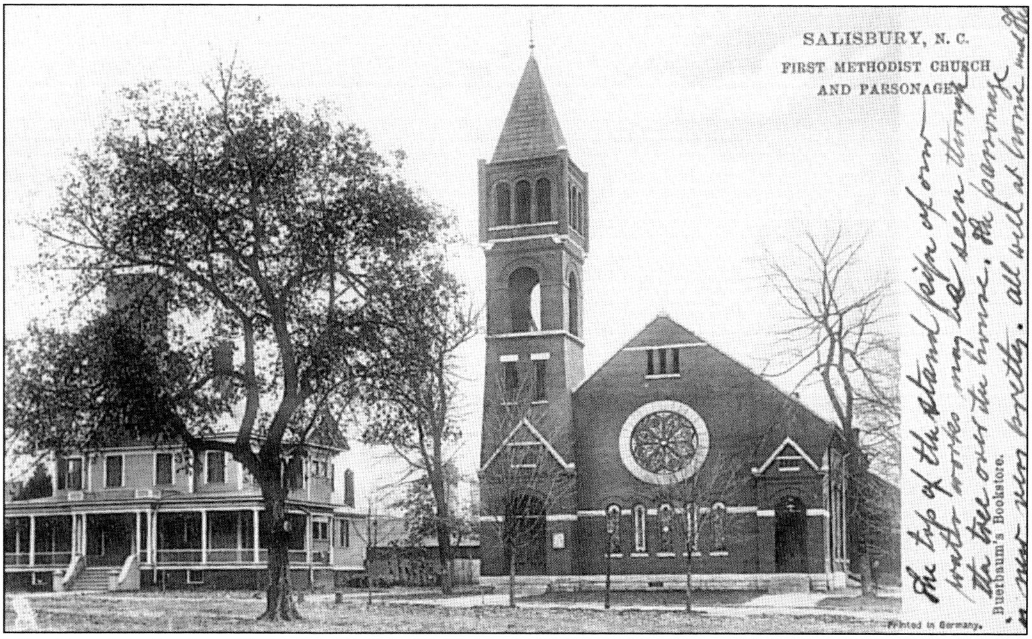

The First Methodist Church and Parsonage in Salisbury were located at the corner of Church and Bank Streets. Erected in 1858, it was torn down in 1918. Postmarked in 1906, this card contains a note by Buerbaum that says, "The top of the stand pipe of our water works may be seen through the tree over the house. The parsonage is new, very pretty. All well at home. Uncle Theo."

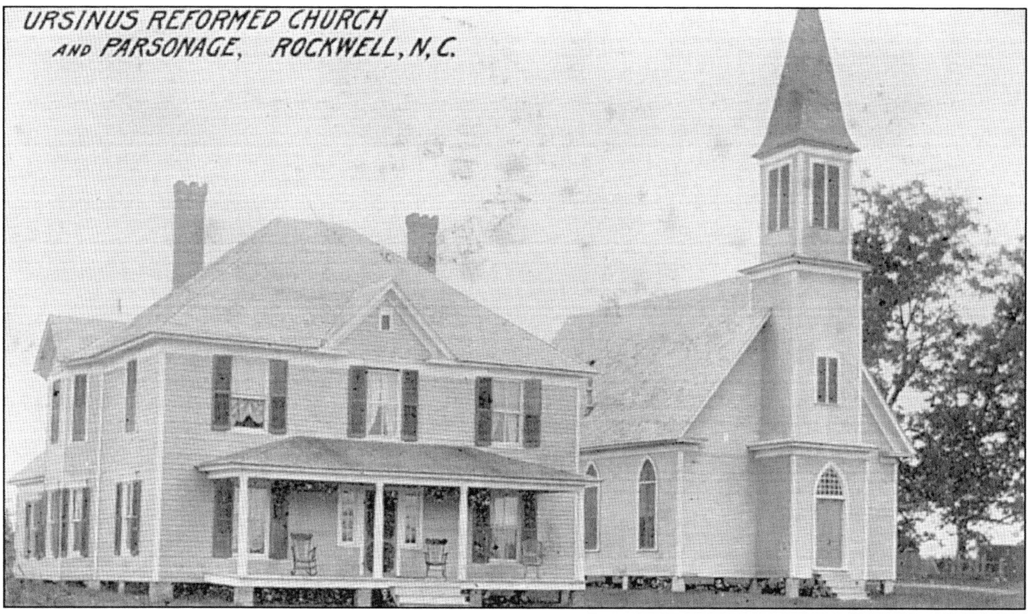

Prior to 1900, no church existed in the immediate vicinity of Rockwell. On a lot donated by Mr. J.W. Peeler, the Ursinus Church building was completed in 1904. The church chose "Ursinus" for its name to honor the author of the Heidelberg Catechism, the official handbook of the Reformed Church. The congregation erected a new building in 1924, and the old church was vacated.

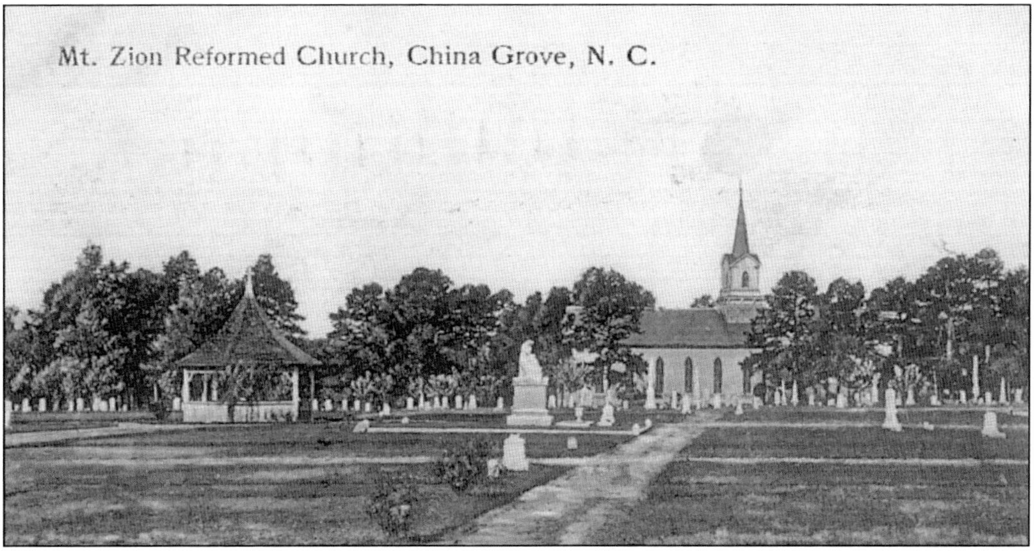

The Mt. Zion Reformed Church in China Grove was organized sometime prior to 1780. The proper name from the beginning was Mt. Zion, but the church was commonly called "Savitz's Church," probably due to an influential family in the area. This name became degraded to "Savage's Church." The second building was painted red, and folklore states that perhaps a superstitious person burned that church to get rid of the devil. The Mt. Zion United Church of Christ is now located on South Main Street in China Grove.

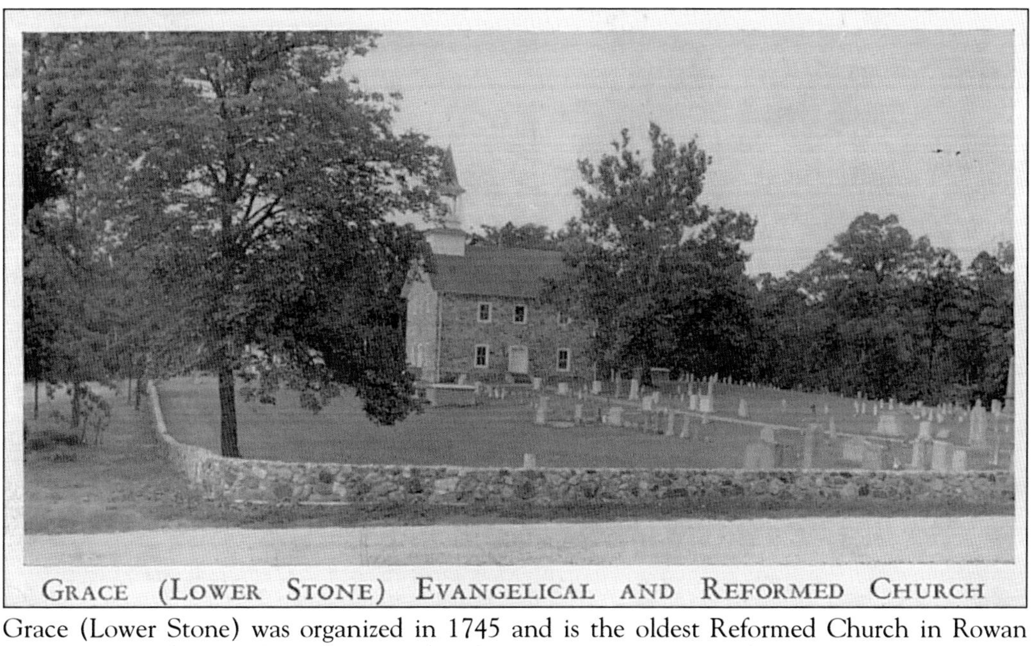

Grace (Lower Stone) was organized in 1745 and is the oldest Reformed Church in Rowan County. It was founded by German settlers from Pennsylvania. The church was erected in 1796 and consecrated in 1810. The structure was built of native granite.

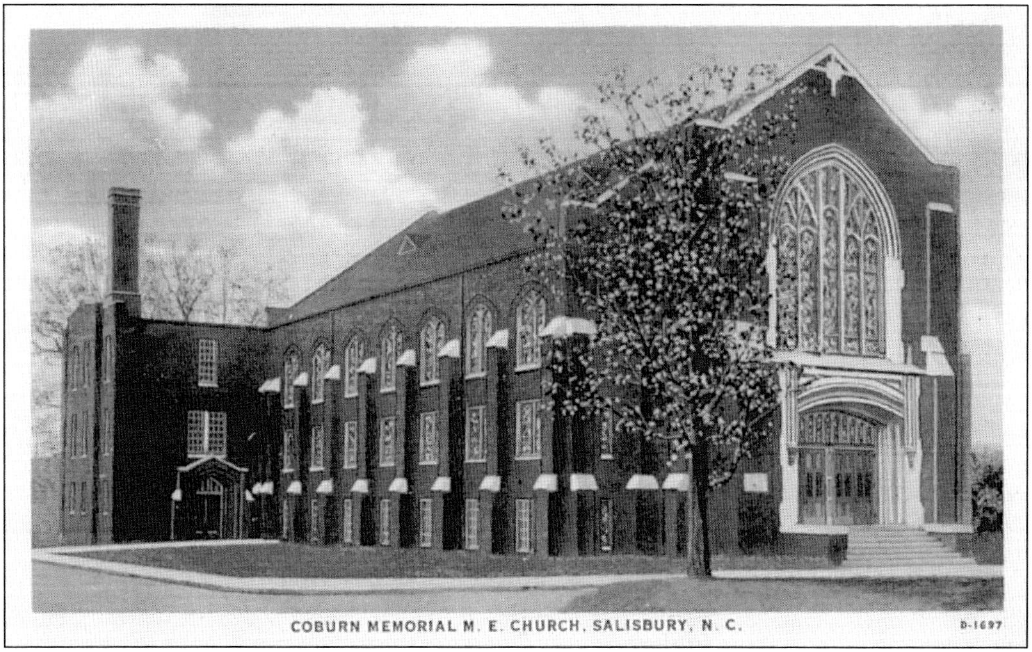

The organizational meeting of Coburn Memorial United Methodist Church was held at the Black farms area (now known as Rowan or Parkdale Mills) under some dogwood trees. The brick church located on South Church Street was started in 1925 and named in honor of its pastor and founder, the Reverend A.L. Coburn.

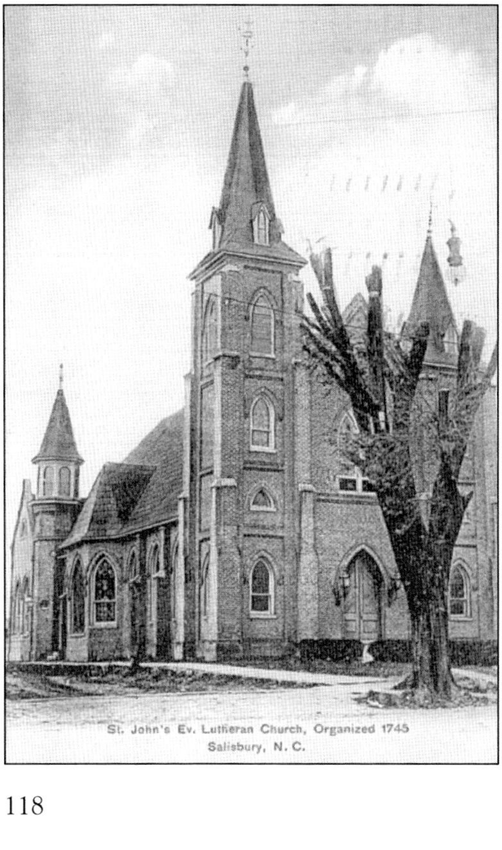

This, the fourth building of St. John's Lutheran Church, was built in 1885 and was located at the corner of North Main and Liberty Streets. Mr. J.D. Small, a local contractor, designed the building. The present structure was erected in 1926 at the corner of Innes and Church Streets.

Faith Reformed Church was located at the corner of West Horah and South Church Streets. The building was constructed in 1897, and the first services were held in 1898. For a number of years, this building was the home of Salisbury's Knights of Pythias. This is now the location of La Cava Restaurant. (Courtesy of the Rowan Public Library.)

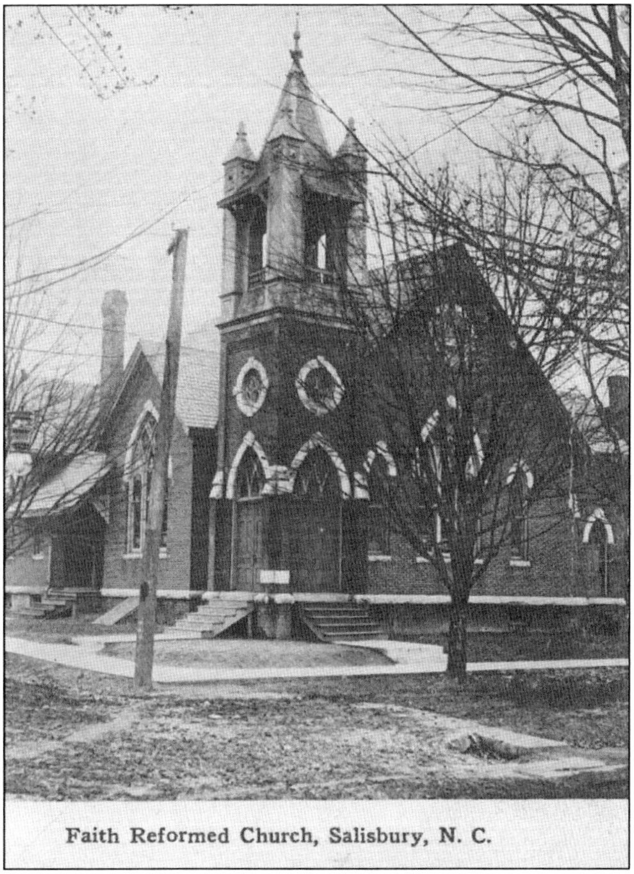

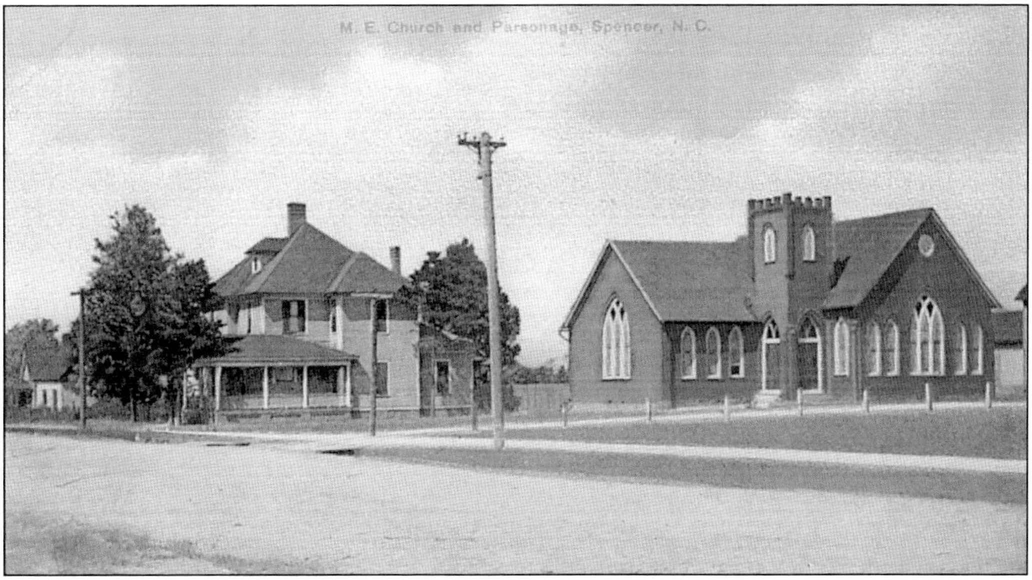

The Central Methodist Church in Spencer erected a brick structure in 1903 that contained a sanctuary and two Sunday school rooms. The building served the congregation until 1914 when it was found to be structurally unsound and was torn down.

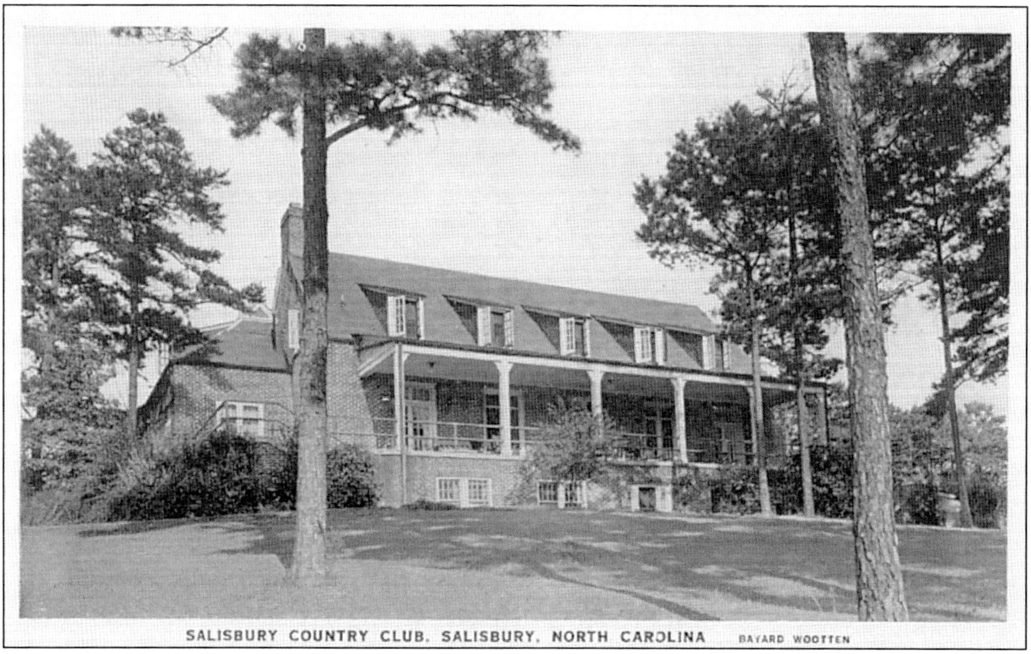

Salisbury's first country club was built in 1927 on Club Drive. The building shown was used until the new club was built in 1989.

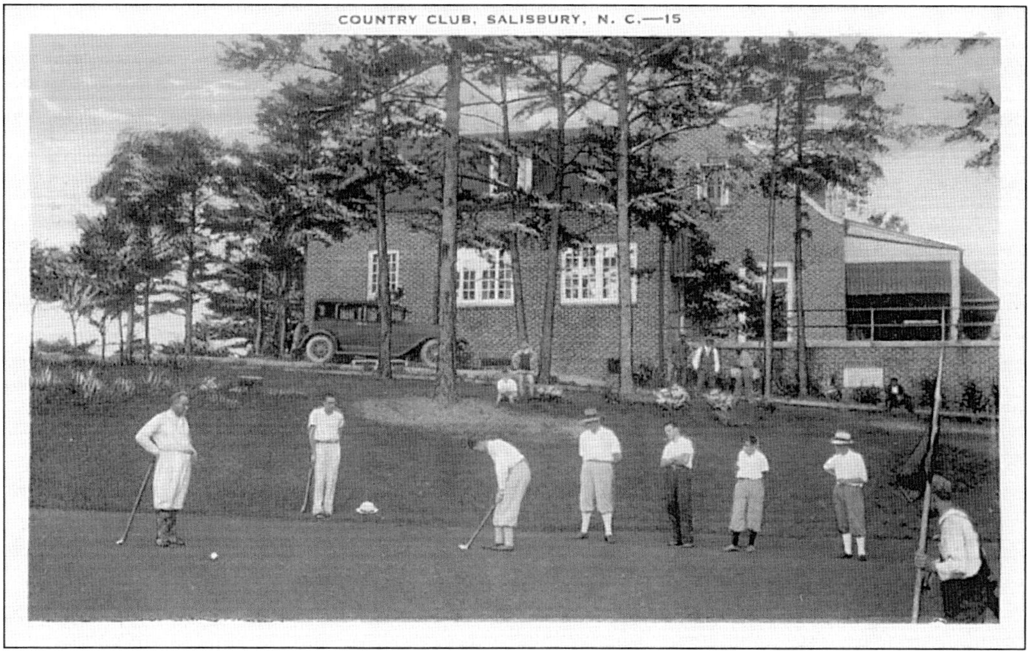

It was Rowan County's golfers who led the way in bringing Salisbury's country club into existence. A nine-hole course was in operation by 1927.

Eight

Community Life and Miscellaneous Views

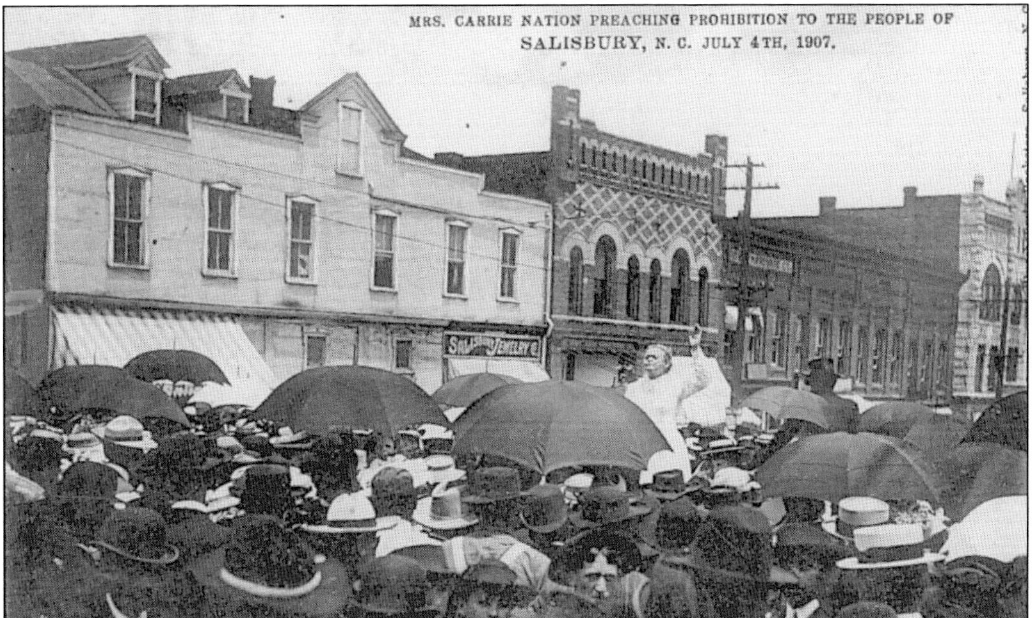

Nearly 6 feet tall and weighing 180 pounds, Carry Nation traveled across the United States preaching prohibition with a hatchet. She chopped bars, kegs, jugs, glasses, and virtually wrecked saloons. She had good reason to visit Salisbury. In 1907, at the age of 60, she lectured and toured eight cities in North Carolina. She attracted a huge Independence Day crowd but did not use her hatchet in Salisbury. She spoke on July 2nd at the Fulton Casino of Fulton Heights. On July 4th, she failed to ride in the parade but spoke to a huge crowd on the square. She sold little gold hatchets as a symbol of attack tools. The Mansion House is the large building to her left. (Courtesy of the Sarah Manning Pope Collection.)

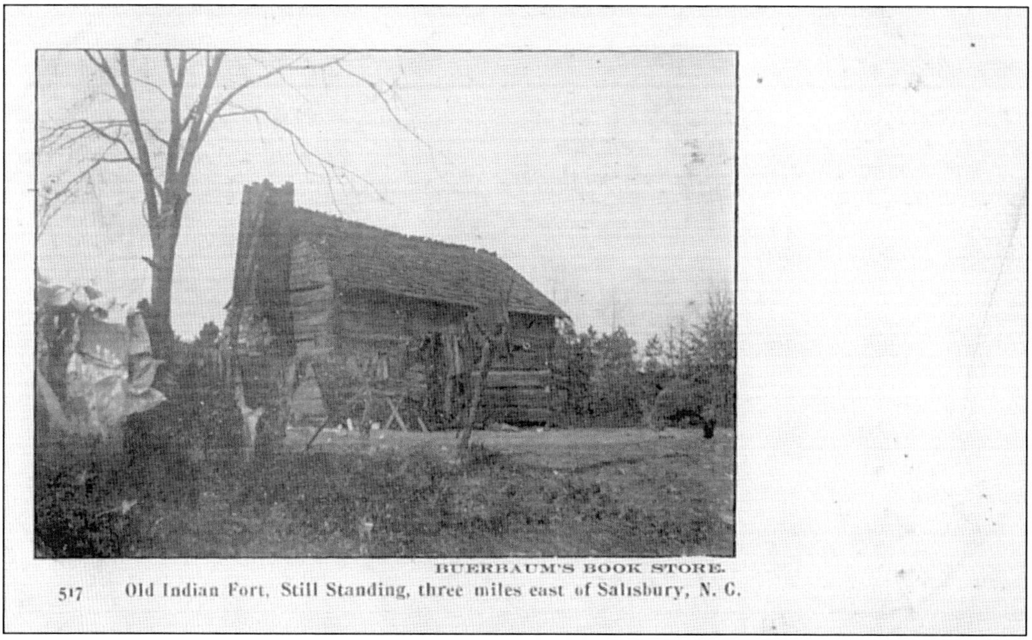

Perhaps Buerbaum fell prey to some local legend or perhaps this really is an old Indian fort, which just happens to look like an ancient log cabin. (Courtesy of the Marian Harter Collection.)

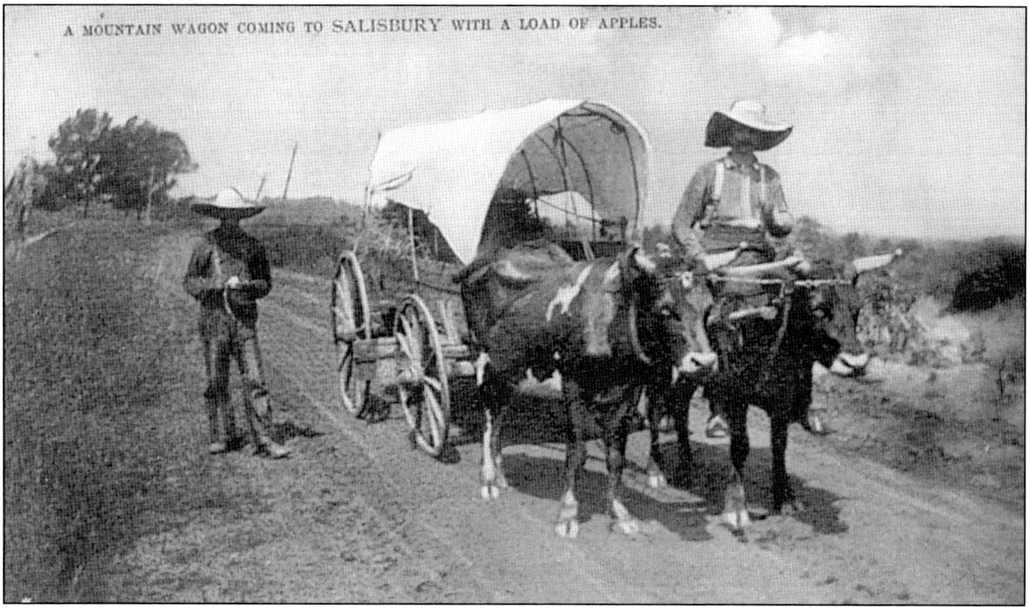

Salisbury was the place for farmers to sell their goods. This covered wagon, much like the wagons used by the early settlers, was delivering a load of apples to Salisbury.

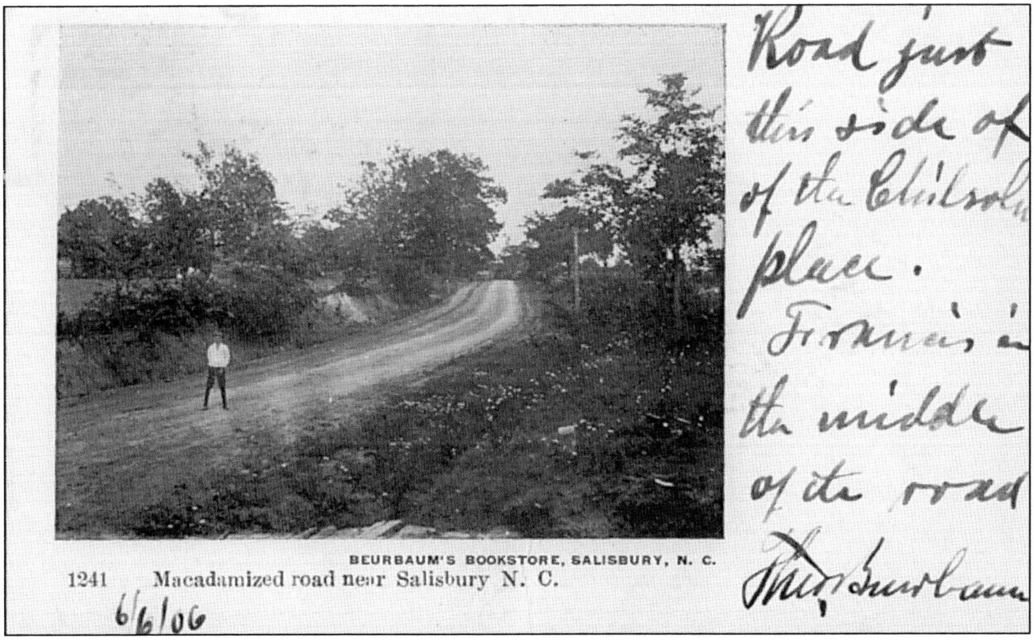

In 1906, few counties in North Carolina were constructing graded macadam roads. The macadamization process involved the compacting into a solid mass a layer of small broken stone on a convex well-drained roadbed. A large number of people did not realize the benefits that a community would derive from these improvements. The state geologist felt there should be state aid to help with the construction to encourage counties to pave their roads. The boy pictured here is Buerbaum's son Francis. (Card from Buerbaum.)

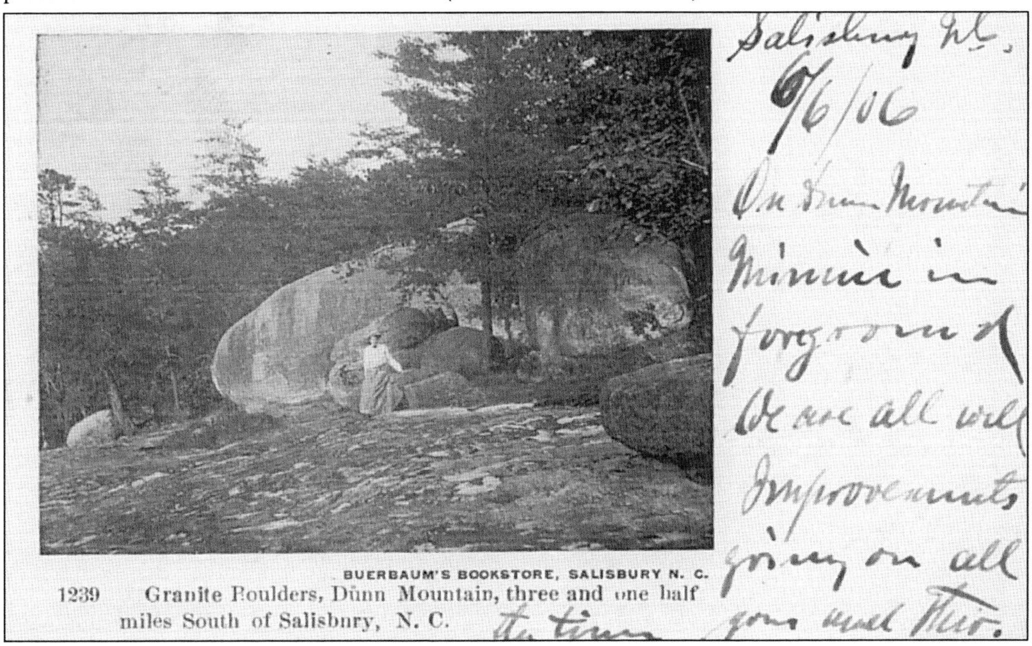

Buerbaum's daughter Minnie is pictured at Dunn's Mountain. This area was named after one of Salisbury's founders, John Dunn, and has been the location of picnics, exploring, and May Day celebrations. (Card from Buerbaum.)

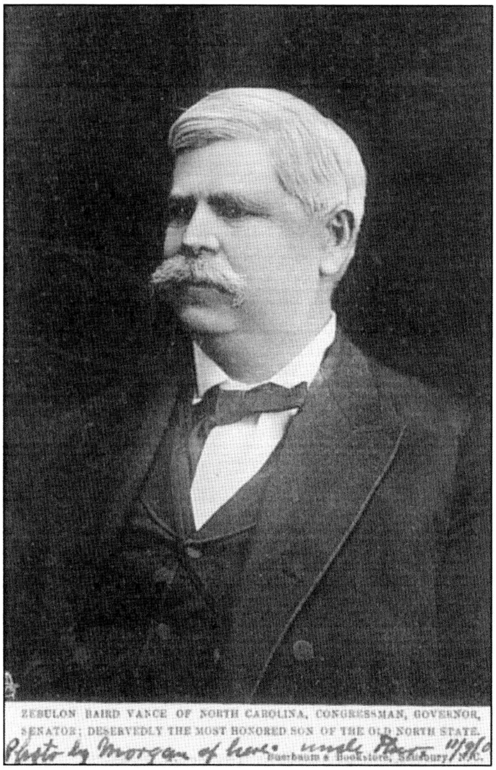

Vance was a Confederate governor of North Carolina and a Democratic U.S. senator. He became governor in 1862 and devoted himself to supplying North Carolina soldiers. Buerbaum's note states, "Photo by Morgan of here. Uncle Theo."

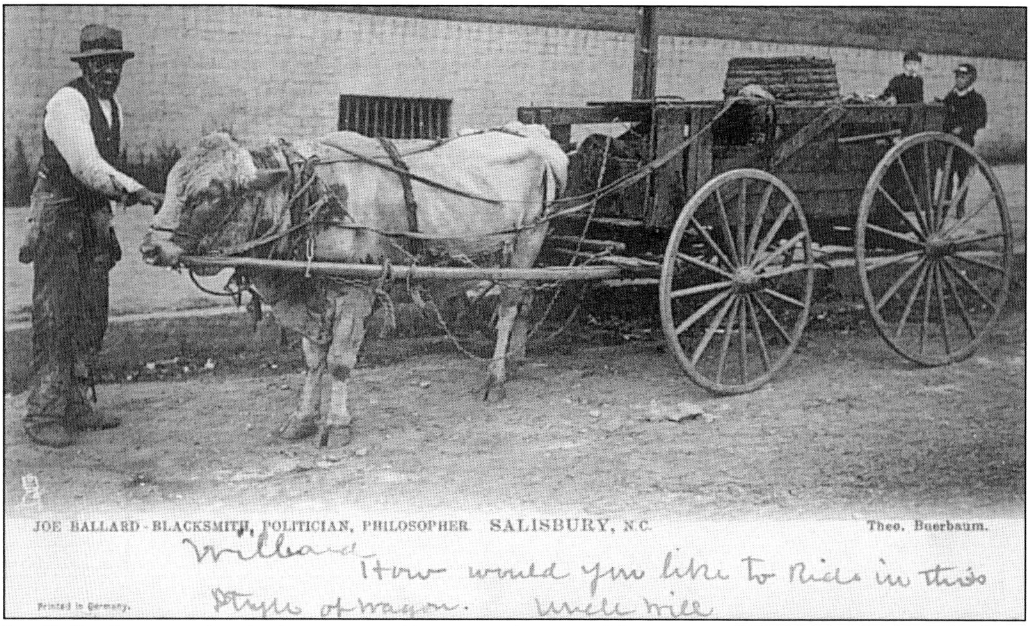

Joe Ballard was an intriguing personality in our history. He was very well known as a politician and storyteller. As chief marshal in the African-American May 30th celebration for many years, he led the parade from Liberty Street down Main Street to the National Cemetery. Ballard's hat was manufactured in 1841 by a local hatter and was worn by Michael Brown, a prominent local shopkeeper. His wagon was drawn by an ox named Prince.

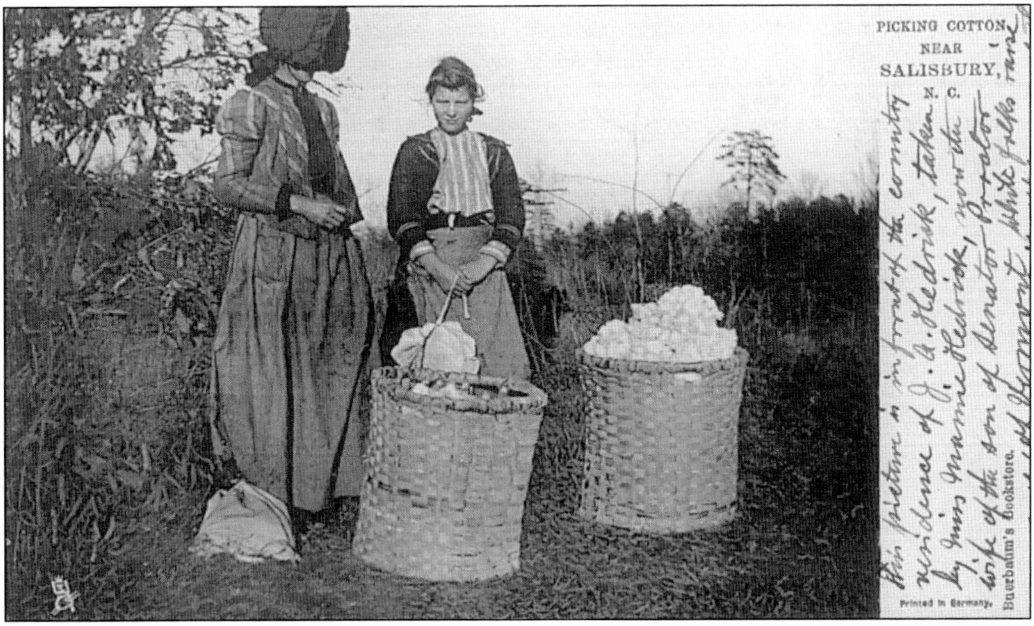

At a revival meeting in 1887, R.G. Pearson proclaimed that the great number of poor and indigent should be helped not with gifts and alms but with the opportunity to make an honest living. His solution was a cotton factory. In coming years, the Salisbury Cotton Mill, Kesler Manufacturing Company, Vance Cotton Mill, Patterson Manufacturing, Linn Mill, Diamond Mills, and others came into existence. Cotton was a major crop until the 1940s. Buerbaum's note says, "This picture is in front of the country residence of J.A. Hedrick, taken by Miss Mamie Hedrick, now the wife of the son of Senator Proctor of Vermont. White folks raise most of the cotton in the South now. Uncle Theo."

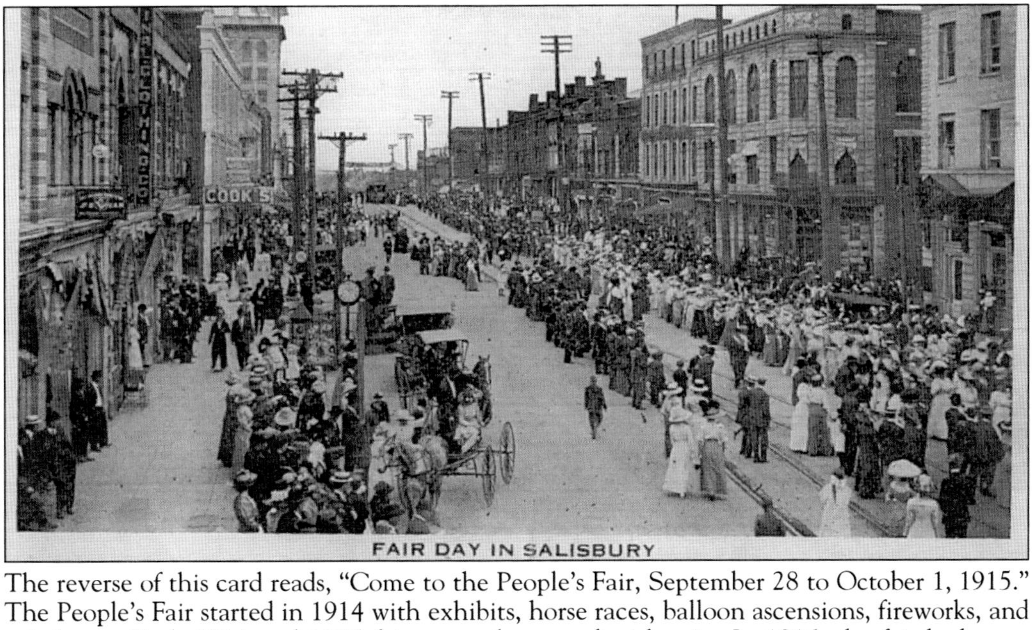

The reverse of this card reads, "Come to the People's Fair, September 28 to October 1, 1915." The People's Fair started in 1914 with exhibits, horse races, balloon ascensions, fireworks, and spiral acts. Both 1914 and 1915 fairs were dampened with rain. In 1916, the fair had great success and included the appearance of Buffalo Bill.

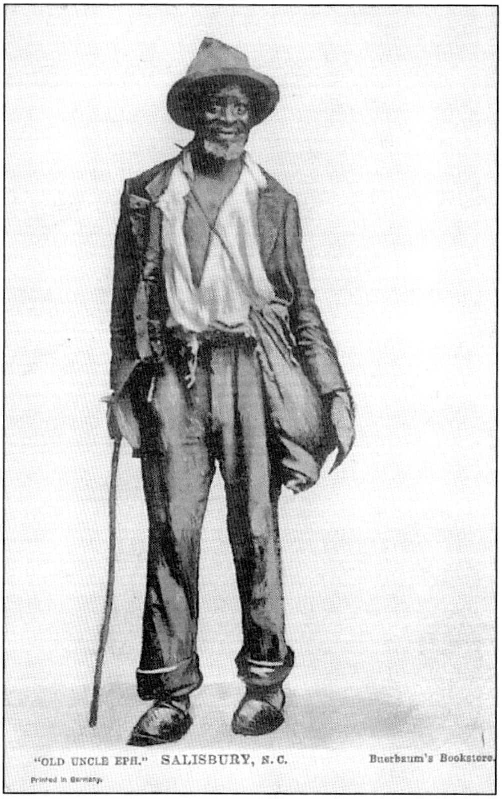

Imagine the stories "Old Uncle Eph" could tell! (Courtesy of the Marian Harter Collection.)

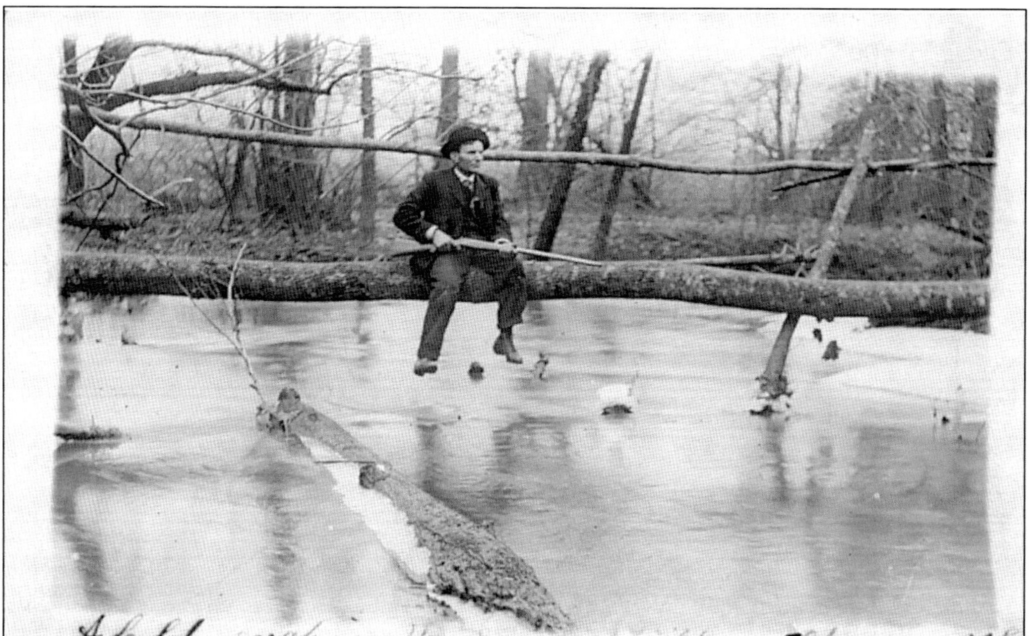

Rowan County's abundant game provided food and sport for many families. This young man appears to be enjoying his solitude in a restful pose over the icy waters.

The Sparks Circus moved to Salisbury in 1910 because of the proximity to the railroad. The circus wintered at the Piedmont Fairground (now the V.A. Hospital property) and endeared itself to the community. Owner Sparks invited local townspeople to visit the circus grounds anytime free of charge. Many local businesses were supported by Sparks. Local seamstresses assisted in making costumes, daily grocery orders were taken, Salisbury Hardware Company ordered special whips and harnesses, and legal work was done by local attorneys. Special events were enhanced by the circus. For example, their camels were used to bring the wise men to the miniature stable at the Community Building on Christmas Eve in 1916. During World War I, Southern Railroad announced an increased demand for transporting troops and army supplies so the use of trains to transport the circus show groups was prohibited. The winter of 1917-1918 was the last for Sparks Circus in Rowan County.

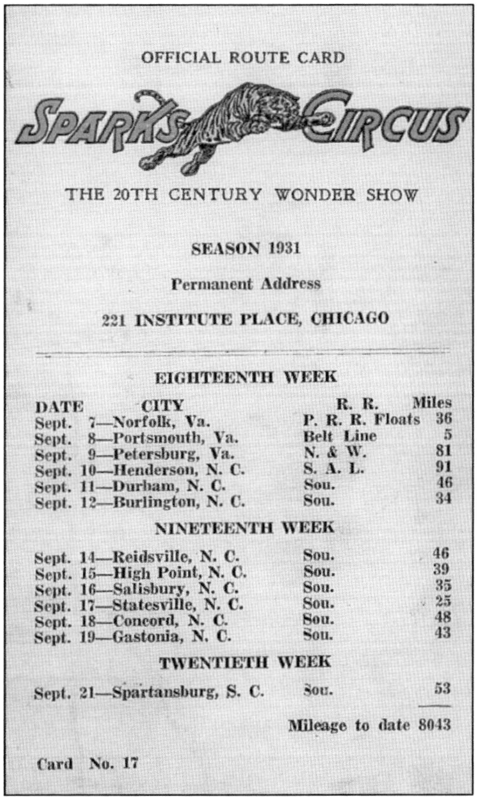

OFFICIAL ROUTE CARD

SPARKS CIRCUS

THE 20TH CENTURY WONDER SHOW

SEASON 1931

Permanent Address

221 INSTITUTE PLACE, CHICAGO

EIGHTEENTH WEEK

DATE	CITY	R. R.	Miles
Sept. 7	Norfolk, Va.	P. R. R. Floats	36
Sept. 8	Portsmouth, Va.	Belt Line	5
Sept. 9	Petersburg, Va.	N. & W.	81
Sept. 10	Henderson, N. C.	S. A. L.	91
Sept. 11	Durham, N. C.	Sou.	46
Sept. 12	Burlington, N. C.	Sou.	34
NINETEENTH WEEK			
Sept. 14	Reidsville, N. C.	Sou.	46
Sept. 15	High Point, N. C.	Sou.	39
Sept. 16	Salisbury, N. C.	Sou.	35
Sept. 17	Statesville, N. C.	Sou.	25
Sept. 18	Concord, N. C.	Sou.	48
Sept. 19	Gastonia, N. C.	Sou.	43
TWENTIETH WEEK			
Sept. 21	Spartansburg, S. C.	Sou.	53

Mileage to date 8043

Card No. 17

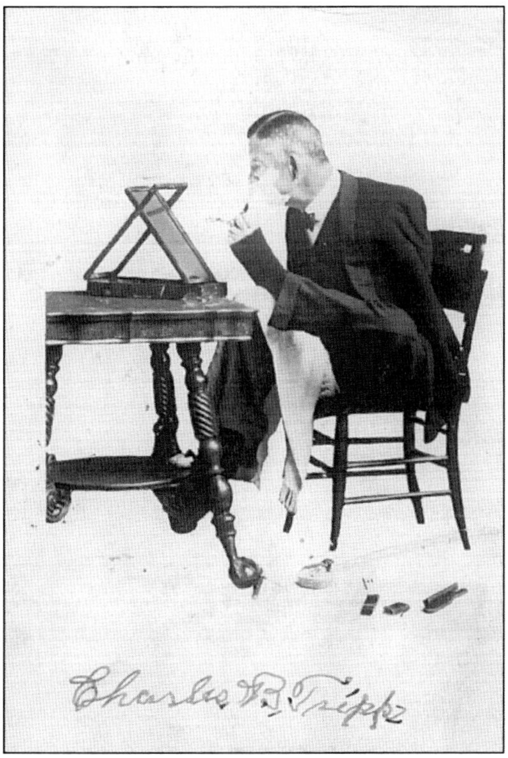

Charles B. Tripp, the "Armless Wonder," traveled with Barnum and Bailey and Ringling Brothers Circus displaying his unusual talents. Born without arms, he learned to feed and dress himself, carve wood, and make furniture, among other things, all with his feet. To shave, as demonstrated on this autographed card, he used a straight razor. During his performances, he would give a speech about self-worth and achieving goals. He wintered in Salisbury and, after retirement, lived here until his death in 1930.

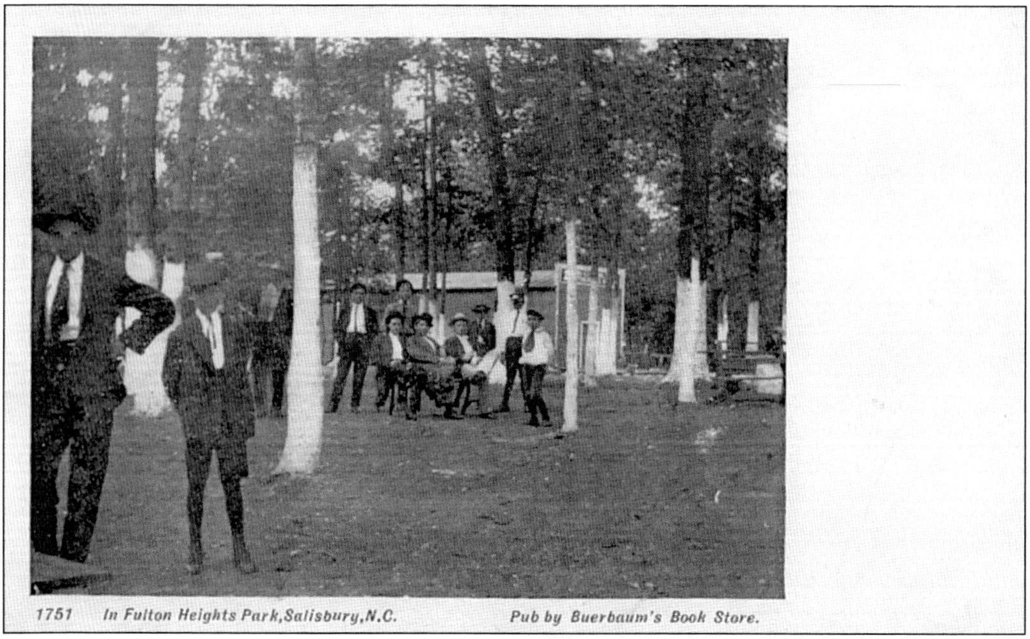

The Southern Development Company was started in 1902 by J.M. Maupin, H.B. Crosby, W. Murdoch Wiley, William Blair, and W.E. Mitchell. The company began buying land to form the Fulton Heights community. Many street names in that area originated with the principles of the Southern Development Company. In 1905, a streetcar line was run down Mitchell Avenue from Chestnut Hill to an amusement park. The park offered recreation, a tent theatre, a skating rink, and a picnic area. It was customary in the early 1900s to whitewash trees to keep them healthy and for cosmetic reasons. The median on Mitchell Avenue was installed when the streetcar line was removed.

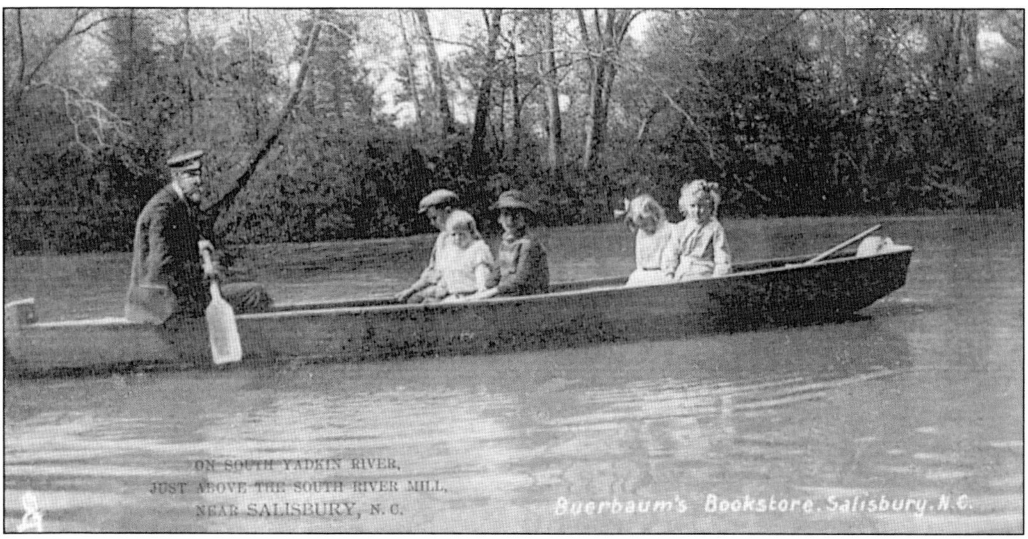

Buerbaum himself is rowing the boat! The children are identified, from left to right, as Francis, Lena, Leman, Beff, and Marion. The date is April 24, 1905, and the occasion is a South River picnic. It is nice to see Theo Buerbaum, the gentleman who left a wonderful photographic legacy for Rowan County, relaxing and enjoying life in his latter years. (Card from Buerbaum.)